Advances in Bioinformatics, Biostatistics and Omic Sciences

Authored by

Luigi Donato, Simona Alibrandi, Rosalia D'Angelo, Concetta Scimone and Antonina Sidoti

Department of Biomedical, Dental Sciences and Morphofunctional Imaging,
Division of Medical Biotechnologies and Preventive Medicine,
University of Messina, Messina 98125,
Italy

&

Alessandra Costa

Department of Economics,
University of Messina, Messina 98125
Italy

Advances in Bioinformatics, Biostatistics and Omic Sciences

Authors: Luigi Donato, Simona Alibrandi, Rosalia D'Angelo,
Concetta Scimone, Antonina Sidoti and Alessandra Costa

ISBN (Online): 978-981-14-8180-2

ISBN (Print): 978-981-14-8178-9

ISBN (Paperback): 978-981-14-8179-6

Published by Bentham Science Publishers Pte. Ltd. Singapore. All Rights Reserved.

need for a court order if at any point you breach any terms of this License Agreement. In no event will any delay or failure by Bentham Science Publishers in enforcing your compliance with this License Agreement constitute a waiver of any of its rights.

3. You acknowledge that you have read this License Agreement, and agree to be bound by its terms and conditions. To the extent that any other terms and conditions presented on any website of Bentham Science Publishers conflict with, or are inconsistent with, the terms and conditions set out in this License Agreement, you acknowledge that the terms and conditions set out in this License Agreement shall prevail.

Bentham Science Publishers Pte. Ltd.
80 Robinson Road #02-00
Singapore 068898
Singapore
Email: subscriptions@benthamscience.net

BENTHAM SCIENCE

CONTENTS

FOREWORD

The ability to analyze the genomes and transcriptomes using NGS techniques was a potential breakthrough in research. These sequencing techniques allow the discovery of unexpected transcripts, high speed, scalability and recently have become highly accessible thanks to a drastic drop in costs. This last condition has enabled the use of sequencing as a clinical tool. However, brute force does not automatically lead to an advancement in knowledge, in fact, the biggest challenge related to the sequencing is processing this huge amount of raw data to assess the differential gene expression, RNA editing, genomic imprinting, new splicing variants, and gene fusions. In this regard, much of the research in Bioinformatics and Biostatistics is developing algorithms and publishing software for filtering, analyzing, and visualizing sequencing data. A few researchers have the necessary skills to create software or understand the algorithms implemented by a tool, so most of them are limited only to the use of the software. These researchers may find themselves disoriented in front of a vastness of software that promises to face the same problem but offers different results. In parallel, technological improvements are providing increasingly long and accurate sequencing allowing direct reading of full-length transcripts and single-cell RNA sequencing. The latter is highly applicable for studying tumor heterogeneity, tracking metastases and deciphering the message carried by even a single extracellular vesicle. In the future, more intelligent programs are expected, that is, capable of comparing sequencing information with all data available in databases and directly providing biologically significant information and translating these findings into clinically actionable results. These will be programs that will speak more and more in biological but also in medical terms. For clinical use, response times are very important. In the case of aggressive diseases, the entire pipeline duration should not exceed a couple of weeks and in the case of aggressive infections, we speak about a few days. All this together will allow for a revolution in science for precision medicine based on personal genome. This book shows various methods for analyzing genomics and transcriptomics data, always keeping in mind the objective of providing really useful information to medicine. Among the different omics applications, it shows the analysis of mitochondrial DNA for the diagnosis of mitochondrial diseases and the improvement of genetic counseling, the prioritization of genes, and the discovery of gene variants. The reader is guided through the use and performance analysis of various programs, data visualization tools are shown and the results of multiple programs are compared for an integrated approach. Through the chapters, we are accompanied in a didactic way, thus bringing non-experts closer to a field usually dominated by bioinformaticians. In the end, the reader understands that sequencing, even if carried out some time before, does not age so quickly, because as new algorithms are produced, we can look at those same data from a new perspective, obtaining new results which provide us with satisfaction of unexpected discovery.

Francesco Piva
Department of Specialistic Clinical and Odontostomatological Sciences
Polytechnic University of Marche
Via Brecce Bianche, Ancona
Italy
E-mail: f.piva@univpm.it

PREFACE

In the last decade, the scientific community assisted in a real revolution determined by the development of technologies that caused a rapid increase in the amount of information usable by researchers. While traditional analytic approaches were based on the study of single molecules, novel technologies permitted a characterization of entire pools of specific biomolecules. Consequently, the term "Omic Sciences" was coined, highlighting the global vision that derives from this kind of study. Among them, genomics, transcriptomics, proteomics and metabolomics represent the most innovative branches that belong to the omic universe. In contrast to the relevance of these methodologies, the common disadvantage of the big amount of data generated and has arisen, hence, its management. Therefore, in order to minimize the "big data" complexity, there was a huge progress of bioinformatic areas, trying to analyse data faster and more accurately. Nowadays, computational sciences are continuously developed, and several tools, based on bioinformatic and biostatistical analysis pipelines, are programmed. Based on this consideration, I think that novel insights in omics experimental procedures and, predominantly, in new strategies for data analysis could provide an interesting and exploitable topic for many researchers. So, the idea for this book series is to realize an integrated approach between all omic sciences, exploiting innovative bioinformatics and biostatistical methodologies able to unveil hidden sides of these scientific areas. This first volume of the proposed book series would face the application of innovative analytic pipelines to obtain the most useful and translational results from genomics and transcriptomics data, with the fundamental support of machine learning algorithms and innovative biostatistical models. Such procedures will be applied to real data coming from human sample analyses, ranging from biopsies to cell cultures. I think that the holistic approach of previously discussed sciences could permit us to advance towards new scenarios, finally trying to see the "big data" as a precious resource rather than a real problem to be faced.

CONSENT FOR PUBLICATION

Not applicable.

CONFLICT OF INTEREST

The authors declare no conflict of interest, financial or otherwise.

ACKNOWLEDGEMENTS

Declared none.

Luigi Donato
Department of Biomedical, Dental Sciences and Morphofunctional Imaging
Division of Medical Biotechnologies and Preventive Medicine
University of Messina, Messina 98125
Italy
E-mail: ldonato@unime.it

New Integrated Mitochondrial DNA Bioinformatics Pipeline to Improve Quality Assessment of Putative Pathogenic Variants from NGS Experiments

Abstract: Mitochondria represents one of the most essential, investigated organelles of eukaryotic cells. Due to the relevance of the functions, especially cellular respiration, mitochondria are subject to continuous oxidative stress stimuli that, over time, can impair this distinct genome, leading, for example, to several neurodegenerative and age-related diseases. Today, the growth of next generation sequencing techniques allows researchers to improve variant detection of mtDNA, increasing, in the meantime, the quantity and complexity of data produced, making molecular diagnosis of mitochondrial diseases more challenging. The main issues that will be faced working with mtDNA high-throughput sequencing deal with detection and interpretation of low heteroplasmy and homoplasmy levels, variants unrelated to exhibited phenotype and identification of variants of unknown significance (VUS). To perform an accurate analysis of mtDNA variants produced by next generation sequencing experiments, we propose an integrated approach that foresees the complementary use of the most recent algorithms applied to mtDNA data, trying to extract the maximum from each one. This workflow foresaw four macro-phases (mitogenome alignment/assembly, variant calling, variant annotation and *in-silico* variant effects predictions), each one characterized by a mixed output coming from several tools and databases rich in complementary information on mtDNA variants. In this way, a superior quality output could be obtained, leading to improved genetic counseling for patients affected by primary mitochondrial pathologies.

Keywords: AVM, CCM, CLC Genomics Workbench, Mitochondria, mtDNA, mtDNA-Server, Mitos2, MitoBreak, MVTools, Mitoweb, MtoolBox, MitoTip, MitImpact 3D, RNA-Seq, RP, SMART2, TRIMITOMICS, VUS, Variants, WES.

INTRODUCTION

Mitochondria are correctly considered one of the most essential and interesting organelles of eukaryotic cells. While well known to act as the powerhouse of the cell, mitochondria are involved in several other fundamental cellular activities, such as induction of apoptosis by the release of cytochrome C following caspase

Luigi Donato, Simona Alibrandi, Rosalia D'Angelo, Concetta Scimone, Antonina Sidoti and Alessandra Costa

activation, storing calcium ions after quickly absorbing and holding them until they are needed, and heat production by non-shivering thermogenesis [1]. Despite these essential functions, the prominent role of mitochondria deals with the production of cellular adenosine triphosphate (ATP) and establishment of membrane potential by oxidative phosphorylation [2]. Such tasks could be accomplished by the involvement of a huge variety of proteins, most of which are encoded by the nuclear genome and then translocated to mitochondria [3]. Nevertheless, the most intriguing aspect of mitochondria lies in the uniqueness of its own genome (mtDNA), distinct from the nuclear one. Human mtDNA consists of a double-stranded circular molecule of about 16,600 nt, structured in nucleoids and associated with proteins, localized in the proximity of the mitochondrial inner membrane, within the mitochondrial matrix [4]. MtDNA codes for only thirteen polypeptides of the oxidative phosphorylation complex (OXPHOS), along with 22 tRNAs and 2 rRNAs (12S and 16S), supporting mitochondrial translational processes. As for the majority of vertebrates, the non-coding portion of DNA is situated within a 1 kb noncoding region (NCR), which represents the most polymorphic site of mtDNA, especially in a hypervariable sub-region called HVR [5]. The latter is frequently sequenced to analyze population genetic lineages through mitochondrial haplogroup assignment [6]. The whole NCR can control both transcription and translation, exerting an important regulatory role within mtDNA, also supported by the mtDNA control region. This portion presents the transcription origin for both strands and the replication origin for one strand and also constitutes the site of mtDNA displacement loop (D-loop) [7]. This region is highly variable and, even if its exact functions are not totally clear, it has already been associated with cancer [8]. Apart from this specific example, it is already known that a lengthy accumulation of lower levels of mtDNA damage and mtDNA copy reduction could be linked to the etiopathogenesis of neurodegenerative and metabolic age-related diseases [9 - 12]. Mitochondrial impairments, with the incidence of about 1:4,300, primarily affect oxidative phosphorylation but, with several mitochondrial proteins encoded by the nuclear genome, the derived pathological phenotypes are greatly heterogeneous [13]. Numerous human pathogenic mtDNA variants, carried by protein coding genes rDNA and tDNA, are continuously updated in the MITOMAP human mitochondrial genome database [14]. Despite an actual number of about 15,000 reported variants, only a few hundred are confirmed as disease-causing. These mutations lead to a wide range of maternally inherited diseases, characterized by high heterogeneity of both clinical phenotype and penetrance, principally deriving from shifts and differences in the mutant load, due to stochastic segregation of mtDNA during cellular divisions. As a consequence of this distribution, the mutation load could range from homoplasmy, with 100% mutant load, to the coexistence of both mutant and wildtype molecules, called heteroplasmy, also varying across different tissues and organs. When the levels of heteroplasmy increase, energy production decreases to the minimum threshold needed for cell physiological homeostasis, leading to the appearance of symptoms [15].

Today, the development of next generation sequencing (NGS) techniques permits efficient analysis of mtDNA, improving sample output and sensitivity of variant detection [16]. Nevertheless, massive parallel sequencing of total mtDNA implies a higher quantity and complexity of data, making molecular diagnosis of mitochondrial diseases more challenging. The main issues that will be faced working with mtDNA high-throughput sequencing deal with detection and interpretation of low heteroplasmy and homoplasmy levels, variants unrelated to exhibited phenotype, and identification of variants of unknown significance (VUS) [17]. Therefore, to perform an accurate analysis of mtDNA variants produced by NGS experiments, we propose an integrated approach that foresees the complementary use of the most recent algorithms applied to mtDNA data, trying to extract the maximum from each one. In this way, a higher quality output can be obtained, leading to improved genetic counseling for people affected by primary mitochondrial pathologies. A schematic workflow of the entire pipeline is reported in Fig. (**1**).

MATERIAL AND METHODS

Samples

To cover the widest range of frequently realized NGS experiments, a heterogeneous group of 26 samples was chosen to perform the whole pipeline. Seven RNA-sequencing outputs, resulting from independent pair-end experiments on the Illumina platform, came from the whole transcriptome analyses of retinal pigmented epithelial (RPE) cells treated with A2E oxidant agent in a follow-up of two time-points (3h and 6h) after basal time (called, respectively, 3h_RPE, 6h_RPE and 0h_RPE), and from biopsies of patients affected by cerebral cavernous angiomas (CCM) (called, respectively, CCM_1, CCM_2 and CCM_CTRL). All RNA-Seq experiments foresaw 3 biological replicates (Total of RNA-Seq samples=18). However, in data analysis outputs, we considered the average results from replicates. The other eight samples consisted of six patients affected by orphan forms of retinitis pigmentosa (RP) (ME_2, ME_3, ME_4, ME_5, RP_8, RP_32), one patient affected by CCM (ME_1) and one patient affected by arteriovenous malformations (ME_6), respectively. These samples underwent whole exome sequencing (WES) in independent pair-end experiments on the Illumina platform. Quality scores for sequenced samples were around 28 across all reads, with mean read length ranging from 100 to 200 bp and with total average read number ranging from about 45 million to 95 million.

MITOGENOME ALIGNMENT/ASSEMBLY	VARIANT CALLING	VARIANT ANNOTATION	*IN-SILICO* VARIANT PREDICTION

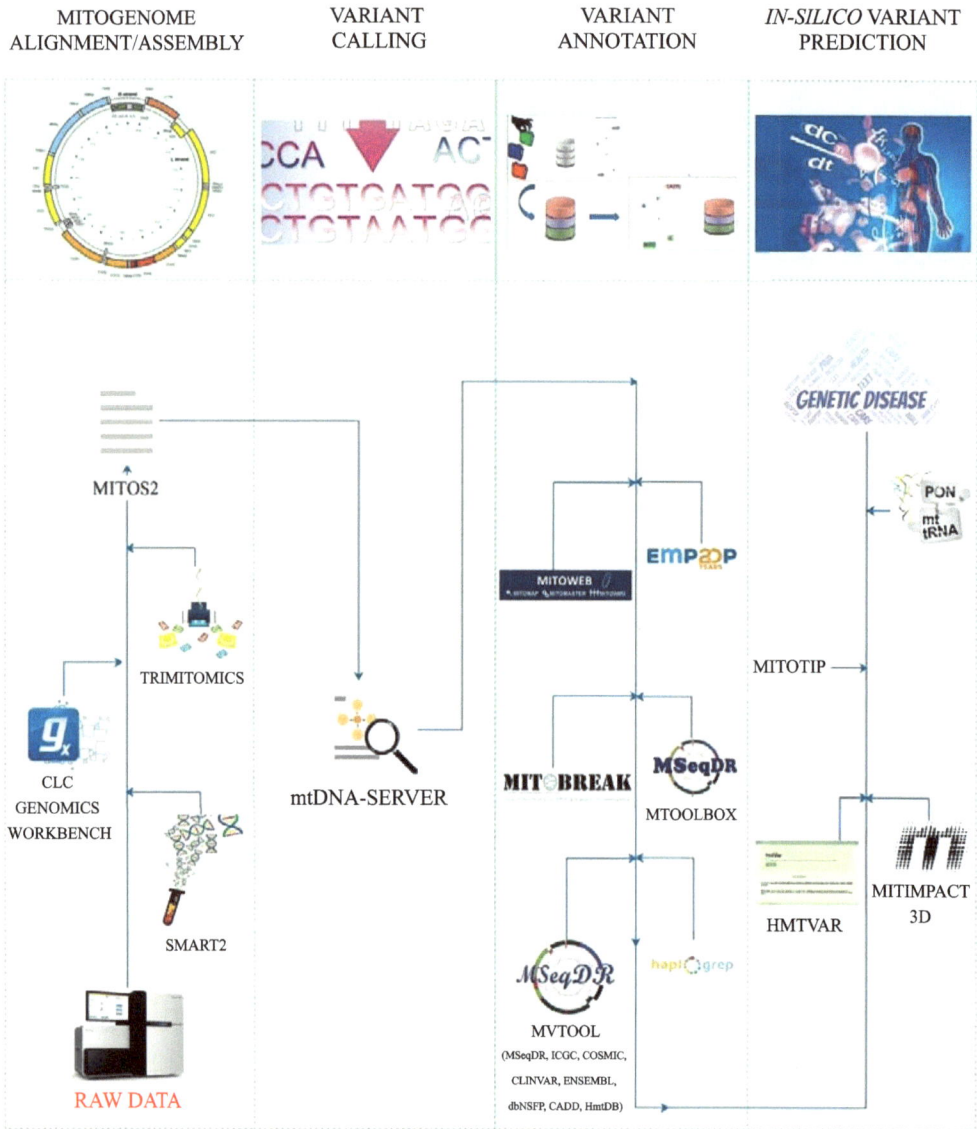

Fig. (1). Diagram of mtDNA variant analysis proposed pipeline. Figure shows main phases of mtDNA variant analysis, listing the single macro-steps with specific tools and databases used.

Mitogenome Assembly/Mapping

Obtained raw sequences were filtered to remove low-quality reads (average per base Phred score < 30) and adaptor sequences. The quality of analyzed data was checked using FastQC (v.0.11.9) (https://www.bioinformatics.babraham.ac.uk/projects/fastqc/) and QualiMap (v.2.2.1) [18], while trimming was realized by Trimmomatic (v.0.39). Filtered data were then assembled/mapped by CLC Genomics Workbench v.20.0.3 (https://digitalinsights.qiagen.com/products-overview/analysis-and-visualization/qiagen-clc-genomics-workbench/), Multi-Sample Statistical Mitogenome Assembly with Repeats (SMART2) [19] and an adapted version of TRIMITOMICS pipeline [20]. All assembly/alignments were realized using the Revised Cambridge Reference Sequence (rCRS), available as sequence number NC_012920 (formerly AC_000021.2) in GenBank's RefSeq database. This specific rCRS is the most commonly used standard comparison sequence for human mtDNA research. It is 16569 bp in length, which includes one spacer at position 3107 to preserve the historical CRS position numbering (Fig. **2**). It is a single reference individual from haplogroup H2a2 and has been used as a standard for reporting variants for over 30 years.

CLC Genomics Workbench is a widely used, cutting edge multifunctional NGS analysis and visualization platform that permits a genome guided assembly after aligning reads to reference and following extraction of consensus sequence from mapped reads. Mapping analysis was conducted using the following settings: quality trim limit = 0.01, ambiguity trim maximum value = 2. Map to annotated reference was as follows: mismatch cost = 2, insertion and deletion costs = 3, minimum length fraction and minimum similarity fraction = 0.8, maximum number of hits for a read = 10, strand-specific = both.

SMART2 is the most recent pipeline in the field that is able to assemble de novo and annotate complete circular mitochondrial genome sequence from whole exome/genome sequencing data even in the presence of repeats. Settings for SMART2 analyses were: automatic selection of number of read pairs per bootstrap, with doubling strategy starting with 100k; number of bootstrap samples=1; minimum seed kmer coverage=20; coverage-based filtering method=intersection; kmer size=31; number of threads=16; genetic code=02-vertebrate.

TRIMITOMICS is a particularly interesting pipeline for the assembly of mitochondrial gene cassettes and whole coding sequences from RNA-Seq reads, based on free algorithms used stepwise, depending on the success of mitogenome assembly in the preceding step. The first step consisted of the NOVOPlasty v.3.8.2 organelle assembler analysis, with the following settings: Genome Range=1-16569; k-mer=31; max memory=16; extend seed directly=no; variance detection=no. If a full or partial mitogenome was not obtained, the RNA-Seq reads were firstly mapped to their respective reference genome with Bowtie2 v.2.4.1 algorithm, using default presets, and then assembled with Trinity v.2.10.0, following genome guided approach with standard settings, except "max intron length=10000". If none of the previously cited methods successfully produced mitogenome, the complete transcriptome was assembled by Velvet v.1.2.10, considering a range of kmer sizes (31, 51, 71). Mitochondrial contigs were then extracted from *de novo* produced transcriptome assemblies by BlastN, using the reference mitogenome. If the complete genome was not retrieved by any of the described approaches, the results were joined or put together as a meta-assembly with MAFFT v.7.464 to improve the output. Raw data are available upon request.

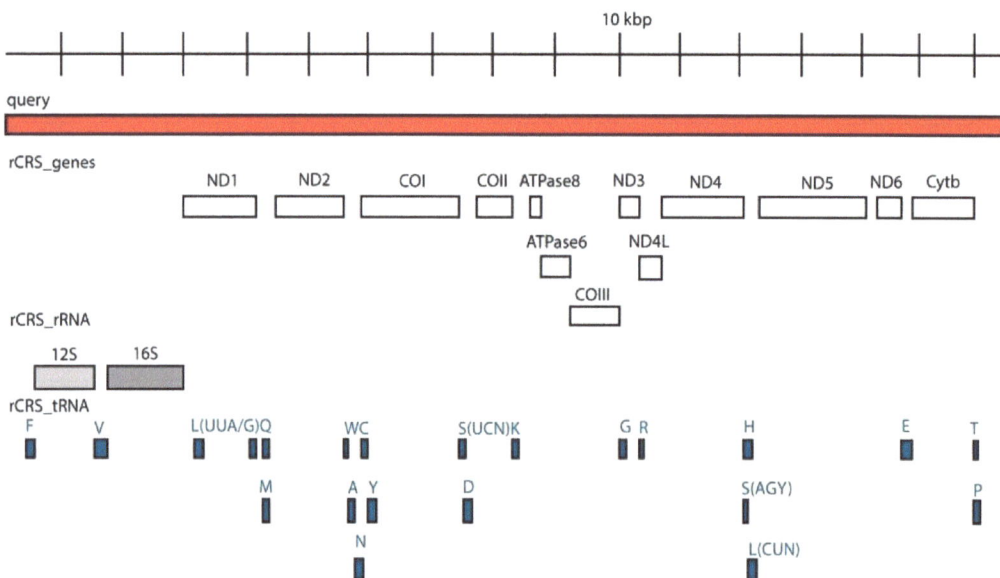

Fig. (2). rCRS reference mitogenome sequence. The figure highlights the genomic features of Revised Cambridge Reference Sequence (rCRS), available as sequence number NC_012920 (formerly AC_000021.2) in the GenBank RefSeq database.

Variant Detection by mtDNA-Server

Once obtained, assembled mitogenomes (in BAM format) were analyzed for variant calling by mtDNA-Server, a highly scalable Hadoop-based server for mtDNA NGS data processing [21]. After input validation and quality control of BAM files, parallel analysis with variant detection was performed. HadoopBAM split the input into several chunks and, for each one, reads were filtered out if the Phred score < 20 and the length < 25, as were reads marked as duplicates. Then, all passed bases for each site were counted per strand (A, C, G, T, N (unknown), d (deletion)). Regarding heteroplasmy detection, several approaches were performed: initially, sites presenting coverage < 10 bases per strand and mitochondrial hotspots around 309, 315 and 3107 were filtered out, according to reference sequence. For survived sites with an allele coverage of 3 bp per strand

and a variant allele frequency (VAF) $\geq$ 1% (strand independent), a machine learning (ML) model was applied, considering sequencing errors per base in each strand. Then, all sites showing a log likelihood ratio (LLR) $\geq$ 5 were tagged as heteroplasmic sites. Additionally, the Wilson and the Agresti-Coull confidence intervals were computed for heteroplasmic variants, and the assigned heteroplasmy level is a weighted mean of heteroplasmy of both strands. An important feature of the mtDNA-Server regards the intra-sample contamination check, based on current phylogeny to avoid erroneous interpretations and conclusions. In the case of contaminations caused by different mtDNA sequences, the two VAF-based profiles generated by the mtDNA-Server (VAF < 50% for the minor, VAF > 50% for the major) lead to different valid haplogroups.

Variant Annotation and Prioritization

This step must be performed very carefully, as it is fundamental for the next interpretation phase of analysis. Thus, it is important to remember several practical rules: I) Explore databases which are continuously updated and specific for mtDNA, II) Evaluate variant frequency not only in the general population, but also in particular haplogroups, III) Pay particular attention to low heteroplasmy levels, IV) Combine additional data supporting the modulation of clinical penetrance, such as mitochondrial haplogroup, V) Consider inter-species nucleotide and/or amino acid conservation. We adopted several dedicated tools for annotations of mtDNA variants, related to the principal, regularly updated, databases.

The most complete tool we used to realize these purposes is the MSeqDR mtDNA Variant Tool set (mvTool), built upon the MSeqDR infrastructure (https://mseqdr.org), which supports all mtDNA nomenclatures, converts variants to standard rCRS- and HGVS-based nomenclatures, and annotates novel mtDNA variants [22]. For previously annotated mtDNA variants, mvTool extracts and provides updated population data and pathogenetic classifications from MSeqDR Consortium members [23], dbNSFP [24], the Human Mitochondrial Database (HmtDB) [25], Mitomap [26], the 1000 Genomes Project data, GeneDx [27], ClinVar [28], with resources coming from around 50,000 germline mitogenomes. If a variant has not been annotated previously, mvTool conducts new predictions by calling Ensembl Variant Effect Predictor (VEP) [29] and stores its genomic annotations in an internal database that mvTool will search first. Furthermore, if the input includes all mtDNA variants of a given sample, exact mtDNA haplogroup assignment can be obtained by Phy-Mer sub-tool.

Nevertheless, variant frequency interpretation of a general population can be challenging, as cited databases include patient data, and due to features of mtDNA genetics (heteroplasmy level, incomplete penetrance, influence of mitochondrial haplogroup background).

To bypass this problem, we made additions to our pipeline analyses performed with tools and databases focusing on haplogroup classification. The already cited Mitomap advises if a variant is identified at >1% in at least one of the macro-lineages or over 10% in the major haplogroups for tRNA variants. Results from this step of prioritization were, then, corroborated by data coming from the forensic database EMPOP v.4/R13 [30], and from other two important and recent updated tools, HaploGrep 2 and MToolBox.

HaploGrep 2 includes a generic rule-based system for immediate quality control (QC), which allows to identify artificial recombinants and missing variants as well as annotating rare and phantom mutations [31].

MToolBox applies a computational strategy to realign already assembled mitochondrial genomes to detect insertions and deletions (indels), and to assess the heteroplasmic fraction (HF) of each variant allele with the related confidence interval (CI), before haplogroup assignment and variant prioritization [32]. This latter step was performed by aligning each sample-specific reconstructed contig against the related macro-haplogroup-specific consensus sequence. This process could identify private variants, through a prioritization process, justifying further clinical investigation. Prioritization also considered the pathogenicity of each mutated allele, computed with different algorithms, and the nucleotide variability of each variant site, while the amino acid variability was considered only if the variant site was codogenic.

Finally, to provide a complete description of the variant, we retrieved data from the Mitobreak database, focusing on mtDNA rearrangements. In detail, MitoBreak provides a complete, quality checked list of breakpoints from circular deleted mtDNAs (deletions), circular partially duplicated mtDNAs (duplications) and linear mtDNAs [33].

In Silico Predictions and Variant Consequences

Today, massive mtDNA screening by NGS has shown a huge number of novel variants of unknown significance (VUS), whose clinical interpretation is more complicated than nuclear VUS, because of the mtDNA characteristics, such as heteroplasmy and high mutation rate not considered in the classical prioritization algorithms, and due to limited guidelines for mtDNA compared to those provided for nuclear VUS.

Thus, it is clear that a combined approach of complementary *in-silico* prediction tools is the best way to obtain reliable results. These tools estimate the functional impact of variants by methods based on structure analysis and/or interspecies sequence conservation.

The most complete and continuously updated tool we used for prediction of mtDNA variants is MitImpact 3D v.3.0.2, a collection of pre-computed pathogenicity predictions for all possible nucleotide changes that determine non-synonymous substitution, in human mitochondrial protein coding genes [34]. The possible effect of these variants was computed by MitImpact 3D through the following missense pathogenicity predictors and machine learning based approach meta-predictors: PolyPhen2 (ver. 2.2.2) [35], SIFT (ver. 5.0.3) [36], FatHmm (ver. 2.2, "weighted" and "unweighted" setting) [37], MutationAssessor (ver. 2.0) [38], PROVEAN (ver. 1.3) [39], EFIN [40], CADD (ver. 1.2) [41], PANTHER [42], PhD-SNP [43], SNAP [44], MutationTaster ver. 2 [45], SNPdryad [46], DEOGEN2 [47], Mitoclass.1 [48], CAROL [49], Condel [50], COVEC (vers. 0.4) [51], Meta-SNP [52], APOGEE (ver. 1.0) [53], dbSNP (ver. 151) [54], ClinVar, PhyloP and PhastCons evolutionary conservation indices (UCSC Gene Tables, group: Comparative Genomics; track: Conservation; tables: phyloP100wayAll and PhastCons100way) [55], SiteVar human mtDNA site-specific variability [56], COSMIC somatic variants (ver. 87) [57], MISTIC Mutual Information scores [58], CHASM [59], TransFIC [60]. Moreover, the tool permitted to evaluate compensated pathogenic deviations (CPDs), amino acid substitutions described as pathogenic in human populations but that appear as wild type residues in non-human ortholog proteins, as well as intra-protein sites that significantly co-variate each other with two different tools, EV Mutation algorithm (https://marks.hms.harvard.edu/evmutation/index.html) and pairwise covariation analyses with the I-COMS resource.

The wide range of data coming from MitImpact 3D was, then, enriched by HmtVAR [61], a free resource which hosts variability and pathogenicity data on human mitochondrial variants, integrated with data coming from several online databases and in-house pathogenicity assessments, based on various evaluation criteria. HmtVAR also presents manually curated tRNA variant attributes manually curated, but the most relevant resources dedicated to mitochondrial tRNAs that we used were MITOTIP and PON-mt-tRNA.

MITOTIP is the most recent tool available through Mitomap that mixes secondary structure information, structural analogies with other tRNA variants and conservation scores, providing the best prediction performances regarding specificity and sensitivity [62].

PON-mt-RNA, instead, is a posterior probability-based algorithm which computes a multifactorial score associating 12 features, including sequence context and evidence of segregation, RNA secondary structure and tertiary interaction, functional assays such as biochemistry and histochemistry, and evolutionary conservation [63].

RESULTS

Alignment and Assembly of mtDNAs

We applied our pipeline to two types of datasets, 8 pair-end WES samples and 6 pair-end RNA-Seq samples. Performed sequencing globally generated about 100 million quality reads (mean mapping quality=28), with a percentage of ~75% uniquely mapped, ranging from a few hundred reads generated from an AVM sample (ME_6) to 35 million reads produced by Illumina pair-end experiment on CCM_1 transcriptome. The big difference between WES and RNA-Seq mapped reads is due to different types of experiments, which consider duplicated reads differently. In transcriptome mapping, duplication is relevant for expression quantification, while WES data might reflect PCR biases. Thus, as shown in Table **1**, filtered reads with quality acceptable features are considerably less than raw ones. Interestingly, the only tool which was able to map mtDNA in all samples was CLC Genomics Workbench, even if the best efficiency was achieved with the SMART2 specific algorithm. Trimitomics adapted workflow, instead, mapped only CCM transcriptomics samples, probably due to a greater depth of initial raw data (not shown), highlighting elevated requirements requested by Bowtie2, NOVOPlasty, Trinity and Velvet algorithms. A detailed report of alignment and assembly statistics is available in Tables **1** & **2**. Once produced, all partial or fully assembled mitogenomes were merged to obtain only one meta-mitogenome for each sample, needed for subsequent steps.

Mitogenome Annotations

De novo annotation with a consistent method is a promising approach to evaluate and improve existing annotations, trying to reduce inconsistencies and errors, such as missing or incorrect information of the reading direction (strand), missing gene annotations, erroneous gene designations, mistaken identity of tRNAs, and inconsistencies in gene names. The MITOchondrial genome annotation Server 2 (MITOS2) uses a novel strategy based on aggregating BLAST searches with previously annotated protein sequences to detect protein coding genes, tRNAs and rRNA. Each structured RNA was annotated using specific covariance models. Annotation of protein coding genes reached the best results in ME_2 and ME_6 detecting 9 and 14 genes, respectively, with high quality score ($\sim 10^6$).

Table 1. Alignment and assembly statistics of WES analyzed samples. The table shows the main features related to mapping and assembly steps performed on WES considered samples by CLC Genomics Workbench and SMART2 algorithms.

	STATISTICS FEATURE	ME_1	ME_2	ME_3	ME_4	ME_5	ME_6	RP_8	RP_32
CLC GENOMICS WORKBENCH	Overall Reads	1,052	3,52	1,086	1,128	1,056	471	4,519	2,841
	Filtered Reads	759	2,542	12	20	7	4	3,777	1,739
	Passed Reads	293	978	1,074	1,108	1,049	467	742	1,102
	Passed FWD Reads	18,163	48,33	57,781	58,553	56,357	28,109	53,711	79,383
	Passed REV Reads	9,486	43,921	46,292	48,35	44,58	16,791	53,716	76,653
	Mapping Quality OK	293	978	1,074	1,108	1,049	467	742	1,102
	Mapping Quality BAD	742	2,512	0	0	0	0	3,706	1,68
	Unmapped Reads	0	0	0	0	0	0	0	0
	Wrong Reference in BAM	17	30	12	20	7	4	71	59
	Base Read Quality OK	27,649	92,251	104,073	106,903	100,937	44,9	107,427	156,036
	Base Read Quality BAD	1,944	6,527	4,401	5,005	5,012	2,267	3,873	9,264
	Bad Alignment	0	0	0	0	0	0	0	0
	Duplicates	0	0	0	0	0	0	0	0
	Short Reads (<25 bp)	0	0	0	0	0	0	0	0

(Table 1) contd.....

SMART2	Filtered mtDNA Read Pairs	872,55	5,174,00	/	1,492,542	789,545	10,847	3,099,482	1,931,744
	Filtered mtDNA Read average length (bp)	100.97	100.75	/	100.97	100.98	100.93	149.67	149.54
	N° of Contigs in Preliminary Assembly	139,66	706,438	/	391,732	130,721	2,762	120,364	357,75
	Longest linear contig in Preliminary Assembly	1,2	4,01	/	1,237	1,331	338	10,964	2,671
	N° of Contigs in Preliminary Filtering	80	95	/	122	76	0	15	103
	Longest linear contig in Preliminary Filtering	526	4,01	/	498	563	0	10,964	2,671
	Aligning mtDNA Reads Pairs	4,092	2,958	/	864	4,958	0	2,614	1,654
	Aligning mtDNA Reads Length (bp)	100.61	99.71	/	100.62	100.71	0	149.40	149.00
	SPAdes N° of Contigs	170	158	/	44	182	0	13	50
	SPAdes Longest linear contig	697	10,699	/	800	640	0	16,538	4,887
	Length of assembled mitogenome	2,244	8,341	/	2,311	1,301	0	16,57	4,935

Table 2. Alignment and assembly statistics of RNA-Seq analyzed samples. Table shows main features related to mapping and assembly step performed on RNA-Seq samples by CLC Genomics Workbench, SMART2 and y TRIMITOMICS algorithms.

	STATISTICS FEATURE	*0h_RPE*	*3h_RPE*	*6h_RPE*	*CCM_CTRL*	*CCM_1*	*CCM_2*
CLC GENOMICS WORKBENCH	**Overall Reads**	11,576,640	6,611,546	7,710,195	3,949,901	34,920,183	8,143,193
	Filtered Reads	11,136,765	6,479,554	7,548,160	6,308	34,148,713	20,006
	Passed Reads	439,875	131,992	162,035	3,943,593	771,47	8,123,187
	Passed FWD Reads	51,913,969	16,056,486	19,301,263	271,265,419	54,688,506	575,414,189
	Passed REV Reads	838,384	205,838	219,486	296,151,473	57,239,947	605,782,207
	Mapping Quality OK	440,014	132,054	162,126	3,943,593	771,47	8,123,187
	Mapping Quality BAD	29,372	10,603	15,517	5,846	36,505	18,526
	Unmapped Reads	0	0	0	0	0	0
	Wrong Reference in BAM	11,107,254	6,468,889	7,532,552	462	34,112,208	1,48
	Base Read Quality OK	52,752,353	16,262,324	19,520,749	567,416,892	111,928,453	1,181,196,396
	Base Read Quality BAD	15,127,187	3,805,671	4,905,387	28,065,651	4,563,517	45,404,841
	Bad Alignment	0	0	0	0	0	0
	Duplicates	0	0	0	0	0	0
	Short Reads (<25 bp)	0	0	0	0	0	0

(Table 2) contd.....

SMART2	Filtered mtDNA Read Pairs	/	/	/	60,538	9,604	85,767
	Filtered mtDNA Read average length (bp)	/	/	/	143.93	101.00	148.30
	N° of Contigs in Preliminary Assembly	/	/	/	38,84	130	57,282
	Longest linear contig in Preliminary Assembly	/	/	/	1,879	2,302	2,446
	N° of Contigs in Preliminary Filtering	/	/	/	227	18	327
	Longest linear contig in Preliminary Filtering	/	/	/	646	1,579	648
	Aligning mtDNA Reads Pairs	/	/	/	1,767	2,013	1,005
	Aligning mtDNA Reads Length (bp)	/	/	/	130.08	100.97	122.46
	SPAdes N° of Contigs	/	/	/	30	9	39
	SPAdes Longest linear contig	/	/	/	1,846	1,646	1,896
	Length of assembled mitogenome	/	/	/	2,037	4,766	2,742

(Table 2) contd.....

	Total Reads	/	/	/	21961017	16867127	36010378
	Paired Reads	/	/	/	21961017 (100.00%)	16867127 (100.00%)	36010378 (100.00%)
	Paired Reads aligned concordantly 0 times	/	/	/	20998795 (95.62%)	16452293 (97.54%)	33173694 (92.12%)
	Paired Reads aligned concordantly exactly 1 time	/	/	/	962222 (4.38%)	414834 (2.46%)	2836684 (7.88%)
	Paired Reads aligned concordantly >1 time	/	/	/	0 (0.00%)	0 (0.00%)	0 (0.00%)
	Pairs aligned concordantly 0 times	/	/	/	20998795	16452293	33173694
TRIMITOMICS	**Pairs aligned discordantly 1 time**	/	/	/	400225 (1.91%)	4969 (0.03%)	519967 (1.57%)
	Pairs aligned 0 times concordantly or discordantly	/	/	/	20598570	16447324	32653727
	Mates make up the pairs	/	/	/	41197140	32894648	65307454
	Mates aligned 0 times	/	/	/	41035881 (99.61%)	32880280 (99.96%)	65083869 (99.66%)
	Mates aligned exactly 1 time	/	/	/	161259 (0.39%)	14368 (0.04%)	223585 (0.34%)
	Mates aligned >1 time	/	/	/	0 (0.00%)	0 (0.00%)	0 (0.00%)
	Overall alignment rate	/	/	/	6.57%	2.53%	9.63%

The worst result was produced by analysis of ME_4 and ME_5 samples, detecting only the origin of heavy strand synthesis (OH). Transcriptome annotations evidenced one gene common to CCM_1 and CCM_2 (*NAD1*), and two genes detected only in CCM_CTRL sample (*COX1* and *LAGLI*). The complete protein plots are shown in Fig. (**3**). ME_1 and ME_4 were the most reliable in rRNA computation (e-values ~ 10^{-30}), while ME_6 showed the highest number of annotated tRNAs, as well as the widest positions covered among mitogenomes. RNA-Seq data annotation highlighted the longest tRNAs in both sample CCM_CTRL and CCM_2, even if with a good but not optimal significance (e-values ~ 10^{-7}). Details on rRNA and tRNA annotations are shown in the non-coding plots of Figs. (**4 - 6**). Interestingly, we were also able to compute the secondary structure of several rRNAs and tRNAs for each sample, the most significant of which are represented in Fig. (**6**). It is clear, especially for rRNAs, how changes in several nucleotides led to different RNA folding.

MtDNA Variant Calling and Annotations

The mtDNA-Server highlighted excellent results from previous alignment/ assembly steps, especially for WES samples, in which the highest coverage is reached around the 2,500 nt position (Fig. **7**). Similar or even better coverages were obtained from analysis of CCM transcriptomes, even if on a different scale, due to expression quantification, as already mentioned (Fig. **8**). Furthermore, CCM transcriptomes were the only ones that showed elevated level of heteroplasmic sites, with the highest peaks reached by *MT-CYB*, *MT-ND5*, *MT-RNR2* and *MT-ATP6* loci (Fig. **9**). WES analysis, instead, highlights only significant homoplasmic sites.

WES analyses evidenced an average value of 8 mtDNA variants throughout all samples, with one, RP32, reaching the highest number (n=16). These RP32 variants were prevalently in protein coding genes (n=15), one of which determining a stop codon gain with high functional impairment, even if the other one seems to be benign or shows a low impact on related encoded proteins. Curiously, the WES samples with the lowest number of identified variants, ME_5 (n=1) and ME_6 (n=2), presented alterations carried only by rRNA genes, exerting a modifier role. Another interesting aspect regards the presence of WES variants in the dbSNP database. Only 3 of them were polymorphic and known in dbSNP, showing that most of the detected variants are new mutations.

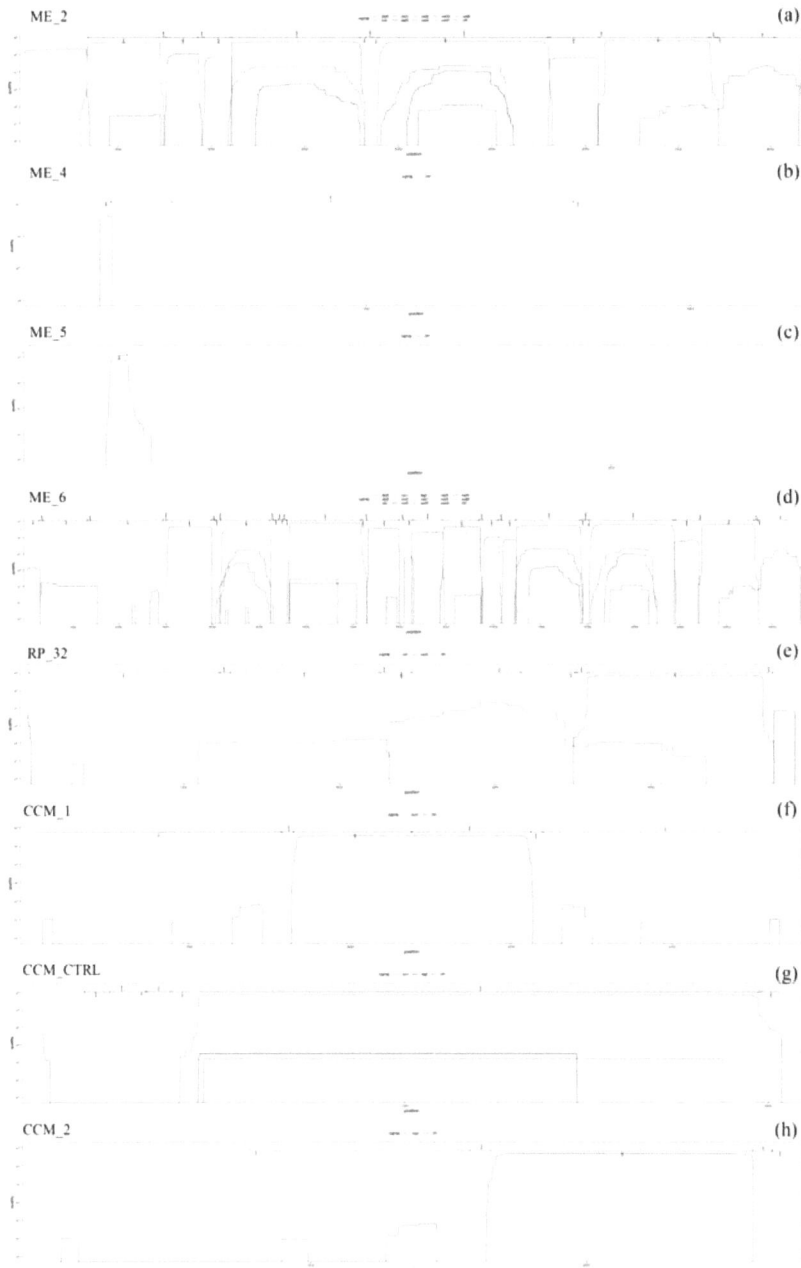

Fig. (3). MITOS2 protein plots. Figure shows MITOS2 annotated protein coding genes after congruences detection in the results of BLASTX searches. The protein plot shows the quality value for each gene and each position if it is above the threshold. Different genes are evidenced by distinctive colors. Briefly, the initial hits used in MITOS2 correspond to the "mountains" in this plot. The lines shown on the top of the plot represent the annotation reported. Quality values are shown on a log scale.

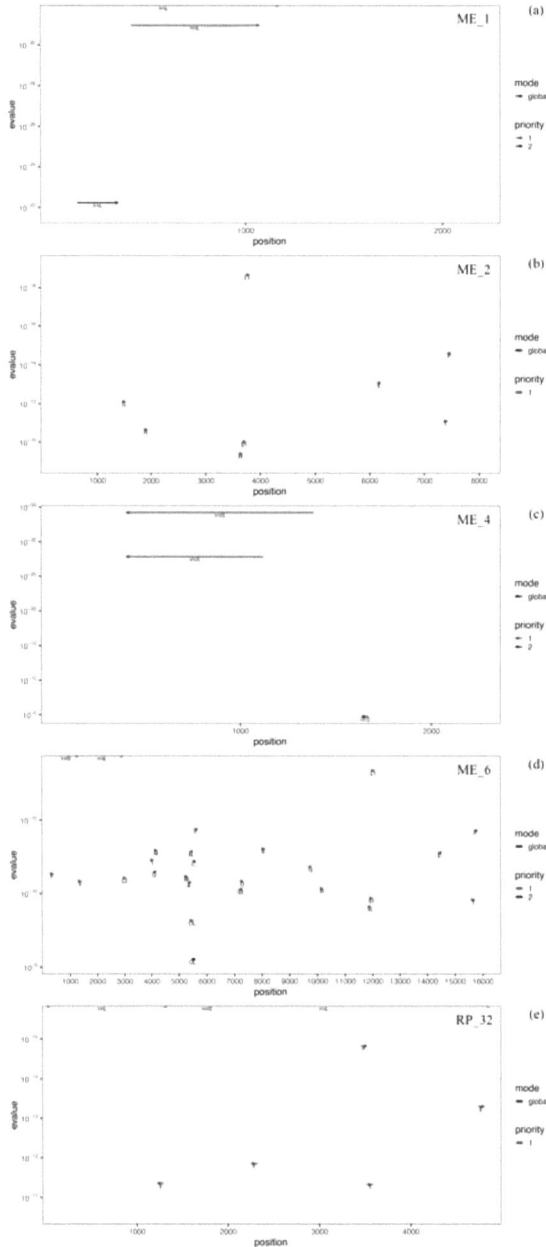

Fig. (4). MITOS2 non-coding RNA plot of WES samples. The non-coding RNA plot shows the hits from computation of rRNAs and tRNAs. The plot differentiates between the hits from the global and local (if present) search by line type. The hits are separated in priorities: priority "1" refers to features set in the first round when MITOS takes the prediction hit of each feature, and priority "2" refers to all other features set afterwards in the remaining unassigned regions. Reverse log scale for the e-value are considered.

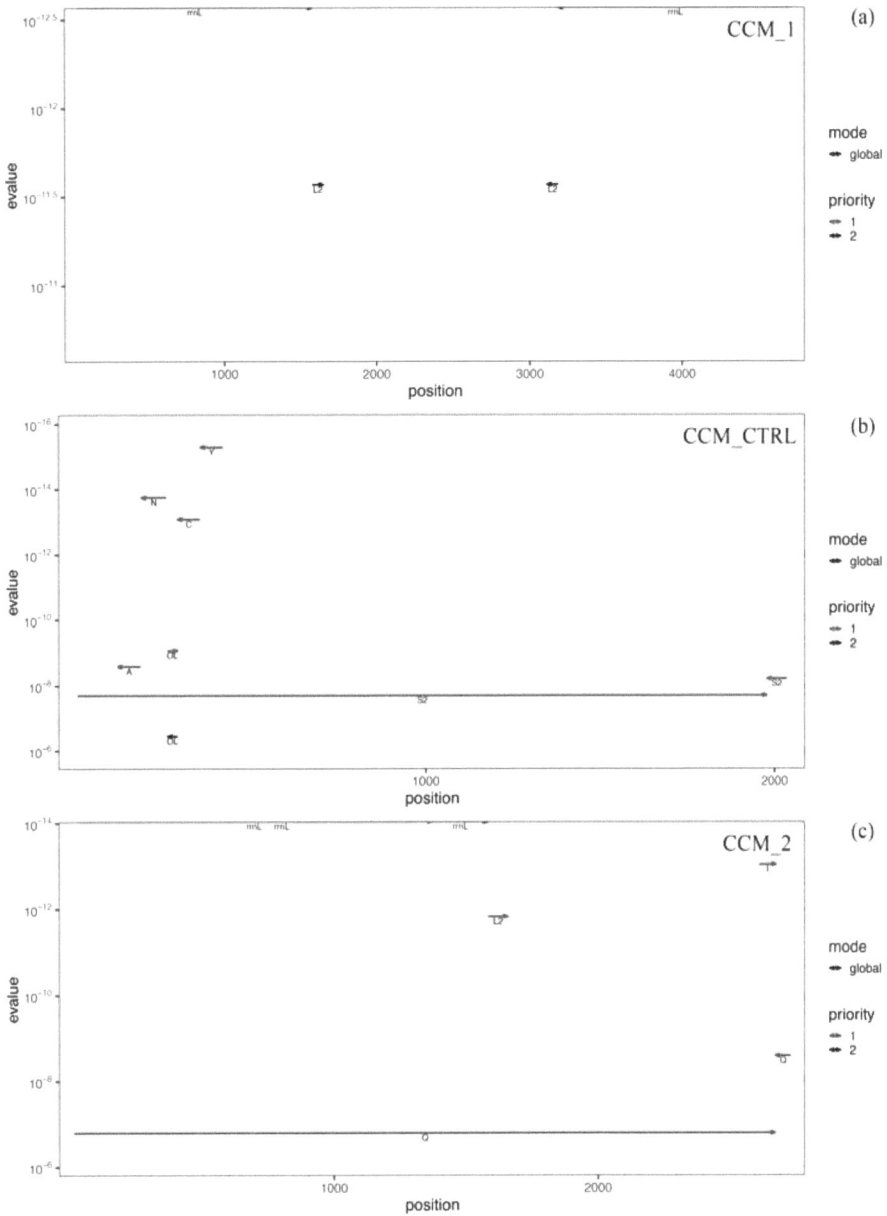

Fig. (5). MITOS2 non-coding RNA plot of RNA-Seq samples. The non-coding RNA plot shows the hits from computation of rRNAs and tRNAs on a sub-set of RNA-Seq samples. The plot differentiates between the hits from the global and local (if present) search by line type. The hits are separated in priorities: priority "1" refers to features set in the first round when MITOS takes the prediction hit of each feature, and priority "2" refers to all other features set afterwards in the remaining unassigned regions. Reverse log scale for the e-value are considered.

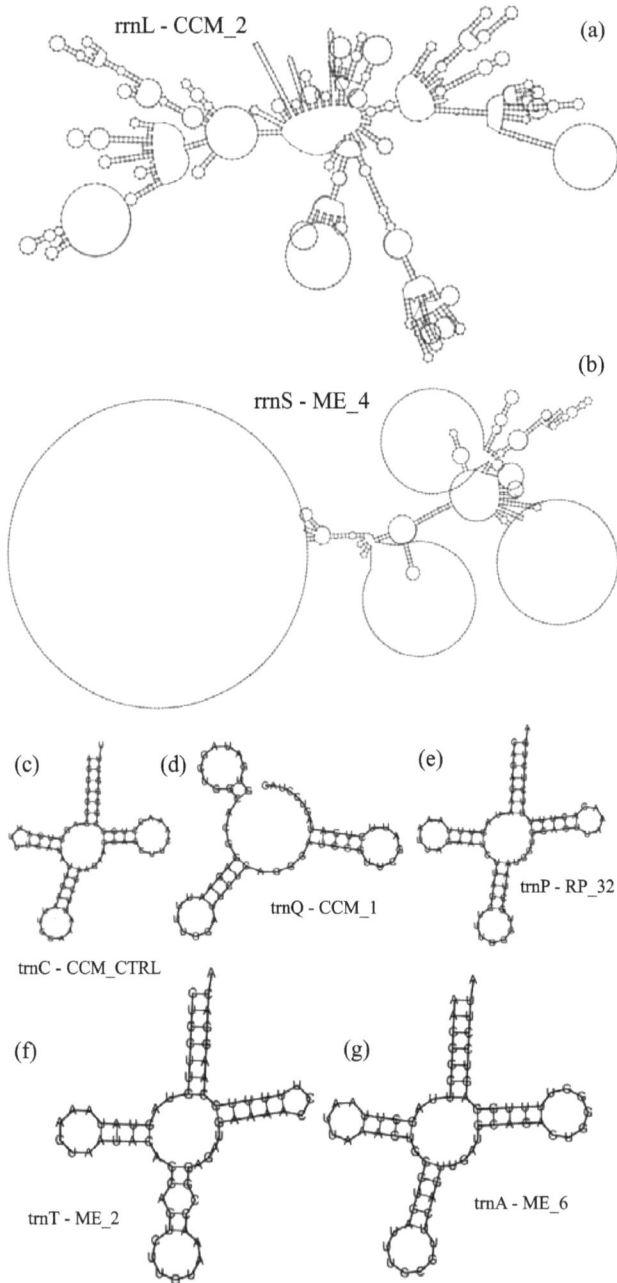

Fig. (6). MITOS2 computation of non-coding RNA secondary structure. Figures represent an example sub-set of computed secondary structures of rRNAs and tRNAs from MITOS2 analyses on both WES (b, e, f, g) and transcriptome (a, c, d) samples.

This scenario is totally opposite to RNA-Seq variant analyses, which identified a higher number of variants (average n=18), but nearly all reported in dbSNP. Thus, transcriptome variants were better annotated than WES ones and might be pathogenic, even if differently defined in relation to possible deleterious functional consequences. Variant annotation summary for both WES and RNA-Seq samples are available in Tables **3** & **4**.

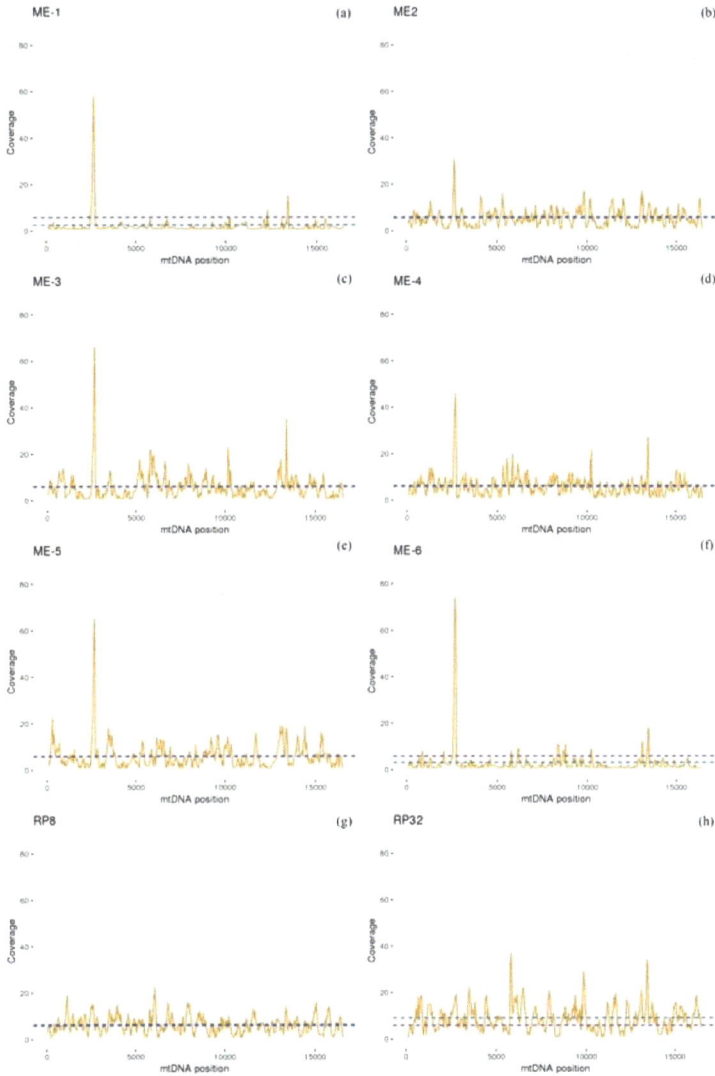

Fig. (7). MtDNA-Server coverage plots for WES samples. Figure shows coverage for each WES sample, which are especially relevant in detecting issues with incorrect concentration of polymerase chain reaction products for the used fragments.

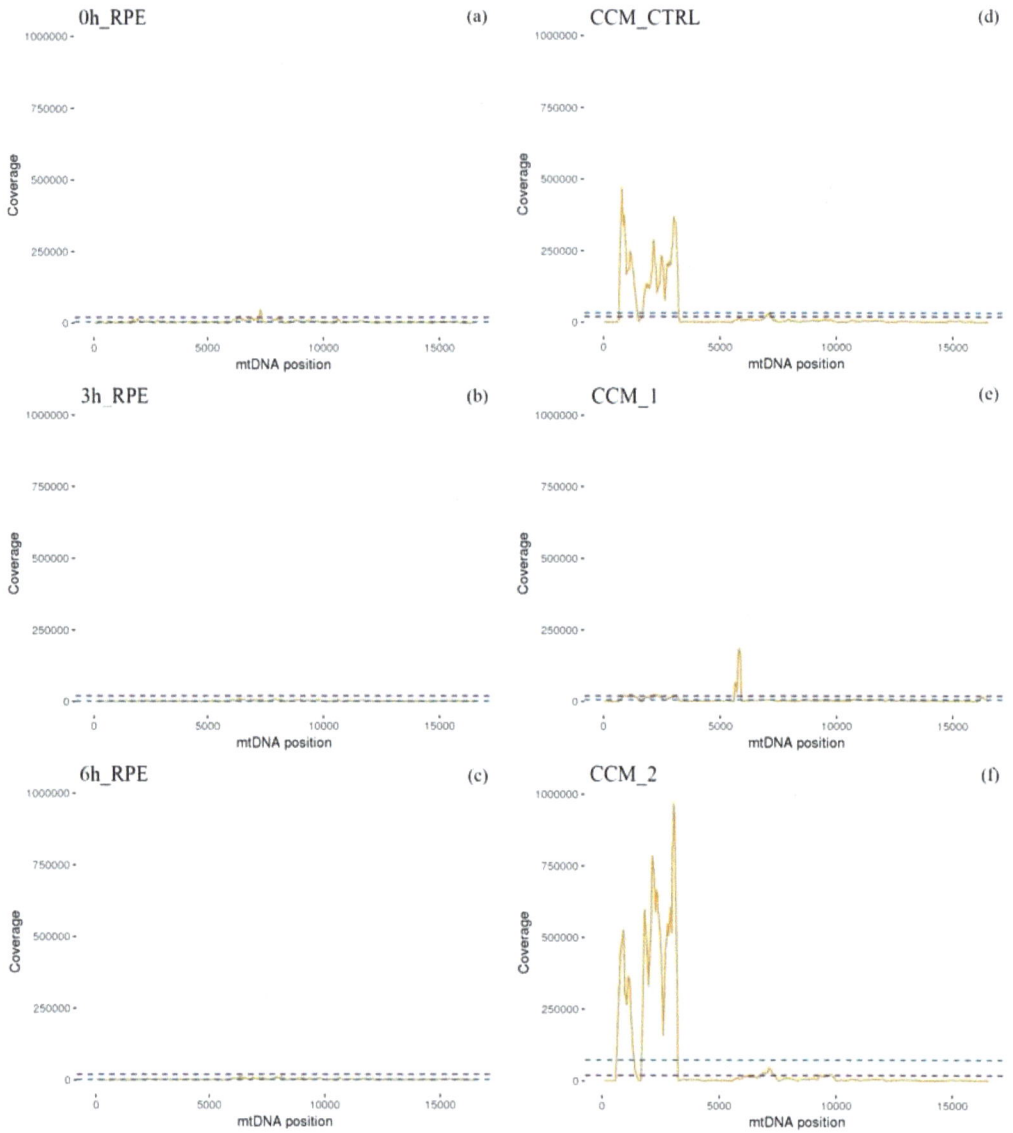

Fig. (8). MtDNA-Server coverage plots for WES samples. Figure shows coverage for each WES sample, which are especially relevant in detecting issues with incorrect concentration of polymerase chain reaction products for the used fragments.

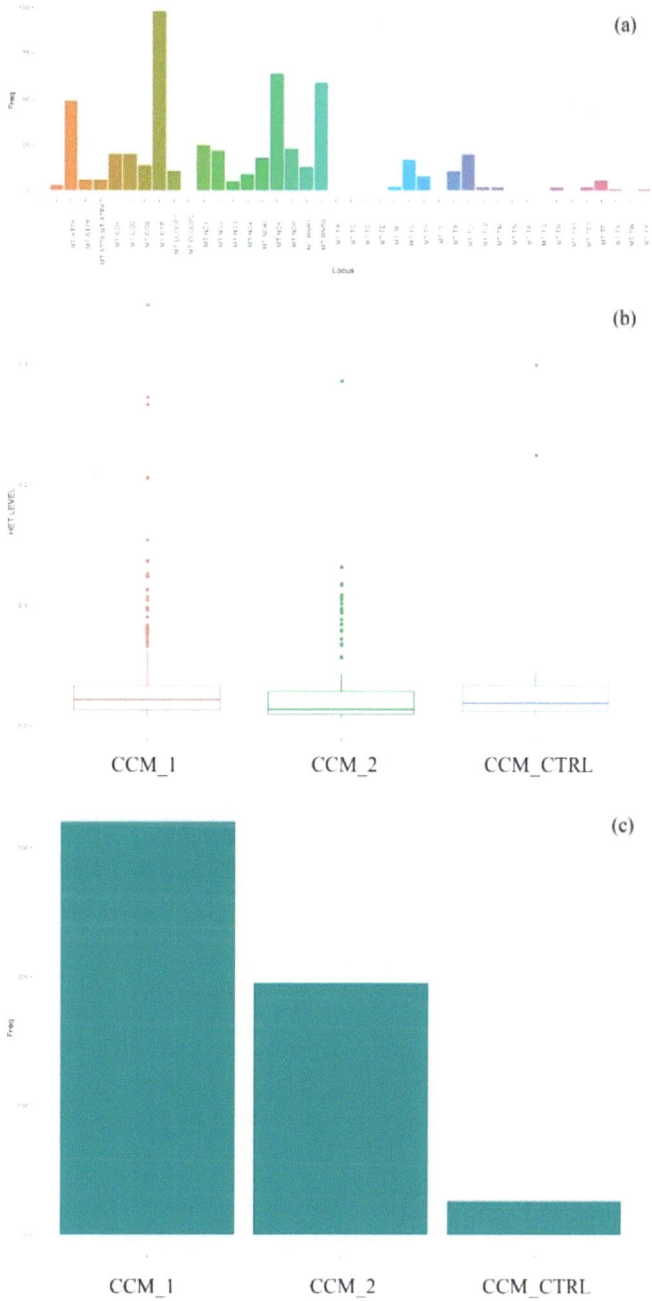

Fig. (9). Results of heteroplasmic analyses by mtDNA-Server. The tool mtDNA-Server found heteroplasmic significant results only in CCM samples. **a)** loci of the heteroplasmic variants on the mitogenomes over all CCM samples. **b)** boxplots of heteroplasmic level per sample. **c)** frequency of heteroplasmic variants as bar plots.

Table 3. WES sample variant annotation summary. Table reports main mitogenome variant annotations from investigated databases, using mvTool, MitoBreak and MitoMaster resources.

			ME_1	ME_2	ME_3	ME_4	ME_5	ME_6	RP_8	RP_32
mvTool	MSeqDR Community Data Population	N° Variants	3	10	10	13	1	2	0	16
		Mitomap Disease	0	0	0	0	0	0	0	0
		Mitomap Status	0	0	0	0	0	0	0	0
		HmtDB Pathogenicity	1 Pending, 1 Likely Benign	1 Pending, 2 Likely Benign	1 Pending, 1 Likely Benign	2 Pathogenic, 2 Likely Benign	0	0	0	3 Pending, 2 Likely Benign
	Disease and Phenotypes	dbSNP	0	0	1	1	0	1	0	3
		MSeqDR Clinical Significance	0	0	0	0	0	0	0	0
		HmtDB Disease	0	0	0	0	0	0	0	0
		COSMIC	0	1	0	0	0	0	0	1
		ICGC	0	1	0	0	0	0	0	2
	VEP	Impact	2 Low, 1 Moderate	7 Low, 2 Moderate, 1 Modifier	7 Low, 1 Moderate, 2 Modifier	11 Low, 4 Moderate, 2 Modifier	1 Modifier	2 Modifier	0	12 Low, 2 Moderate, 1 Modifier, 1 High
		Biotype	3 Protein Coding	9 Protein Coding, 1 mt_rRNA	8 Protein Coding, 2 mt_rRNA	11 Protein Coding, 2 mt_rRNA	1 mt_rRNA	2 mt_rRNA	0	15 Protein Coding, 1 mt_rRNA
		Consequence Terms	2 Synonymous, 1 Missense	5 Synonymous, 2 Missense	4 Synonymous, 1 Missense	6 Synonymous, 4 Missense	0	0	0	10 Synonymous, 2 Missense, 1 Stop Gained, 1 Non-coding Transcript Exon
	CADD	Raw Raknscore	0	0	0	0	0	0	0	0
	HmtDB Patho Table	N° Variants	0	0	0	0	0	0	0	0
		Pathogenicity	0	0	0	0	0	0	0	0
MitoBreak		N° Deletions	0	0	0	1	0	0	0	0
		Healthy Tissue	0	0	0	0	0	0	0	0
		Del of replication origins	0	0	0	None	0	0	0	0
		Location of the deleted regions	0	0	0	Inside the major arc	0	0	0	0

(Table 3) contd.....

MitoMaster	N° Variants	2 Transitions, 1 Transversion	9 Transitions, 1 Transversion	8 Transitions, 2 Transversion	11 Transitions, 2 Transversion	1 Transitions	2 Transitions	0	15 Transitions, 1 Transversion
	Mut Type	3 Coding	9 Coding, 1 rRNA	8 Coding, 2 rRNA	11 Coding, 2 rRNA	1 rRNA	2 rRNA	0	15 Coding, 1 rRNA
	Patient Report	0	0	0	0	0	0	0	0

Table 4. RNA-Seq sample variant annotation summary. Table reports main mitogenome variant annotations from investigated databases, using mvTool, MitoBreak and MitoMaster resources.

			0h_RPE	3h_RPE	6h_RPE	CCM_CTRL	CCM_1	CCM_2
mvTool	MSeqDR Community Data Population	N° Variants	20	21	21	13	8	24
		Mitomap Disease	4	4	4	0	1	4
		Mitomap Status	3 Reported, 1 Conflicting	3 Reported, 1 Conflicting	3 Reported, 1 Conflicting	0	Conflicting	Reported
		HmtDB Pathogenicity	8 Pending, 4 Benign	8 Pending, 4 Benign	9 Pending, 4 Benign	6 Pending, 2 Benign, 1 Likely Benign, 1 Pathogenic	5 Pending, 2 Benign	13 Pending, 2 Benign, 1 Likely Pathogenic, 1 Polymorphic tRNA
	Disease and Phenotypes	dbSNP	17	17	18	8	7	22
		MSeqDR Clinical Significance	4 Likely Pathogenic, 2 Not Provided	4 Likely Pathogenic, 2 Not Provided	4 Likely Pathogenic, 2 Not Provided	1 Likely Pathogenic, 1 Benign, 3 Not Provided	1 Likely Pathogenic, 1 Likely Benign 2 Not Provided	3 Likely Pathogenic, 1 Benign, 2 Not Provided
		HmtDB Disease	4	4	4	3	2	6
		COSMIC	1	1	1	0	0	1
		ICGC	2	2	2	1	0	3
	VEP	Impact	11 Low, 4 Moderate, 5 Modifier	11 Low, 5 Moderate, 5 Modifier	11 Low, 4 Moderate, 5 Modifier	3 Low, 4 Moderate, 6 Modifier	1 Low, 2 Moderate, 5 Modifier	12 Low, 3 Moderate, 9 Modifier
		Biotype	20 Protein Coding	21 Protein Coding	20 Protein Coding, 1 mt_rRNA	10 Protein Coding, 3 mt_rRNA	6 Protein Coding, 2 mt_rRNA	21 Protein Coding, 2 mt_tRNA, 1 mt_rRNA
		Consequence Terms	11 Synonymous, 3 Missense, 4 Upstream	11 Synonymous, 5 Missense, 4 Upstream	11 Synonymous, 3 Missense, 4 Upstream, 1 Non-coding Transcript Exon	12 Synonymous, 3 Missense, 5 Upstream, 3 Non-coding Transcript Exon	1 Synonymous, 2 Missense, 2 Upstream, 1 Non-coding Transcript Exon	3 Synonymous, 4 Missense, 2 Upstream, 2 Non-coding Transcript Exon
	CADD	Raw Raknscore	1	1	1	1	0	1
	HmtDB Patho Table	N° Variants	3	3	3	4	4	5
		Pathogenicity	1	1	1	1	2	2

(Table 4) contd.....

MitoBreak	N° Deletions	0	1	0	0	0	1
	Healthy Tissue	0	Aged Tissues	0	0	0	Unfertilized oocytes, arrested(...)
	Del of replication origins	0	None	0	0	0	None
	Location of the deleted regions	0	Inside the major arc	0	0	0	Inside the major arc
MitoMaster	N° Variants	20 Transitions	20 Transitions, 1 Transversion	21 Transitions	12 Transitions, 1 Transversion	8 Transitions	24 Transitions
	Mut Type	15 Coding, 5 Non-coding	17 Coding, 4 Non-coding	16 Coding, 5 Non-coding	7 Coding, 3 Non-coding, 3 rRNA	5 Coding, 3 Non-coding	17 Coding, 6 Non-coding, 1 rRNA
	Patient Report	4	4	4	0	1	4

In Silico Functional Consequences and Pathogenicity Predictions

The last step of performed pipeline foresaw the use of *in silico* predictions, to clarify the possible consequences of identified variants, especially ones which lack certain effects such as VUS. WES results highlighted a prevalence of deleterious consequences among the 25 unique variants identified by mvTool and MITIMPACT 3D, as evidenced by Polyphen2 (15/25), Provean (19/25), Panther (22/25), Phd-SNP (17/25), SNAP (17/25), and Meta-SNP (17/25). Interestingly, HmtVAR detected a further 5 unique variants (30), and most of the 30 identified were found in protein coding sequences (26/30), even if only 2 were pathogenic. Almost all variants (24) were computed by EVmutation, quantifying simultaneously the effects of multiple mutations by explicitly modeling interactions between all the pairs of residues in proteins (and bases in RNAs). The impact of the latter analysis is further corroborated by the total absence of CPD, which increases the probability that hypothesized effects of detected variants are truly positive. The scenario could also represent an important discovery as all variants seem to be new mutations, given their absence both in dbSNP and CLINVAR (Table **5**).

Table 5. *In silico* prediction analyses report. Table shows principal results on pathogenicity prediction of identified variants through all samples. The main macro-resources used are highlighted in red.

MitImpact 3D		ME_1	ME_2	ME_3	ME_4	ME_5	ME_6	RP_8	RP_32	0h_RPE	3h_RPE	6h_RPE	CCM_CTRL	CCM_1	CCM_2
N° Variants		3	10	10	13	1	2	0	16	20	21	21	13	8	24
PolyPhen 2	Benign	1	3	1	2				3	7	7	7	4	2	4
	Probably damaging	0	2	2	5				6	4	5	4	1	0	5

(Table 5) contd.....

SIFT	Neutral	1	5	3	7			9	9	9	9	5	2	7
	Deleterious	0	0	0	0			0	2	3	2	0	0	2
FatHmm	Neutral	1	4	2	5			7	8	8	8	3	2	5
	Deleterious	0	1	1	2			2	3	4	3	2	0	4
PROVEAN	Neutral	1	1	1	2			1	7	8	7	3	1	2
	Deleterious	0	4	2	5			8	4	4	4	2	1	7
Mutation Assessor	Neutral Impact	1	2	1	2			2	4	3	4	1	1	1
	Low impact	0	2	0	0			2	2	2	2	1	0	2
	Medium impact	0	1	0	2			1	2	2	2	1	1	3
	High impact	0	0	2	3			4	2	3	2	1	0	2
EFIN_SP	Neutral	1	4	2	3			5	9	10	9	5	2	7
	Damaging	0	1	1	4			4	2	2	2	0	0	2
EFIN_HD	Neutral	1	5	2	3			6	9	9	9	4	2	7
	Damaging	0	0	1	4			3	2	3	2	1	0	2
CADD	Neutral	1	2	1	2			2	5	4	5	3	2	3
	Deleterious	0	3	2	5			7	6	8	6	2	0	6
PANTHER	Neutral	0	0	0	2			1	6	7	6	4	2	5
	Disease	1	5	3	5			8	3	3	3	1	0	4
PhD-SNP	Neutral	1	2	1	2			2	5	4	5	2	1	1
	Disease	0	3	2	5			7	6	8	6	3	1	8
SNAP	Neutral	1	2	1	2			2	4	3	4	2	1	3
	Disease	0	3	2	5			7	5	7	5	3	1	6
Meta-SNP	Neutral	1	1	1	3			1	6	6	6	3	1	3
	Disease	0	4	2	4			8	5	6	5	2	1	6
CAROL	Neutral	1	4	1	2			4	6	6	6	4	2	5
	Deleterious	0	1	2	5			5	3	4	3	1	0	4
Condel	Neutral	0	2	2	5			4	3	4	3	1	0	4
	Deleterious	1	3	1	2			5	8	8	8	4	2	5
COVEC_WMV	Neutral	1	4	1	2			4	6	6	6	4	2	5
	Deleterious	0	1	2	5			5	3	4	3	1	0	4
MToolBox	Neutral	1	2	1	2			2	5	5	5	3	2	4
	Deleterious	0	3	2	5			7	6	7	6	2	0	5
APOGEE	N	1	3	1	3			5	9	10	9	4	2	5
	P	0	2	2	4			4	2	2	2	1	0	4
Mutation Taster	Polymorphism	1	3	2	7			4	7	7	7	3	2	8
	Disease Causing	0	2	1	0			5	2	3	2	2	0	1
dbSNP	SNP	0	0	0	0			0	4	4	4	2	2	4
	New Mutation	1	5	3	7			9	7	8	7	3	0	5
CLINVAR	Yes	0	0	0	0			0	2	2	2	1	1	1
	No	1	5	3	7			9	9	10	9	4	1	8
Mitomap	Yes	0	0	0	0			0	0	0	0	0	0	2
	No	1	5	3	7			9	9	10	9	5	2	7
Mitoclass1	Neutral	1	4	1	2			4	8	7	8	3	2	3
	Damaging	0	1	2	5			5	3	5	3	2	0	6
DDG_Intra	Yes	0	0	0	2			0	6	6	6	4	2	6
	No	1	5	3	5			9	5	6	5	1	0	3
DDG_Inter	Yes	0	0	0	1			0	1	1	1	1	0	0
	No	1	5	3	6			9	8	9	8	4	2	9

(Table 5) contd.....

EV_Mutation	Yes	1	5	3	7				8	5	5	5	4	1	7
	No	0	0	0	0				1	6	7	6	1	1	2
CPD	Yes	0	0	0	0				0	1	1	1	0	0	0
	No	1	5	3	7				9	10	11	10	5	2	9
HmtVAR	N° Variants	0	10	3	9	1			7	0	16	1	13	3	14
	CDS	0	9	2	9	0			6	0	13	0	7	1	8
	Regulatory	0	0	0	0	0			0	0	3	0	3	1	4
	rRNA	0	1	1	0	1			1	0	0	1	3	1	0
	tRNA	0	0	0	0	0			0	0	0	0	0	0	2
	Polymorphic	0	0	0	0	0			0	0	2	0	2	0	0
	Likely Polymorphic	0	2	0	2	0			0	0	0	0	1	0	1
	Likely Pathogenic	0	0	0	0	0			0	0	0	0	0	0	2
	Pathogenic	0	0	0	2	0			0	0	1	0	1	0	0
Pon-mt-tRNA	N° Variants	0	0	0	0				0	0	0	0	0	0	2
	Classification	/	/	/	/				/	/	/	/	/	/	Likely Neutral

Yet again, the situation is drastically different in RNA-Seq samples where, even if 50 variants were detected by mvTool and MITIMPACT 3D throughout all transcriptomes, just a few databases assigned a damaging role to only about half of the variants. These databases were CADD (28/50), PhD-SNP (32/50), SNAP (27/50), Condel (35/50) and MToolBox (26/50). Also EVmutation outputted results for only 27/50, limiting the cumulative impact of multiple variants. Again, the low number of variants involved in CPD (3/50) evidenced the consistency of obtained data. Curiously, HmtVAR classified most of the identified variants as CDS (29/50) and regulatory (11/50), providing important evidence on the different kinds of impact probably determined by these variants, as corroborated by the presence of two of them in the Pon-mt-tRNA database. This time, however, several variants were found on CLINVAR (9/50), but most of the total ones were also present on dbSNP, suggesting the polymorphic nature of identified variants (Table **5**).

Regarding haplogroup classification, as highlighted in Table **6**, most of the WES samples probably belonged to H2a2a1 haplogroup, as seen from both the mtDNA-Server and HaploGrep2. RPE cell transcriptomes, instead, showed a putative assignment to U5b1b1+@16192 haplogroup, as outputted by both the mtDNA-Server and EMPOP database. Additionally, the latter evidenced geographical distribution of haplogroup-related variants, suggesting that most of them are typically from Central Europe, Latin America and South-Central Asia (Fig. **10**). Furthermore, HaploGrep2 analysis provided the phylogenetic trees of haplogroup-related variants that are only represented for two samples of each NGS analyzed categories, due to the large space that the representation of such data requires (Fig. **11**). However, several samples failed haplogrouping, probably due to the lack of the whole mitogenome sequence.

Fig. (10). EMPOP geographic map of query haplogroups distribution. Figure is a screenshot of an interactive map that depicts the sampled populations within the query range (red) and matches in the sampled populations (green) for haplogrouping analysis in EMPOP.

Table 6. Haplogrouping analyses result summary. Table presents main outcomes produced by mtDNA-Server, MToolBox, Haplogrep2 and EMPOP analyses.

	mtDNA-Server Haplogroups	MToolBox Best Predicted Haplogroups	EMPOP Haplogrouping (Best Rank)	Haplogrep2 Haplogroups
ME_1	H2a2a1	/	/	/
ME_2	H2a2a1	120	/	H2a2a1
ME_3	H2a2a1	/	/	/
ME_4	H2a2a1	1508	/	/
ME_5	H2a2a1	822	/	/
ME_6	H2a2a1	H72	/	H2a2a1
RP_8	/	/	/	/
RP_32	H2a2a1	/	/	H2a2a1
0h_RPE	U5b1b1+@16192	/	U5b1b1+@16192	/
3h_RPE	U5b1b1+@16192	/	U5b1b1+@16192	/
6h_RPE	U5b1b1+@16192	/	U5b1b1+@16192	/
CCM_CTRL	H5'36	/	U5b1b1+152	/
CCM_1	H2a1a	/	U5b1b1+152	H2a2a1
CCM_2	K1a1b1	L2'3'4'5'6	U5b1b1+152	H2a2a1

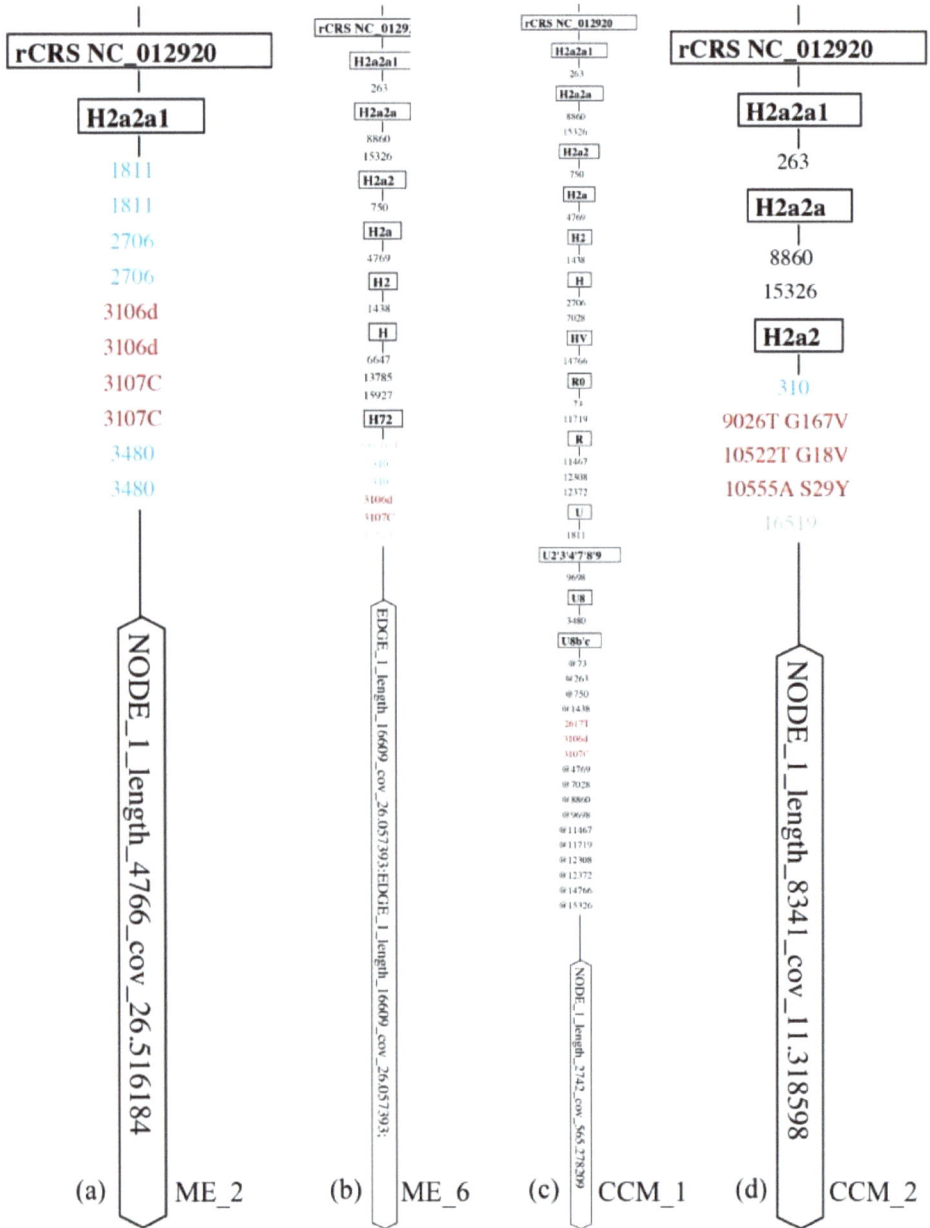

Fig. (11). Haplogrep2 graphical phylogenetic tree of a sub-group of identified variants. Polymorphisms in the tips of the phylogeny are candidates for new haplogroups. Polymorphisms marked in red do not occur in phylogenetic tree and may require further attention, whereas mutations in blue are private polymorphisms for this group, already known by Phylotree. The annotation of amino acid changes and mutational hotspots (green) can be defined by the user.

DISCUSSION

With the advent of "omics" sciences and the development of specific bioinformatics algorithms, the analysis of mitochondrial DNA and its linkage to related diseases became systematic. mtDNA variants could be classified into four different categories: protein mutations, tRNA and rRNA variants which determine impairments in polypeptide synthesis, rearrangement mutations and mutations carried by the regulatory region that could alter mtDNA transcription and replication [64]. Among disorders already known to be determined by such variants, we could cite Lactic acidosis, Kearns-Sayre Syndrome (KSS), Mitochondrial Encephalopathy, Pearson syndrome, Stroke-like episodes (MELAS), Leigh syndrome, Myoclonus Epilepsy with Ragged Red Fibers, Leber Hereditary Optic Neuropathy (LHON) [65]. Moreover, impairments in mitochondrial function could be involved in the etiopathology of cancer, as well as in etiology of metabolic diseases such as fatty liver diseases, adipose tissue inflammation, type-2 diabetes and cardiovascular diseases [66]. However, the best characterized mitochondrial link with diseases consists of oxidative stress induced pathologies, such as Parkinson's, Alzheimer's, and other neurodegenerative diseases [67].

Thus, we analyzed 15 samples from patients affected by pathologies potentially induced by oxidative stress damage to unveil what nowadays remains very challenging: the putative role of still unknown mtDNA variants in onset and progression of disease not yet linked to mitochondria. Our purpose was to develop a new analytic pipeline able to mix the advantages of the most recently developed tools and updated databases, to improve output and minimize their biases.

First of all, we decided to consider the most analyzed type of samples in NGS experiments, such as WES and RNA-Seq, to maximize the usefulness of the pipeline to the widest fields of genomics. As already evidenced, analyses on two distinct kinds of samples provided radically different results, starting from the initial step of mitogenome assembly to variant identification and annotation.

The most complete alignment/assembly algorithm was the CLC Genomics Workbench proprietary one which, while producing the best results with WES samples, overestimated RNA-Seq ones. As already mentioned, this could be an intrinsic factor due to the expression counts from transcriptomes analyses, that cannot be totally removed by the standard pipeline of commercial tools. More reliable assemblies were retrieved from SMART2 outputs, which highlighted very good results on nearly all samples, focusing more on assembly parameter optimization. This algorithm reduced RNA-Seq overestimation, probably thanks to its peculiarity of working in the presence of repeats. Only RPE cell transcriptomes failed the assembly phase, probably due to the highest number of wrongly reference-aligned reads in BAM produced files. Thus, we tried to face the RNA-Seq challenge by applying the specific meta-algorithm TRIMITOMICS, which combined three different methods (NOVOPlasty, Bowtie2/Trinity and Velvet) of mt genome recovery from transcriptome data. Also in this case, we did not obtain perfect results, but we were able to improve mitogenome assemblies, as evidenced by data shown in Bowtie2 output. Once data was obtained from all algorithms, we assembled them into a metamitogenome (one for each sample), to retrieve the most possible mt genome and annotated it with MITOS. The latter, thanks to a mixed approach based on multi-BLASTed searches, permitted to bypass the necessity for a built-in database of specifically curated protein, tRNA and rRNA mitochondrial models, drastically improving the consistence of assembled mitogenomes.

Then, we performed variant calling and annotation, using mtDNA-Server and several continuously updated databases. The importance of analyses realized by mtDNA-Server lies in the possibility to detect homoplasmic and heteroplasmic variants in a secure and reproducible way, also detecting within-sample contamination on the basis of mitochondrial haplogroups. This level of accuracy is fundamental as, while higher error rates within NGS can be balanced by higher sequencing depth for variant detection, interpretation of results is very delicate when it is necessary to analyze VAF < 10%, which is also one of the most serious limits of Sanger sequencing.

Database explorations are more critical, especially regarding population and clinical data. The frequency of mtDNA variants in a general population is not available in typical exome/genome related databases such as GNOMAD, so it is necessary to look at dedicated resources. Among them, the most updated are Mitomap and HmtDB, containing essential information on the mitochondrial reference sequence, along with an extensive compilation of mtDNA variants. Even if they are quite complete, several aspects are not totally covered, such as mtDNA rearrangements with related breakpoints. Thus, we improved this flaw adding data from MitoBreak, probably the most complete database in the field, frequently used to discover mitochondrial DNA deletion breakpoints in mtDNA related diseases [68]. Curiously, only variants from transcriptome analyses were found in the three cited databases, probably due to higher expression of carrying genes. In the meantime, the absence of data on variants detected by WES could be seen as some interesting information, which might be novel mutations related to diseases of interest. However, before investigating clinical databases, we had to tackle several aspects of mtDNA genetics.

The first was to assess the threshold effect, a phenomenon for which a huge number of mtDNA variants only cause clinical manifestations when present in a given tissue at a certain heteroplasmy level [69]. A common assumption is that mutation levels above 70% are generally more likely to manifest with mitochondrial disease symptoms, though several mutations manifest with severe disease even at much lower mtDNA mutation levels, probably in relation to impact on encoded protein function.

Furthermore, pathogenic interpretation of variant frequency throughout a general population is more challenging as previously cited databases do not consider variant frequency within a peculiar haplogroup, which might lead to misinterpretation due to underrepresentation of several groups. Many ethnic backgrounds do not show symptoms of mtDNA disease mutations exhibited by other ethnic groups. This has led to the hypothesis that the haplogroup might play a role in modulating variant pathogenicity [70]. To overcome this problem, we added results retrieved from haplogrouping analyses carried out by the mtDNA-Server itself, MToolBox, HaploGrep2 and the forensic database EMPOP, which highlighted common haplogroups for WES samples (H2a2a1) and RNA-Seq ones (U5b1b1), giving strength to identified variants.

Given the particular biology of mtDNA discussed above, mtDNA variant pathogenicity assessment might be challenging, especially for new mutations or VUS, frequently inconsistence between different databases and diagnostic laboratories. Benign variants are by definition irrelevant to disease; however, they can be present at variable levels in different tissues. This condition increases suspicion of its pathogenicity, especially if the above-mentioned threshold effect is exceeded. Furthermore, even if several guidelines for mtDNA variant pathogenicity classification have been suggested [71], currently none is extensively followed. Clinical databases combining mtDNA variants and clinical information such as CLINVAR, COSMIC and ENSEMBL are available. However, as already cited, mtDNA specific data, such as haplogroup frequency and heteroplasmy, are not systematically reported in each database, especially if not mitochondrial specialized. This scenario increases the necessity to develop pipeline collecting information from multiple resources to provide a complete description of the variants.

Thus, we used multiple dedicated web-based resources and databases developed to support the clinical assessment of mtDNA variants in individuals with suspected mitochondrial disease. Analyses with these *in silico* prediction tools, frequently based on approaches assessing interspecies sequence conservation and/or structure analysis, permitted to evaluate the functional impact of mitogenome variations. The widest collection of structurally and evolutionary annotated pathogenicity predictions is MitImpact 3D. As already shown in the results section, outcomes from this database, combined with those from MSeqDR, HmtVar, MToolBox, Mitotip and Pon-mt-tRNA, could offer useful insights into the susceptibility of non-synonymous mutations in mitochondrial protein-coding genes, despite major inconsistencies deriving from different algorithms they were based on.

Analyses of WES and RNA-Seq samples showed a trend similar to the one already evidenced in the annotation step involving known variants, with a higher number of predicted variants that characterized transcriptome outputs, but with a global prevalence of pathogenicity within exome produced data. Thus, all the data produced by the entire pipeline permitted to obtain robust and reliable data, useful for further biological interpretations.

CONCLUSION AND PERSPECTIVES

Thanks to continuously updated and improved next generation sequencing technologies, we now have access to the entire mtDNA sequencing data, which is constantly being increased. However, the complexity of mtDNA interpretation is exponentially growing, requiring better and more specific analytic pipelines to assess mtDNA variant pathogenicity or additional information, such as mitochondrial haplogroups, identification of helper or synergistic mutations and co-occurrences of variants. These powerful results, along with further pathway analyses to decrypt the biological role of involved genes, should be incorporated into clinical diagnostic settings, as they are hypothesized to modulate the phenotypic expression of mtDNA pathogenic variants. In this way, an integrative analysis of the mitochondrial genome, together with the nuclear genome, could drastically improve the field of precision molecular medicine, with the final goal to improve patients' healthcare.

REFERENCES

[1]   van der Bliek AM, Sedensky MM, Morgan PG. Cell biology of the mitochondrion. Genetics 2017; 207(3): 843-71.
      [http://dx.doi.org/10.1534/genetics.117.300262] [PMID: 29097398]

[2]   Agrawal A, Mabalirajan U. Rejuvenating cellular respiration for optimizing respiratory function: targeting mitochondria. Am J Physiol Lung Cell Mol Physiol 2016; 310(2): L103-13.
      [http://dx.doi.org/10.1152/ajplung.00320.2015] [PMID: 26566906]

[3]   Dennerlein S, Wang C, Rehling P. Plasticity of mitochondrial translation. Trends Cell Biol 2017; 27(10): 712-21.
      [http://dx.doi.org/10.1016/j.tcb.2017.05.004] [PMID: 28606446]

[4]   Yan C, Duanmu X, Zeng L, Liu B, Song Z. Mitochondrial DNA: Distribution, mutations, and elimination. Cells 2019; 8(4): E379.
      [http://dx.doi.org/10.3390/cells8040379] [PMID: 31027297]

[5]   Farge G, Falkenberg M. Organization of DNA in mammalian mitochondria. Int J Mol Sci 2019;

20(11): E2770.
[http://dx.doi.org/10.3390/ijms20112770] [PMID: 31195723]

[6]   Lalueza-Fox C, Sampietro ML, Gilbert MT, *et al.* Unravelling migrations in the steppe: Mitochondrial DNA sequences from ancient central Asians. Proc Biol Sci 2004; 271(1542): 941-7.
[http://dx.doi.org/10.1098/rspb.2004.2698] [PMID: 15255049]

[7]   Yasukawa T, Yang MY, Jacobs HT, Holt IJ. A bidirectional origin of replication maps to the major noncoding region of human mitochondrial DNA. Mol Cell 2005; 18(6): 651-62.
[http://dx.doi.org/10.1016/j.molcel.2005.05.002] [PMID: 15949440]

[8]   Nicholls TJ, Minczuk M. In D-loop: 40 years of mitochondrial 7S DNA. Exp Gerontol 2014; 56: 175-81.
[http://dx.doi.org/10.1016/j.exger.2014.03.027] [PMID: 24709344]

[9]   Donato L, D'Angelo R, Alibrandi S, Rinaldi C, Sidoti A, Scimone C. Effects of A2E-induced oxidative stress on retinal epithelial cells: New insights on differential gene response and retinal dystrophies. Antioxidants 2020; 9(4): E307.
[http://dx.doi.org/10.3390/antiox9040307] [PMID: 32290199]

[10]   Donato L, Scimone C, Alibrandi S, *et al.* Discovery of *GLO1* new related genes and pathways by RNA-Seq on A2E-stressed retinal epithelial cells could improve knowledge on retinitis pigmentosa. Antioxidants 2020; 9(5): E416.
[http://dx.doi.org/10.3390/antiox9050416] [PMID: 32413970]

[11]   Donato L, Scimone C, Alibrandi S, Rinaldi C, Sidoti A, D'Angelo R. Transcriptome analyses of lncRNAs in A2E-stressed retinal epithelial cells unveil advanced links between metabolic impairments related to oxidative stress and retinitis pigmentosa. Antioxidants 2020; 9(4): E318.
[http://dx.doi.org/10.3390/antiox9040318] [PMID: 32326576]

[12]   Nissanka N, Moraes CT. Mitochondrial DNA damage and reactive oxygen species in neurodegenerative disease. FEBS Lett 2018; 592(5): 728-42.
[http://dx.doi.org/10.1002/1873-3468.12956] [PMID: 29281123]

[13]   El-Hattab AW, Craigen WJ, Scaglia F. Mitochondrial DNA maintenance defects. Biochim Biophys Acta Mol Basis Dis 2017; 1863(6): 1539-55.
[http://dx.doi.org/10.1016/j.bbadis.2017.02.017] [PMID: 28215579]

[14]   Brandon MC, Lott MT, Nguyen KC, *et al.* MITOMAP: a human mitochondrial genome database-2004 update. Nucleic Acids Res 2005; 33(Database issue): D611-3.
[http://dx.doi.org/10.1093/nar/gki079] [PMID: 15608272]

[15]   Chinnery PF, Hudson G. Mitochondrial genetics. Br Med Bull 2013; 106: 135-59.
[http://dx.doi.org/10.1093/bmb/ldt017] [PMID: 23704099]

[16]   Duan M, Chen L, Ge Q, *et al.* Evaluating heteroplasmic variations of the mitochondrial genome from whole genome sequencing data. Gene 2019; 699: 145-54.
[http://dx.doi.org/10.1016/j.gene.2019.03.016] [PMID: 30876822]

[17]   Carroll CJ, Brilhante V, Suomalainen A. Next-generation sequencing for mitochondrial disorders. Br J Pharmacol 2014; 171(8): 1837-53.
[http://dx.doi.org/10.1111/bph.12469] [PMID: 24138576]

[18]   Okonechnikov K, Conesa A, García-Alcalde F. Qualimap 2: Advanced multi-sample quality control for high-throughput sequencing data. Bioinformatics 2016; 32(2): 292-4.
[PMID: 26428292]

[19]   Alqahtani F, Măndoiu II. Statistical mitogenome assembly with repeats. J Comput Biol 2020; 27(9): 1407-21.
[http://dx.doi.org/10.1089/cmb.2019.0505] [PMID: 32048871]

[20]   Plese B, Rossi ME, Kenny NJ, Taboada S, Koutsouveli V, Riesgo A. Trimitomics: An efficient pipeline for mitochondrial assembly from transcriptomic reads in nonmodel species. Mol Ecol Resour

2019; 19(5): 1230-9.
[http://dx.doi.org/10.1111/1755-0998.13033] [PMID: 31070854]

[21]   Weissensteiner H, Forer L, Fuchsberger C, *et al.* mtDNA-Server: next-generation sequencing data analysis of human mitochondrial DNA in the cloud. Nucleic Acids Res 2016; 44(W1): W64-9.
[http://dx.doi.org/10.1093/nar/gkw247] [PMID: 27084948]

[22]   Shen L, Attimonelli M, Bai R, *et al.* MSeqDR mvTool: A mitochondrial DNA Web and API resource for comprehensive variant annotation, universal nomenclature collation, and reference genome conversion. Hum Mutat 2018; 39(6): 806-10.
[http://dx.doi.org/10.1002/humu.23422] [PMID: 29539190]

[23]   Shen L, Diroma MA, Gonzalez M, *et al.* MSeqDR: A centralized knowledge repository and bioinformatics web resource to facilitate genomic investigations in mitochondrial disease. Hum Mutat 2016; 37(6): 540-8.
[http://dx.doi.org/10.1002/humu.22974] [PMID: 26919060]

[24]   Liu X, Wu C, Li C, Boerwinkle E. dbNSFP v3.0: A one-stop database of functional predictions and annotations for human nonsynonymous and splice-site SNVs. Hum Mutat 2016; 37(3): 235-41.
[http://dx.doi.org/10.1002/humu.22932] [PMID: 26555599]

[25]   Clima R, Preste R, Calabrese C, *et al.* HmtDB 2016: data update, a better performing query system and human mitochondrial DNA haplogroup predictor. Nucleic Acids Res 2017; 45(D1): D698-706.
[http://dx.doi.org/10.1093/nar/gkw1066] [PMID: 27899581]

[26]   Ruiz-Pesini E, Lott MT, Procaccio V, *et al.* An enhanced MITOMAP with a global mtDNA mutational phylogeny. Nucleic Acids Res 2007; 35(Database issue): D823-8.
[http://dx.doi.org/10.1093/nar/gkl927] [PMID: 17178747]

[27]   Belsare S, Levy-Sakin M, Mostovoy Y, *et al.* Evaluating the quality of the 1000 genomes project data. BMC Genomics 2019; 20(1): 620.
[http://dx.doi.org/10.1186/s12864-019-5957-x] [PMID: 31416423]

[28]   Landrum MJ, Lee JM, Benson M, *et al.* ClinVar: improving access to variant interpretations and supporting evidence. Nucleic Acids Res 2018; 46(D1): D1062-7.
[http://dx.doi.org/10.1093/nar/gkx1153] [PMID: 29165669]

[29]   Yates A, Akanni W, Amode MR, *et al.* Ensembl 2016. Nucleic Acids Res 2016; 44(D1): D710-6.
[http://dx.doi.org/10.1093/nar/gkv1157] [PMID: 26687719]

[30]   Huber N, Parson W, Dür A. Next generation database search algorithm for forensic mitogenome analyses. Forensic Sci Int Genet 2018; 37: 204-14.
[http://dx.doi.org/10.1016/j.fsigen.2018.09.001] [PMID: 30241075]

[31]   Weissensteiner H, Pacher D, Kloss-Brandstätter A, *et al.* HaploGrep 2: mitochondrial haplogroup classification in the era of high-throughput sequencing. Nucleic Acids Res 2016; 44(W1): W58-63.
[http://dx.doi.org/10.1093/nar/gkw233] [PMID: 27084951]

[32]   Calabrese C, Simone D, Diroma MA, *et al.* MToolBox: a highly automated pipeline for heteroplasmy annotation and prioritization analysis of human mitochondrial variants in high-throughput sequencing. Bioinformatics 2014; 30(21): 3115-7.
[http://dx.doi.org/10.1093/bioinformatics/btu483] [PMID: 25028726]

[33]   Damas J, Carneiro J, Amorim A, Pereira F. MitoBreak: the mitochondrial DNA breakpoints database. Nucleic Acids Res 2014; 42(Database issue): D1261-8.
[http://dx.doi.org/10.1093/nar/gkt982] [PMID: 24170808]

[34]   Castellana S, Rónai J, Mazza T. MitImpact: an exhaustive collection of pre-computed pathogenicity predictions of human mitochondrial non-synonymous variants. Hum Mutat 2015; 36(2): E2413-22.
[http://dx.doi.org/10.1002/humu.22720] [PMID: 25516408]

[35]   Adzhubei I, Jordan DM, Sunyaev SR. Predicting functional effect of human missense mutations using PolyPhen-2. Curr Protoc Hum Genet. 2013;Chapter 7:Unit7 20.

[http://dx.doi.org/10.1002/0471142905.hg0720s76]

[36] Vaser R, Adusumalli S, Leng SN, Sikic M, Ng PC. SIFT missense predictions for genomes. Nat Protoc 2016; 11(1): 1-9.
[http://dx.doi.org/10.1038/nprot.2015.123] [PMID: 26633127]

[37] Rogers MF, Shihab HA, Mort M, Cooper DN, Gaunt TR, Campbell C. FATHMM-XF: accurate prediction of pathogenic point mutations *via* extended features. Bioinformatics 2018; 34(3): 511-3.
[http://dx.doi.org/10.1093/bioinformatics/btx536] [PMID: 28968714]

[38] Reva B, Antipin Y, Sander C. Predicting the functional impact of protein mutations: application to cancer genomics. Nucleic Acids Res 2011; 39(17): e118.
[http://dx.doi.org/10.1093/nar/gkr407] [PMID: 21727090]

[39] Choi Y, Chan AP. PROVEAN web server: a tool to predict the functional effect of amino acid substitutions and indels. Bioinformatics 2015; 31(16): 2745-7.
[http://dx.doi.org/10.1093/bioinformatics/btv195] [PMID: 25851949]

[40] Zeng S, Yang J, Chung BH, Lau YL, Yang W. EFIN: predicting the functional impact of nonsynonymous single nucleotide polymorphisms in human genome. BMC Genomics 2014; 15: 455.
[http://dx.doi.org/10.1186/1471-2164-15-455] [PMID: 24916671]

[41] Rentzsch P, Witten D, Cooper GM, Shendure J, Kircher M. CADD: predicting the deleteriousness of variants throughout the human genome. Nucleic Acids Res 2019; 47(D1): D886-94.
[http://dx.doi.org/10.1093/nar/gky1016] [PMID: 30371827]

[42] Tang H, Thomas PD. PANTHER-PSEP: predicting disease-causing genetic variants using position-specific evolutionary preservation. Bioinformatics 2016; 32(14): 2230-2.
[http://dx.doi.org/10.1093/bioinformatics/btw222] [PMID: 27193693]

[43] Capriotti E, Calabrese R, Casadio R. Predicting the insurgence of human genetic diseases associated to single point protein mutations with support vector machines and evolutionary information. Bioinformatics 2006; 22(22): 2729-34.
[http://dx.doi.org/10.1093/bioinformatics/btl423] [PMID: 16895930]

[44] Bromberg Y, Yachdav G, Rost B. SNAP predicts effect of mutations on protein function. Bioinformatics 2008; 24(20): 2397-8.
[http://dx.doi.org/10.1093/bioinformatics/btn435] [PMID: 18757876]

[45] Schwarz JM, Rödelsperger C, Schuelke M, Seelow D. MutationTaster evaluates disease-causing potential of sequence alterations. Nat Methods 2010; 7(8): 575-6.
[http://dx.doi.org/10.1038/nmeth0810-575] [PMID: 20676075]

[46] Wong KC, Zhang Z. SNPdryad: predicting deleterious non-synonymous human SNPs using only orthologous protein sequences. Bioinformatics 2014; 30(8): 1112-9.
[http://dx.doi.org/10.1093/bioinformatics/btt769] [PMID: 24389653]

[47] Raimondi D, Tanyalcin I, Ferté J, *et al.* DEOGEN2: prediction and interactive visualization of single amino acid variant deleteriousness in human proteins. Nucleic Acids Res 2017; 45(W1): W201-6.
[http://dx.doi.org/10.1093/nar/gkx390] [PMID: 28498993]

[48] Martín-Navarro A, Gaudioso-Simón A, Álvarez-Jarreta J, Montoya J, Mayordomo E, Ruiz-Pesini E. Machine learning classifier for identification of damaging missense mutations exclusive to human mitochondrial DNA-encoded polypeptides. BMC Bioinformatics 2017; 18(1): 158.
[http://dx.doi.org/10.1186/s12859-017-1562-7] [PMID: 28270093]

[49] Lopes MC, Joyce C, Ritchie GR, *et al.* A combined functional annotation score for non-synonymous variants. Hum Hered 2012; 73(1): 47-51.
[http://dx.doi.org/10.1159/000334984] [PMID: 22261837]

[50] Yuan X, Bai J, Zhang J, Yang L, Duan J, Li Y, *et al.* CONDEL: Detecting copy number variation and genotyping deletion zygosity from single tumor samples using sequence data. Bioinform 2020; 17(4): 1141-53.

[51]   Frousios K, Iliopoulos CS, Schlitt T, Simpson MA. Predicting the functional consequences of non-synonymous DNA sequence variants--evaluation of bioinformatics tools and development of a consensus strategy. Genomics 2013; 102(4): 223-8.
[http://dx.doi.org/10.1016/j.ygeno.2013.06.005] [PMID: 23831115]

[52]   Capriotti E, Altman RB, Bromberg Y. Collective judgment predicts disease-associated single nucleotide variants. BMC Genomics 2013; 14 (Suppl. 3): S2.
[http://dx.doi.org/10.1186/1471-2164-14-S3-S2] [PMID: 23819846]

[53]   Castellana S, Fusilli C, Mazzoccoli G, et al. High-confidence assessment of functional impact of human mitochondrial non-synonymous genome variations by APOGEE. PLOS Comput Biol 2017; 13(6): e1005628.
[http://dx.doi.org/10.1371/journal.pcbi.1005628] [PMID: 28640805]

[54]   Sherry ST, Ward MH, Kholodov M, et al. dbSNP: the NCBI database of genetic variation. Nucleic Acids Res 2001; 29(1): 308-11.
[http://dx.doi.org/10.1093/nar/29.1.308] [PMID: 11125122]

[55]   Ramani R, Krumholz K, Huang YF, Siepel A. PhastWeb: a web interface for evolutionary conservation scoring of multiple sequence alignments using phastCons and phyloP. Bioinformatics 2019; 35(13): 2320-2.
[http://dx.doi.org/10.1093/bioinformatics/bty966] [PMID: 30481262]

[56]   Accetturo M, Santamaria M, Lascaro D, et al. Human mtDNA site-specific variability values can act as haplogroup markers. Hum Mutat 2006; 27(9): 965-74.
[http://dx.doi.org/10.1002/humu.20365] [PMID: 16865696]

[57]   Tate JG, Bamford S, Jubb HC, et al. COSMIC: The catalogue of somatic mutations in cancer. Nucleic Acids Res 2019; 47(D1): D941-7.
[http://dx.doi.org/10.1093/nar/gky1015] [PMID: 30371878]

[58]   Simonetti FL, Teppa E, Chernomoretz A, Nielsen M, Marino Buslje C. MISTIC: Mutual information server to infer coevolution. Nucleic Acids Res 2013; 41(Web Server issue): W8-14.

[59]   Carter H, Karchin R. Predicting the functional consequences of somatic missense mutations found in tumors. Methods Mol Biol 2014; 1101: 135-59.
[http://dx.doi.org/10.1007/978-1-62703-721-1_8] [PMID: 24233781]

[60]   Gonzalez-Perez A, Deu-Pons J, Lopez-Bigas N. Improving the prediction of the functional impact of cancer mutations by baseline tolerance transformation. Genome Med 2012; 4(11): 89.
[http://dx.doi.org/10.1186/gm390] [PMID: 23181723]

[61]   Preste R, Vitale O, Clima R, Gasparre G, Attimonelli M. HmtVar: a new resource for human mitochondrial variations and pathogenicity data. Nucleic Acids Res 2019; 47(D1): D1202-10.
[http://dx.doi.org/10.1093/nar/gky1024] [PMID: 30371888]

[62]   Sonney S, Leipzig J, Lott MT, et al. Predicting the pathogenicity of novel variants in mitochondrial tRNA with MitoTIP. PLOS Comput Biol 2017; 13(12): e1005867.
[http://dx.doi.org/10.1371/journal.pcbi.1005867] [PMID: 29227991]

[63]   Niroula A, Vihinen M. PON-mt-tRNA: A multifactorial probability-based method for classification of mitochondrial tRNA variations. Nucleic Acids Res 2016; 44(5): 2020-7.
[http://dx.doi.org/10.1093/nar/gkw046] [PMID: 26843426]

[64]   Otten ABC, Sallevelt SCEH, Carling PJ, et al. Mutation-specific effects in germline transmission of pathogenic mtDNA variants. Hum Reprod 2018; 33(7): 1331-41.
[http://dx.doi.org/10.1093/humrep/dey114] [PMID: 29850888]

[65]   Stewart JB, Chinnery PF. The dynamics of mitochondrial DNA heteroplasmy: Implications for human health and disease. Nat Rev Genet 2015; 16(9): 530-42.
[http://dx.doi.org/10.1038/nrg3966] [PMID: 26281784]

[66]   Li H, Slone J, Fei L, Huang T. Mitochondrial DNA variants and common diseases: A mathematical model for the diversity of age-related mtDNA mutations. Cells 2019; 8(6): E608.
[http://dx.doi.org/10.3390/cells8060608] [PMID: 31216686]

[67]   Cruz ACP, Ferrasa A, Muotri AR, Herai RH. Frequency and association of mitochondrial genetic variants with neurological disorders. Mitochondrion 2019; 46: 345-60.
[http://dx.doi.org/10.1016/j.mito.2018.09.005] [PMID: 30218715]

[68]   Hjelm BE, Rollins B, Morgan L, *et al.* Splice-Break: Exploiting an RNA-seq splice junction algorithm to discover mitochondrial DNA deletion breakpoints and analyses of psychiatric disorders. Nucleic Acids Res 2019; 47(10): e59.
[http://dx.doi.org/10.1093/nar/gkz164] [PMID: 30869147]

[69]   Rossignol R, Faustin B, Rocher C, Malgat M, Mazat JP, Letellier T. Mitochondrial threshold effects. Biochem J 2003; 370(Pt 3): 751-62.
[http://dx.doi.org/10.1042/bj20021594] [PMID: 12467494]

[70]   Bhatti S, Aslam Khan M, Abbas S, *et al.* Problems in mitochondrial DNA forensics: While interpreting length heteroplasmy conundrum of various Sindhi and Baluchi ethnic groups of Pakistan. Mitochondrial DNA A DNA Mapp Seq Anal 2018; 29(4): 501-10.
[http://dx.doi.org/10.1080/24701394.2017.1310853] [PMID: 28391756]

[71]   Hume S, Nelson TN, Speevak M, *et al.* CCMG practice guideline: Laboratory guidelines for next-generation sequencing. J Med Genet 2019; 56(12): 792-800.
[http://dx.doi.org/10.1136/jmedgenet-2019-106152] [PMID: 31300550]

CHAPTER 2

Variant Calling on RNA Sequencing Data: State of Art and Future Perspectives

Abstract: In recent decades, scientific research has marked an important change in the conceptualization of studies. The development of new analytical technologies, capable of generating large amounts of data, led to the transition from the reductionist scientific model to the holistic one. Among these "high-throughput" technologies, next-generation sequencing (NGS) has exponentially increased the amount of knowledge about complex living systems. Bioinformatics and biostatistics are two disciplines developed together with the NGS platforms in order to allow more accurate analysis and data management. NGS technology can be equally applied to both emerging DNA and RNA, originally, for the detection of variants and the analysis of gene expression, respectively. However, in recent years, the possibility of calling variants from the RNA-seq analysis has become increasingly concrete. Here we discuss the different analytical conceptualizations that distinguish DNA from the analysis of RNA sequencing data, highlighting the informative potential of RNA-seq data, not only in relation to the quantification of gene expression. Therefore, the application of the variant calling pipeline analysis to transcriptome data is discussed. Furthermore, the possibility of identifying single nucleotide variants starting from RNA samples, allows characterizing two important mechanisms of regulation of gene expressions such as RNA editing and genomic imprinting. The study of these two biological mechanisms is probably the most stimulating resource obtained from RNA-seq and clearly requires highly adequate bioinformatics support, which is now being developed.

Keywords: Alignment, ABRA2, CaSpER, Diploid-SQUID, eSNV-Detect, Edit-ome, Epigenetics, GATK, Imprinting, JACUSA, RNA sequencing, Transcriptome analysis, SNP discovery, RNA editing, SAMtools, RNAIndel, RVboost, SNPiR, VaDiR, Variant calling.

INTRODUCTION

The "omic" sciences include those fields of investigation whose output is a massive amount of data and which find wide application for the description of complex biological systems. Although their development has increased significantly in recent decades, the first term containing the suffix "ome" was "genome", coined in the 1920s by Hans Winkler [1] to describe the entire genetic set of an organism and probably derived from Sanskrit "OM", Indication of total-

Luigi Donato, Simona Alibrandi, Rosalia D'Angelo, Concetta Scimone, Antonina Sidoti and Alessandra Costa

ity. Subsequently, in 1986, "genomics" was introduced to indicate the analytical approach that allows studying the DNA of an organism globally.

In the last decades, with the introduction of high-throughput technologies, further *omic* disciplines have expanded in the field of life sciences and these include transcriptome, proteome, metabolome, lipidome, referring to the study of the entire RNA, protein, metabolites, pools lipid present in a cell, a tissue or an organism, respectively [2]. This rapid development has distorted the conventional reductionist scientific model towards the new holistic model. The link between the *omic* disciplines, in fact, led to the beginning of "systems biology", a new branch in which the integration of data allows defining models to be translated for understanding the living system [3]. Nucleic acids and proteins or metabolites use two analytical approaches that differ in both procedure and data output. The techniques based on mass spectrometry are conventional for the global determination of the spectra of proteins or metabolites [4 - 7]. Instead, sequencing-based technologies were developed to obtain the correct nucleotide sequence of both DNA and RNA molecules [8]. Independently proposed by Maxam and Gilbert [9] and Sanger [10], initially, DNA sequencing strategies allowed to obtain nucleotide sequences of small fragments. Nowadays, next-generation sequencing (NGS) platforms mainly use the sequencing-by-synthesis principle originally proposed by Sanger but rapidly generate gigabases as output. Therefore, the big challenge is the appropriate analysis and interpretation of the results. This requirement has encouraged the progress of analytical algorithms and pipelines, suitable for managing the large amount of data generated [11]. Although NGS technologies are equally applied to both DNA and RNA sequencing, as explained below, their pipeline analyses require substantial different approaches. Variant calling (VC) is the process by which it is possible to identify nucleotide variants and is the most popular goal of DNA sequencing [12]. The transcriptome analysis instead aims to evaluate differential gene expression among tissues or under varying biological conditions [13]. Due to this different experimental conception, these two application fields were considered collateral but not-superimposable. Therefore, here we want to discuss a very controversial topic, related to the possibility of performing VC analysis on transcriptome-generated data.

NEXT-GENERATION SEQUENCING

DNA sequencing by NGS platforms provides several areas of application, of which the most common is the discovery of nucleotide variants. From this field, known as "genomics", further applications have been developed. These include the assembly of the de novo genome [14], metagenomics [15], epigenomics [16], and chromatin immunoprecipitation [17].

However, these applications are not the subject of this thesis. The use of NGS for the discovery of mutations and variants has determined a greater availability of information usable for the identification of genes that cause rare diseases, as well as for the detection of genetic susceptibility factors involved in the onset of multifactorial diseases. Both single nucleotide variants, structural and copy number variations can be identified [18 - 20]. Variant calling is a qualitative analysis. However, sequencing-by-synthesis workflow can introduce biases risking to increase error and, then, false-positive [21]. So, variant caller algorithms use statistic-based models in order to avoid basic miscalling.

RNA sequencing instead allows obtaining the picture of genes expressed within a cell or a tissue in a given time-lapse (before and after pharmacological treatment) or under a specific condition (oxidative stress, disease) [22, 23]. The entire RNA pool sequenced is known as transcriptome and it represents a measurement of gene expression. Therefore, transcriptome analysis is a quantitative evaluation that requires a comparison among two or more conditions to detect differentially expressed genes and give them the correct biological significance in relation to the condition object of the study.

With RNAseq, it is possible to characterize canonical coding RNAs, alternative transcripts and non-coding RNAs [24 - 26]. A new branch of transcriptome analysis is "RNA degradomics". As the name suggests, "degradomics" refers to the study of post-transcriptional regulation mechanisms that occur within cells, with the aim of regulating transcription levels. To date, the degradomics of RNA has been characterized in plants [27].

Although genome and transcriptome analyses aim at different goals, the first analytical steps of raw data are the same. Each analysis pipeline can be divided into three different phases. The first and the second are common to all NGS processing data. In detail, sequence run output is a massive set of fragments, called reads that are stored in FASTQ format. The FASTQ format results from the base call and combines a confidence score for each sequenced nucleotide [28].

The confidence score indicates the probability of calling an incorrect base and this process represents the primary analytical step. Based on the score value, the read quality check is performed and low-quality reads are discarded. Only filtered reads will be mapped to a reference genome (secondary analysis). The format of the file issued following mapping is called SAM (Sequence Alignment / Map). However, due to its large size, it is compressed into a binary format (BAM). From this phase, tertiary analysis begins, and it will be different for the two pipelines, as will be discussed below. These differences are the reason why the conventional variant calling process is not appliable to RNA-seq data.

Variant Calling

As mentioned above, the greatest challenge of genome analysis is the most reliable discrimination between effective sequence variants and the false-positive derived from base miscalling. Several factors influence variant calling and, among them, duplicate reads, depth and coverage are the most important for our purpose.

In a sequencing experiment, duplicate reads derive from clonal amplification bias, such as over-amplification, and they must be removed following mapping [29]. Depth refers to the number of times that a precise nucleotide is effectively sequenced. Coverage is the portion of the genome effectively sequenced. When a given number of reads are outputted by a DNA sequencing, these reads can be mapped to few genome regions and, in this case, the result is low coverage and high depth [30 - 32]. In contrast, the same number of reads can map on a larger genome region, resulting in a higher coverage but a lower depth being the reads distributed on a wider region. Therefore, statistical models applied to variant calling take particularly into account these parameters and, for each base, they aim to reduce the probability of miscalling rate. More rarely, heuristic models can be applied to variant calling [33]. Variant attribution is based on Fisher's Exact Test application, inherent within the algorithm. So, this approach first requires knowledge about the distribution and variance of allele calls at heterozygous loci. This knowledge is assumed by the allele ratio, indicating the ratio between reads counting wild-type and mutated nucleotide. Therefore, it is well evident as polyclonal, or other PCR biases can affect variant detection.

Differential Gene Expression Analysis

Differential gene expression (DGE) is a quantitative analysis to identify both coding and non-coding genes, differentially expressed among two or more conditions. Transcription level of a given genome region was attributed by counting the total reads mapped on the region itself. The more mapping reads, the higher the expression level. Again, duplicate reads can lead to an overestimation of gene expression and false positive results [34, 35]. Another important aspect to consider in DGE analysis is the length of the transcription to the extent that fewer reads are produced for longer transcriptions. Data normalization with respect to depth and length transcription, prior to the quantification of gene expression, helps improve data reliability [36]. Because of the discrete nature of the read count values, DGE is performed by modeling the RNAseq data on a Poisson or on a negative binomial distribution. However, the comparison of gene expression is often referred to as the ratio of expression between the two groups compared. In this perspective, expression values take on the functionality of continuous variables that follow a normal distribution. Therefore, the null hypothesis to test is the absence of a statistically significant difference between the average read count of a given gene, between the two groups. T-test and ANOVA are the most common parametric tests applied to calculate pValue. Non-parametric methods, on the other hand, use Fisher's exact test to assign the pValue [37].

VARIANT CALLING FROM RNA-SEQ DATA: WHAT'S THE NEW?

The opportunity to characterize global gene expression of cell and tissue at specific times or conditions represented a turning point in understanding different physio-pathological transitions. Together with the possibility to build complex molecular signalling networks, expression analysis also allows to formulate targeted therapies in a highly selective way. Hybridization-based strategies as microarray platforms have been largely used since 1995, quantifying gene expression by binding single-stranded cDNA molecules to complementary target probes, immobilized on a chip [38]. This approach has the important limitation of being applicable only to annotated genes. Therefore, in recent years, this technology has been more frequently replaced by RNA sequencing. By mapping the reads on a reference genome, in fact, the analysis of the transcriptome allows to identify new functional chromosomal regions as well as a new class of RNA molecules with regulatory characteristics, alternative coding transcripts and fusion transcripts [39, 40]. However, transcriptome analysis can also be considered as a partial exome sequencing, limited to transcriptionally active chromosomal regions. Based on this assumption, the ability to make variant calling from RNAseq data is a challenge that has not yet been resolved unambiguously.

The first successful attempt was published by Chepelev *et al.*, in 2009 [41]. Their approach was based on removing redundant reads (introduced by PCR biases) and overlapping but non-coincident reads maintenance in order to reduce false-positive rate. The workflow was found valid for the identification of both novel variants and annotated SNPs, also occurring in splice junctions.

However, several other factors influence the identification of variants by the RNAseq analysis.These inlcude mapping and coverage. Mapping can interfere in two ways. The first is related to exon boundary-spanning that, in cDNA reads, is continuous. The second concerns the uniquely read mapping. Certainly, it improves the output but read alignment to high-identity sequence regions as paralog genes, can increase false positives [42]. About coverage, false negative variant risk is related to the expression level. The variant calling a statistical attribution, variants within low expressed genes will be less likely to be discovered. Despite these technical limitations, the variant calling to RNAseq datasets has been more widely applied, in particular, in zootechnical and agrifood research [43, 44]. Several comparative studies were performed in order to draw the most specific analysis pipeline, highlighting the importance of read mapping and the impact of paralogues and pseudogenes [45]. A strategy based on double duplicate removal was proposed by Quinn and colleagues [46]. This approach considers a double, pre-alignment and post-alignment, duplicate reads' removal. Variant calling produced comparable data for SAMtools and Genome Analysis Toolkit (GATK), for coverage ≥10x. For lower coverage levels, SAMtools resulted in increased sensitivity but reduced specificity in SNP detection.

The biases in variant calling applied to the RNAseq datasets are mainly related to the tools applied to the analysis. GATK and SAMtools are designed for genome data and consider parameters such as depth, strand bias, mapping qualities and variant position bias towards the end of the reads. The GATK variant quality score recalibration is based on HapMap variants to prioritize both novel and known variants. This tool was integrated by Wang and colleagues [47], who implemented the tool to obtain a boosting method, called RNA Variant Boosting (RVboost), optimized for transcriptome variant prioritization. At the same time, the eSNV-Detect tool was developed by Tang and colleagues.

However, this method implements variant calling together with functional variant annotation in a clinical-specific context [48]. In the last three years, several other tools have been developed; these include the HaplotypeCaller GATK (https://gatk.broadinstitute.org/hc/en-us/articles/360035531192?id=4067), the *Opossum* that pre-processes RNA-seq reads prior to variant calling [49], the MapReduce implementation *Halvade* that runs in parallel STAR, Picard and GATK on data subsets [50]. The RVboost, together with the other two variant callers SNPiR and MuTect2, was recently integrated with the novel Variant Detection in RNA (*VaDiR*) [51].

Given the very recent release of these tools, only few comparative studies have been performed [52, 53]. However, nowadays, the possibility of using transcriptome data for SNP detection is considered very rare and is mainly related to cancer research. The first proposal to use RNAseq data for molecular diagnosis of monogenic diseases was published in June and focused on genetic diagnosis in genodermatoses [54].

However, together with SNPs, another important technical challenge is related to structural variants. Tools for structural variant detection on RNA-seq data are now available in 2020 and include ABRA2 [55], CaSpER [56], RNAIndel [57], and Diploid-SQUID [58].

WHERE VARIANT CALLING ON DNA DOES NOT ARRIVE: RNA EDITING AND IMPRINTING PROFILES

As mentioned above, the first aim of variant calling analysis is genotyping and variant detection. We discussed the very recent approaches proposed to apply this strategy to transcriptome data. Fig. (**1**) shows the most validated analysis pipeline for RNA-seq data.

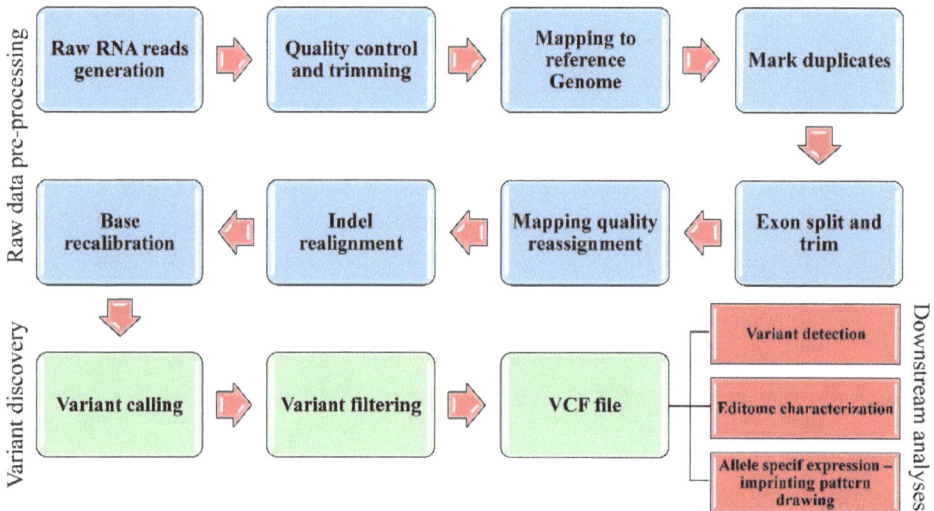

Fig. (1). Analysis phases for RNA-sequencing data processing.

However, if we think of SNPs on cDNA reads, a very legitimate question regards the meaning of SNPs and, in particular, if they are really mutated nucleotides or derive from editing modification. RNA editing includes post-transcriptional RNA changes that occur in one or more nucleotides. Editing modifications include insertions and deletions or nucleotide substitutions. In both cases, the edited RNA differs from the encoding DNA, so the process is considered a genetic recoding.

Given these differences, variant calling applied to transcriptome data can provide important findings about RNA editing modifications [59]. Very interestingly, Peng and colleagues [60] developed a pipeline analysis aimed at annotating the Human RNA "editome", as the entire editing sites set, identified in terms of genome-transcriptome differences. More recently, the JACUSA software, instead, has been developed in order to be usable for RNA-RNA comparison [61]. An outstanding advantage of this implementation is the possibility to compare editing events across samples, conditions or time points.

Since 2008, the whole transcriptome analysis has also been applied to the discovery of new imprinted genes [62, 63]. Imprinting is an exceptional specific allele expression and consists of permanent epigenetic modifications that occur in the zygote. These modifications lead to the selective inactivation of some autosomal alleles, in relation to their parental inheritance pattern. The transcriptome-based print profile is based on the ability to call variants by cDNA reads. When a transcriptome profile is obtained from a sample, the expressed SNPs are selected and genotyped in both parents in order to elaborate the inheritance pattern.

A pipeline analysis developed for plants has been published by Zou and colleagues [64]. Imprinting is not the only allele specific expression mechanism. Other conditions, as allele expression imbalance, show epigenetic inactivation of an allelic copy however, in this case, the mechanism is independent of parental origin. In the context of imprinting pattern characterization, these phenomena can be confounding factors. The *AEI-Imprinting-Joint test* (AIJ) is a statistical model proposed in order to discriminate imprinting-allele expression from non-imprinting one [65]. It was released in October 2019 and no literature data are available about its application. Even more recently, a new statistical approach to detect imprinting by mapping expression quantitative trait loci (eQTL) has been proposed by Deng and colleagues [66]. The conventional analysis of eQTL, in fact, does not allow the characterization of the imprinting profile and the estimation of the dominance effect. Again, there are no additional references, having been the method published in April 2020. Currently, parental genome sequencing combined with progeny transcriptome analysis (trios) is the most accepted approach for identification of imprinted genes in animals [67, 68]. In Human, several trios studies are conducting in order to clarify gene expression regulation occurring during embryo development and in malignant transformation [69 - 71].

CONCLUDING REMARKS

The development of next-generation sequencing has rapidly changed the traditional research approach that was based on the observation of single events. The possibility to obtain a wide instantaneous picture of cell life, during a specific time frame or condition, has greatly increased knowledge. At the same time, data reliability is mostly dependent on *ad hoc* algorithms designed in order to minimize false results and biases introduced during wet laboratory phase. Among all NGS applications, RNA-seq is clearly one of the most informative and stimulating approaches. Although conceived for quantifying gene expression, it is used for the detection of variants. This innovative concept allows characterizing important features of gene expression regulation, such as RNA editing and genome imprinting. In these fields, applications so far are not common due to the few bioinformatic sources available for data analysis. However, based on the latest sources of literature briefly discussed here, in the near future, the analysis of transcriptomes will be able to provide important insights into the finest mechanisms related to regulation of gene expression, clearly not limited to coding transcripts.

REFERENCES

[1]　Winkler H. Verbreitung und ursache der parthenogenesis im pflanzen- und tierreiche. Jena: G. Fischer, German 1920.
[http://dx.doi.org/10.5962/bhl.title.1460]

[2]　MacKenzie S. High-throughput interpretation of pathways and biology. Drug News Perspect 2001; 14(1): 54-7.
[PMID: 12819809]

[3]　Alon U. An introduction to systems biology: design principles of biological circuits. London: Chapman & Hall/CRC 2007.

[4]　Davoli E, Zucchetti M, Matteo C, Ubezio P, D'Incalci M, Morosi L. The space dimension at the micro level: mass spectrometry imaging of drugs in tissues. Mass Spectrom Rev 2020.
[http://dx.doi.org/10.1002/mas.21633] [PMID: 32501572]

[5]　Pauter K, Szultka-Młyńska M, Buszewski B. Determination and identification of antibiotic drugs and bacterial strains in biological samples. Molecules 2020; 25(11): E2556.
[http://dx.doi.org/10.3390/molecules25112556] [PMID: 32486359]

[6]　Yukihiro Y, Zaima N. Application of mass spectrometry imaging for visualizing food components. Foods 2020; 9(5): E575.
[http://dx.doi.org/10.3390/foods9050575] [PMID: 32375379]

[7]　Cipollo JF, Parsons LM. Glycomics and glycoproteomics of viruses: Mass spectrometry applications and insights toward structure-function relationships. Mass Spectrom Rev 2020; 39(4): 371-409.
[http://dx.doi.org/10.1002/mas.21629] [PMID: 32350911]

[8]　ten Bosch JR, Grody WW. Keeping up with the next generation: massively parallel sequencing in clinical diagnostics. J Mol Diagn 2008; 10(6): 484-92.
[http://dx.doi.org/10.2353/jmoldx.2008.080027] [PMID: 18832462]

[9]　Maxam AM, Gilbert W. A new method for sequencing DNA. Proc Natl Acad Sci USA 1977; 74(2): 560-4.
[http://dx.doi.org/10.1073/pnas.74.2.560] [PMID: 265521]

[10]　Sanger F, Nicklen S, Coulson AR. DNA sequencing with chain-terminating inhibitors. Proc Natl Acad Sci USA 1977; 74(12): 5463-7.
[http://dx.doi.org/10.1073/pnas.74.12.5463] [PMID: 271968]

[11]　Mahdavi MA. Bioinformatics Trends and Methodologies. London, UK: Intechopen 2011.
[http://dx.doi.org/10.5772/786]

[12]　Harismendy O, Ng PC, Strausberg RL, *et al.* Evaluation of next generation sequencing platforms for population targeted sequencing studies. Genome Biol 2009; 10(3): R32.
[http://dx.doi.org/10.1186/gb-2009-10-3-r32] [PMID: 19327155]

[13]　Xiao J, Jin X, Jia X, *et al.* Transcriptome-based discovery of pathways and genes related to resistance against Fusarium head blight in wheat landrace Wangshuibai. BMC Genom 2013; 14: 197.
[http://dx.doi.org/10.1186/1471-2164-14-197] [PMID: 23514540]

[14]　Wang W, Wang F, Hao R, *et al.* First de novo whole genome sequencing and assembly of the bar-

headed goose. PeerJ 2020; 8: e8914.
[http://dx.doi.org/10.7717/peerj.8914] [PMID: 32292659]

[15] Kumar Awasthi M, Ravindran B, Sarsaiya S, *et al.* Metagenomics for taxonomy profiling: tools and approaches. Bioengineered 2020; 11(1): 356-74.
[http://dx.doi.org/10.1080/21655979.2020.1736238] [PMID: 32149573]

[16] Basil P, Li Q, McAlonan GM, Sham PC. Genome-wide DNA methylation data from adult brain following prenatal immune activation and dietary intervention. Data Brief 2019; 26: 104561.
[http://dx.doi.org/10.1016/j.dib.2019.104561] [PMID: 31667312]

[17] Coutte L, Antoine R, Slupek S, *et al.* Combined RNAseq and ChIPseq analyses of the BvgA virulence regulator of Bordetella pertussis. mSystems 2020; 5(3): e00208-20.
[http://dx.doi.org/10.1128/mSystems.00208-20] [PMID: 32430408]

[18] Scimone C, Donato L, Alafaci C, *et al.* High-throughput sequencing to detect novel likely gene-disrupting variants in pathogenesis of sporadic Brain Arteriovenous Malformations. Front Genet 2020; 11: 146.
[http://dx.doi.org/10.3389/fgene.2020.00146] [PMID: 32184807]

[19] Gong T, Hayes VM, Chan EKF. Detection of somatic structural variants from short-read next-generation sequencing data. Brief Bioinform 2020; 7: bbaa056.

[20] Anwar T, Rufail ML, Djomehri SI, *et al.* Next-generation sequencing identifies recurrent copy number variations in invasive breast carcinomas from Ghana. Mod Pathol 2020; 33(8): 1537-45.
[http://dx.doi.org/10.1038/s41379-020-0515-2] [PMID: 32152520]

[21] Wakeling MN, Laver TW, Colclough K, Parish A, Ellard S, Baple EL. Misannotation of multiple-nucleotide variants risks misdiagnosis. Wellcome Open Res 2019; 4: 145.
[http://dx.doi.org/10.12688/wellcomeopenres.15420.1] [PMID: 31976378]

[22] Donato L, D'Angelo R, Alibrandi S, Rinaldi C, Sidoti A, Scimone C. Effects of A2E-induced oxidative stress on retinal epithelial cells: new insights on differential gene response and retinal dystrophies. Antioxidants 2020; 9(4): 307.
[http://dx.doi.org/10.3390/antiox9040307] [PMID: 32290199]

[23] Mencucci MV, Flores LE, Gagliardino JJ, Abba MC, Maiztegui B. Integrative transcriptomic analysis of pancreatic islets from patients with prediabetes/type 2 diabetes. Diabetes Metab Res Rev 2020; 4: e3359.
[http://dx.doi.org/10.1002/dmrr.3359] [PMID: 32500584]

[24] Howlader J, Robin AHK, Natarajan S, *et al.* Transcriptome analysis by RNA-seq reveals genes related to plant height in two sets of parent-hybrid combinations in Easter lily (*Lilium longiflorum*). Sci Rep 2020; 10(1): 9082.
[http://dx.doi.org/10.1038/s41598-020-65909-x] [PMID: 32494055]

[25] Wang Y, Xu J, Ge M, Ning L, Hu M, Zhao H. High-resolution profile of transcriptomes reveals a role of alternative splicing for modulating response to nitrogen in maize. BMC Genomics 2020; 21(1): 353.
[http://dx.doi.org/10.1186/s12864-020-6769-8] [PMID: 32393171]

[26] Wang H, Zhong J, Zhang C, *et al.* The whole-transcriptome landscape of muscle and adipose tissues reveals the ceRNA regulation network related to intramuscular fat deposition in yak. BMC Genomics 2020; 21(1): 347.
[http://dx.doi.org/10.1186/s12864-020-6757-z] [PMID: 32381004]

[27] Li YF, Zhao M, Wang M, *et al.* An improved method of constructing degradome library suitable for sequencing using Illumina platform. Plant Methods 2019; 15: 134.
[http://dx.doi.org/10.1186/s13007-019-0524-7] [PMID: 31832076]

[28] Van der Auwera GA, Carneiro MO, Hartl C, *et al.* From FastQ data to high confidence variant calls: the Genome Analysis Toolkit best practices pipeline. Curr Protoc Bioinformatics 2013; 43: 11.10.1-33.

[29] Smith EN, Jepsen K, Khosroheidari M, *et al.* Biased estimates of clonal evolution and subclonal

heterogeneity can arise from PCR duplicates in deep sequencing experiments. Genome Biol 2014; 15(8): 420.
[http://dx.doi.org/10.1186/s13059-014-0420-4] [PMID: 25103687]

[30] Kim K, Seong MW, Chung WH, *et al.* Effect of next-generation exome sequencing depth for discovery of diagnostic variants. Genomics Inform 2015; 13(2): 31-9.
[http://dx.doi.org/10.5808/GI.2015.13.2.31] [PMID: 26175660]

[31] Parks M, Lambert D. Impacts of low coverage depths and post-mortem DNA damage on variant calling: a simulation study. BMC Genomics 2015; 16: 19.
[http://dx.doi.org/10.1186/s12864-015-1219-8] [PMID: 25613391]

[32] Kishikawa T, Momozawa Y, Ozeki T, *et al.* Empirical evaluation of variant calling accuracy using ultra-deep whole-genome sequencing data. Sci Rep 2019; 9(1): 1784.
[http://dx.doi.org/10.1038/s41598-018-38346-0] [PMID: 30741997]

[33] Mielczarek M, Szyda J. Review of alignment and SNP calling algorithms for next-generation sequencing data. J Appl Genet 2016; 57(1): 71-9.
[http://dx.doi.org/10.1007/s13353-015-0292-7] [PMID: 26055432]

[34] Parekh S, Ziegenhain C, Vieth B, Enard W, Hellmann I. The impact of amplification on differential expression analyses by RNA-seq. Sci Rep 2016; 6: 25533.
[http://dx.doi.org/10.1038/srep25533] [PMID: 27156886]

[35] Salzberg AC, Hu J, Conroy EJ, *et al.* Effects of duplicated mapped read PCR artifacts on RNA-seq differential expression analysis based on qRNA-seq. bioRxiv.
[http://dx.doi.org/10.1101/301259]

[36] Abrams ZB, Johnson TS, Huang K, Payne PRO, Coombes K. A protocol to evaluate RNA sequencing normalization methods. BMC Bioinformatics 2019; 20 (Suppl. 24): 679.
[http://dx.doi.org/10.1186/s12859-019-3247-x] [PMID: 31861985]

[37] Li WV, Li JJ. Modeling and analysis of RNA-seq data: a review from a statistical perspective. Quant Biol 2018; 6(3): 195-209.
[http://dx.doi.org/10.1007/s40484-018-0144-7] [PMID: 31456901]

[38] Schena M, Shalon D, Davis RW, Brown PO. Quantitative monitoring of gene expression patterns with a complementary DNA microarray. Science 1995; 270(5235): 467-70.
[http://dx.doi.org/10.1126/science.270.5235.467] [PMID: 7569999]

[39] Kumar S, Vo AD, Qin F, Li H. Comparative assessment of methods for the fusion transcripts detection from RNA-Seq data. Sci Rep 2016; 6: 21597.
[http://dx.doi.org/10.1038/srep21597] [PMID: 26862001]

[40] Shang Q, Yang Z, Jia R, Ge S. The novel roles of circRNAs in human cancer. Mol Cancer 2019; 18(1): 6.
[http://dx.doi.org/10.1186/s12943-018-0934-6] [PMID: 30626395]

[41] Chepelev I, Wei G, Tang Q, Zhao K. Detection of single nucleotide variations in expressed exons of the human genome using RNA-Seq. Nucleic Acids Res 2009; 37(16): e106.
[http://dx.doi.org/10.1093/nar/gkp507] [PMID: 19528076]

[42] Cirulli ET, Singh A, Shianna KV, *et al.* Screening the human exome: a comparison of whole genome and whole transcriptome sequencing. Genome Biol 2010; 11(5): R57.
[http://dx.doi.org/10.1186/gb-2010-11-5-r57] [PMID: 20598109]

[43] Cánovas A, Rincon G, Islas-Trejo A, Wickramasinghe S, Medrano JF. SNP discovery in the bovine milk transcriptome using RNA-Seq technology. Mamm Genome 2010; 21(11-12): 592-8.
[http://dx.doi.org/10.1007/s00335-010-9297-z] [PMID: 21057797]

[44] Mueller JC, Kuhl H, Timmermann B, Kempenaers B. Characterization of the genome and transcriptome of the blue tit Cyanistes caeruleus: polymorphisms, sex-biased expression and selection signals. Mol Ecol Resour 2016; 16(2): 549-61.

[http://dx.doi.org/10.1111/1755-0998.12450] [PMID: 26220359]

[45]   Atak ZK, Gianfelici V, Hulselmans G, *et al.* Comprehensive analysis of transcriptome variation uncovers known and novel driver events in T-cell acute lymphoblastic leukemia. PLoS Genet 2013; 9(12): e1003997.
[http://dx.doi.org/10.1371/journal.pgen.1003997] [PMID: 24367274]

[46]   Quinn EM, Cormican P, Kenny EM, *et al.* Development of strategies for SNP detection in RNA-seq data: application to lymphoblastoid cell lines and evaluation using 1000 Genomes data. PLoS One 2013; 8(3): e58815.
[http://dx.doi.org/10.1371/journal.pone.0058815] [PMID: 23555596]

[47]   Wang C, Davila JI, Baheti S, *et al.* RVboost: RNA-seq variants prioritization using a boosting method. Bioinformatics 2014; 30(23): 3414-6.
[http://dx.doi.org/10.1093/bioinformatics/btu577] [PMID: 25170027]

[48]   Tang X, Baheti S, Shameer K, *et al.* The eSNV-detect: a computational system to identify expressed single nucleotide variants from transcriptome sequencing data. Nucleic Acids Res 2014; 42(22): e172.
[http://dx.doi.org/10.1093/nar/gku1005] [PMID: 25352556]

[49]   Oikkonen L, Lise S. Making the most of RNA-seq: Pre-processing sequencing data with Opossum for reliable SNP variant detection. Wellcome Open Res 2017; 2: 6.
[http://dx.doi.org/10.12688/wellcomeopenres.10501.2] [PMID: 28239666]

[50]   Decap D, Reumers J, Herzeel C, Costanza P, Fostier J. Halvade-RNA: Parallel variant calling from transcriptomic data using MapReduce. PLoS One 2017; 12(3): e0174575.
[http://dx.doi.org/10.1371/journal.pone.0174575] [PMID: 28358893]

[51]   Neums L, Suenaga S, Beyerlein P, *et al.* VaDiR: an integrated approach to Variant Detection in RNA. Gigascience 2018; 7(2): 1-13.
[http://dx.doi.org/10.1093/gigascience/gix122] [PMID: 29267927]

[52]   Dharshini SAP, Taguchi YH, Gromiha MM. Identifying suitable tools for variant detection and differential gene expression using RNA-seq data. Genomics 2020; 112(3): 2166-72.
[http://dx.doi.org/10.1016/j.ygeno.2019.12.011] [PMID: 31862361]

[53]   Wrzeszczynski KO, Felice V, Abhyankar A, *et al.* Analytical validation of clinical whole-genome and transcriptome sequencing of patient-derived tumors for reporting targetable variants in cancer. J Mol Diagn 2018; 20(6): 822-35.
[http://dx.doi.org/10.1016/j.jmoldx.2018.06.007] [PMID: 30138725]

[54]   Saeidian AH, Youssefian L, Vahidnezhad H, Uitto J. Research techniques made simple: whole-transcriptome sequencing by RNA-seq for diagnosis of monogenic disorders. J Invest Dermatol 2020; 140(6): 1117-1126.e1.
[http://dx.doi.org/10.1016/j.jid.2020.02.032] [PMID: 32446329]

[55]   Mose LE, Perou CM, Parker JS. Improved indel detection in DNA and RNA *via* realignment with ABRA2. Bioinformatics 2019; 35(17): 2966-73.
[http://dx.doi.org/10.1093/bioinformatics/btz033] [PMID: 30649250]

[56]   Serin Harmanci A, Harmanci AO, Zhou X. CaSpER identifies and visualizes CNV events by integrative analysis of single-cell or bulk RNA-sequencing data. Nat Commun 2020; 11(1): 89.
[http://dx.doi.org/10.1038/s41467-019-13779-x] [PMID: 31900397]

[57]   Hagiwara K, Ding L, Edmonson MN, *et al.* RNAIndel: discovering somatic coding indels from tumor RNA-Seq data. Bioinformatics 2020; 36(5): 1382-90.
[http://dx.doi.org/10.1093/bioinformatics/btaa247] [PMID: 31593214]

[58]   Qiu Y, Ma C, Xie H, Kingsford C. Detecting transcriptomic structural variants in heterogeneous contexts *via* the Multiple Compatible Arrangements Problem. Algorithms Mol Biol 2020; 15: 9.
[http://dx.doi.org/10.1186/s13015-020-00170-5] [PMID: 32467720]

[59]   Martínez-Montes AM, Fernández A, Pérez-Montarelo D, *et al.* Using RNA-Seq SNP data to reveal

potential causal mutations related to pig production traits and RNA editing. Anim Genet 2017; 48(2): 151-65.
[http://dx.doi.org/10.1111/age.12507] [PMID: 27642173]

[60]   Peng Z, Cheng Y, Tan BC, *et al.* Comprehensive analysis of RNA-Seq data reveals extensive RNA editing in a human transcriptome. Nat Biotechnol 2012; 30(3): 253-60.
[http://dx.doi.org/10.1038/nbt.2122] [PMID: 22327324]

[61]   Piechotta M, Wyler E, Ohler U, Landthaler M, Dieterich C. JACUSA: site-specific identification of RNA editing events from replicate sequencing data. BMC Bioinformatics 2017; 18(1): 7.
[http://dx.doi.org/10.1186/s12859-016-1432-8] [PMID: 28049429]

[62]   Babak T, Deveale B, Armour C, *et al.* Global survey of genomic imprinting by transcriptome sequencing. Curr Biol 2008; 18(22): 1735-41.
[http://dx.doi.org/10.1016/j.cub.2008.09.044] [PMID: 19026546]

[63]   Wang X, Sun Q, McGrath SD, Mardis ER, Soloway PD, Clark AG. Transcriptome-wide identification of novel imprinted genes in neonatal mouse brain. PLoS One 2008; 3(12): e3839.
[http://dx.doi.org/10.1371/journal.pone.0003839] [PMID: 19052635]

[64]   Zou J, Xiang D, Datla R, Wang E. A protocol for epigenetic imprinting analysis with RNA-seq data. Methods Mol Biol 2018; 1751: 199-208.
[http://dx.doi.org/10.1007/978-1-4939-7710-9_14] [PMID: 29508299]

[65]   Chen DP, Zhang FY, Lin SL. AIJ: joint test for simultaneous detection of imprinting and non-imprinting allelic expression imbalance. Math Biosci Eng 2019; 17(1): 366-86.
[http://dx.doi.org/10.3934/mbe.2020020] [PMID: 31731356]

[66]   Deng S, Hardin J, Amos CI, Xiao F. Joint modeling of eQTLs and parent-of-origin effects using an orthogonal framework with RNA-seq data. Hum Genet 2020; 139(8): 1107-17.
[http://dx.doi.org/10.1007/s00439-020-02162-2] [PMID: 32270270]

[67]   Zhuo Z, Lamont SJ, Abasht B. RNA-seq analyses identify frequent allele specific expression and no evidence of genomic imprinting in specific embryonic tissues of chicken. Sci Rep 2017; 7(1): 11944.
[http://dx.doi.org/10.1038/s41598-017-12179-9] [PMID: 28931927]

[68]   Ahn B, Choi MK, Yum J, Cho IC, Kim JH, Park C. Analysis of allele-specific expression using RNA-seq of the Korean native pig and Landrace reciprocal cross. Asian-Australas J Anim Sci 2019; 32: 1816-25.
[http://dx.doi.org/10.5713/ajas.19.0097] [PMID: 31208168]

[69]   Zhabotynsky V, Inoue K, Magnuson T, Mauro Calabrese J, Sun W. A statistical method for joint estimation of cis-eQTLs and parent-of-origin effects under family trio design. Biometrics 2019; 75(3): 864-74.
[http://dx.doi.org/10.1111/biom.13026] [PMID: 30666629]

[70]   Jadhav B, Monajemi R, Gagalova KK, *et al.* RNA-Seq in 296 phased trios provides a high-resolution map of genomic imprinting. BMC Biol 2019; 17(1): 50.
[http://dx.doi.org/10.1186/s12915-019-0674-0] [PMID: 31234833]

[71]   Pilvar D, Reiman M, Pilvar A, Laan M. Parent-of-origin-specific allelic expression in the human placenta is limited to established imprinted loci and it is stably maintained across pregnancy. Clin Epigenetics 2019; 11(1): 94.
[http://dx.doi.org/10.1186/s13148-019-0692-3] [PMID: 31242935]

CHAPTER 3

An Innovative Gene Prioritization Pipeline for DNA-Sequencing Analyses

Abstract: In recent decades, the development of next-generation sequencing (NGS) technologies has made it possible to understand molecular mechanisms at the basis of various genetic diseases. The huge amount of data obtained from these experiments must be carefully analyzed. One of the most sensitive steps consists of gene prioritization, already performed by several widely used computational tools such as Endeavour, ToppGene, and Candid, to obtain only the genes that are most probably associated with the disease of interest. Furthermore, among these genes, it is important to choose those that show the highest statistical significance, to obtain a more reliable result. This represents one of the major limitations for many researchers. In this work, we propose an innovative method that could help researchers reduce a large amount of data by applying filters before the prioritization process that is carried out by Toppgene, today considered the most powerful tool. We performed prioritization of candidate genes obtained by whole-exome sequencing (WES) on a patient affected by an orphan form of retinitis pigmentosa. We obtained new mutations and polymorphic variants in known associated/causative and yet unrelated genes. The upstream application of different filters allowed us to work with a smaller number of genes and therefore, to produce a lower statistical bias. Furthermore, Toppgene has proven to be a complete, reliable tool for carrying out the prioritization process.

Keywords: Bioinformatics, Biostatistics, Candid, Conditional Formatting, CLC Genomics Workbench, Disease Ontology, DNA, DNASTAR Lasergene Suite, Excel, Gene Prioritization, GO, Human Phenotype, Mouse Phenotype, Molecular Function, NGS, Pipeline, ToppGene, RP, WGS, WES.

INTRODUCTION

Since the completion of the Human Genome project in 2003, a growing interest in high-throughput omics techniques such as microarrays, next-generation sequencing (NGS), whole genome sequencing (WGS) and whole-exome sequencing (WES), has led to extraordinary progress in the study of Mendelian disorders, and also helped researchers to comprehend the pathophysiological mechanisms of rare genetic diseases.

Luigi Donato, Simona Alibrandi, Rosalia D'Angelo, Concetta Scimone, Antonina Sidoti and Alessandra Costa

Knowledge of molecular networks and, consequently, disease mechanisms is very important to develop effective therapies.

Thus, the advent of NGS technologies has led to a considerably growth of different genomic research sectors, such as metagenomics, pharmacogenomics and pharmacokinetics. In addition, this scenario has allowed to perform experiments reducing time and costs compared to the past.

Despite these advantages, high-throughput genome-wide studies are not enough to identify the most promising candidate genes responsible for the disease of interest. Most hereditary diseases are polygenic and multifactorial and express different clinical phenotypes that are often the result of genetic, environmental and physiological interactions [1]. WES and WGS-based experiments are helpful for classification and characterization, but these approaches generate a huge number of potential candidate genes, many of which have no connection with the disease of interest since they are very unlikely to exert a functional effect at a protein and/or systemic level. Resequencing, together with a pathway or expression analyses, might be necessary to identify and validate the best candidate genes, but this option is expensive and time-consuming. For these reasons, it is convenient to restrict the large quantity of genomic data to a small number, which, however, turns out to be promising. This process is defined as "Gene prioritization".

Recent studies evidenced that prioritization aids researchers not only in selecting promising candidate genes but also in discovering novel genes of interest for several diseases.

In this work, we performed prioritization of candidate genes, obtained by WES, on a patient affected by an orphan form of retinitis pigmentosa (RP) (data under publication) using the ToppGene tool, to demonstrate its reliability and validity. In the meantime, we developed a complex analytic pipeline, to better manage data produced by the up-stream step of DNA-Sequencing.

MATERIALS AND METHODS

The whole process of prioritization consists of several steps (Fig. **1**):

1. The first step consists of an omics experiment (microarray, NGS, WGS, WES). The obtained raw data are analyzed through an informatics pipeline by appropriate software such as CLC Genomics Workbench, DNASTAR Lasergene Suite, Genomatix Software Suite, Torrent Suite, and Illumina BaseSpace. Software choice is crucial, and the quality of the entire analysis

depends on it.

2. The second step foresees the application of the first prioritization filters to the data obtained in step 1. The choice of filter is variable and depends on the final result that has to be obtained.

3. In the third step, the data is prioritized by several computational tools such as ToppGene, Endeavour, Suspect and Pinta. The correct choice is critical to obtain the best results.

4. The fourth step consists of the statistical evaluation of results produced, the analysis of pathways and the validation of variants obtained from the prioritization process through Sanger sequencing.

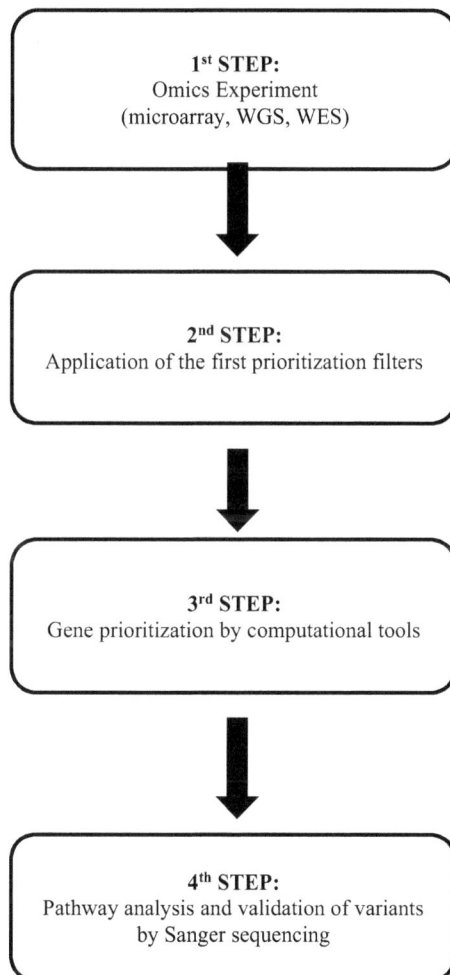

1st STEP:
Omics Experiment
(microarray, WGS, WES)

2nd STEP:
Application of the first prioritization filters

3rd STEP:
Gene prioritization by computational tools

4th STEP:
Pathway analysis and validation of variants
by Sanger sequencing

Fig. (1). Prioritization of NGS big data. Workflow chart shows the main steps required for data analysis.

Currently, 46 prioritization tools are available, including Suspects [2], Gene Distiller [3], Gene Wanderer, Posmed, Endeavour, Pinta, Candid [4] and ToppGene (https://toppgene.cchmc.org/prioritization.jsp). The common goal of these tools is to highlight promising genes from large genomic data produced by OMIC experiments. This selection is obtained by the application of computational algorithms that evaluate specific connections, such as genotype-phenotype relationships, homology between different species, and gene expression data. Thus, gene prioritization is based on the strength of these connections. This approach, known as "semantic similarity", is used to produce previously cited associations. Semantic similarity evaluates the rate of association between genes or of a gene to a disease based on similarity in the meaning of their annotations, which refer to ontologies such as gene ontology (GO), human phenotype (HPO) and disease ontology (DO) [5].

Gene Ontology contains a specific vocabulary of terms, called GO Terms. It can be divided into three domains: Molecular Function (MF), Biological Process and Cellular Component [6].

Molecular Function describes the biochemical activity of a single gene product or molecular complexes made of multiple gene products. However, this domain does not specify when and where the action occurs. An example of a molecular function is "catalytic activity".

The location where the biochemical event takes place is described by cellular component, which refers only to cellular anatomy such as "mitochondrion", "nuclear membrane" or "Golgi apparatus".

Lastly, the *Biological Process* refers to all molecular activities carried out by a gene product. These processes are often involved in a chemical or physical transformation. Examples of biological process terms are "cell growth" and "maintenance of signal transduction".

All terms of each domain are expressed by a name and a GO ID that is represented as a unique seven-digit identifier prefixed by GO. For example, in Table **1**, three possible annotation terms of the *RHO* gene are listed.

Table 1. GO annotation terms for *RHO* gene. This table shows the main categories of gene ontology: Biological process, Molecular function, Cellular component.

	GO ID	Qualified Go term
Biological Process	GO:0001523	retinoid metabolic process
Molecular Function	GO:0004930	G protein-coupled receptor activity
Cellular Component	GO:0000139	Golgi membrane

Human Phenotype is a standardized, controlled vocabulary that gives phenotype information about product genes and their relationships. Thus, it is a computational bridge between genome biology and clinical medicine. HPO contains 13,000 terms describing human disease-related phenotypic abnormalities. Each term is assigned to one of the following five sub-ontologies: phenotypic abnormality, mode of inheritance, clinical modifier, clinical course, frequency.

Disease Ontology, on the other hand, enables cross-referencing among disease concepts, genes contributing to disease, and the host of symptoms, findings and signs. DO semantically integrates and connects over 46,000 diseases and medical vocabulary terms through extensive cross-reference mappings (MeSH, ICD, NCI's thesaurus, SNOMED and OMIM) [7].

Gene ontology, human ontology and disease ontology data can be represented by a directed acyclic graph (DAG). This graph contains nodes and edges. Nodes represent the terms, and edges represent the relationships among terms [8].

For example, the graph below (Fig. **2**) shows the possible interactions of the molecular function term GO:0004930. "G protein-coupled receptor activity term" has two parents: "G protein-coupled receptor signaling pathway" and "transmembrane signaling receptor activity". This reflects the fact that the G protein-coupled receptor is a subtype of the transmembrane receptor and the G protein-coupled receptor activity is a subtype of the signaling pathway.

Although all computational software tools follow the same principle to perform the classification of candidate genes, actually they differ in the strategy used to calculate the similarity. ToppGene uses a combination of fuzzy measure and the Pearson correlation, while other tools such as Endeavour use Fisher's omnibus analysis and the Pearson correlation as well. Furthermore, another difference that characterizes the different tools is the data source used [9]. Most software computes gene prioritization based on the combination of a few data sources. Compared to other tools, ToppGene offers better performance, is more complete and its database resources are not limited to KEGG, but result from the combination of six data sources (KEGG, BioCarta, BioCyc, Reactome, GenMAPP, MsigDb). A peculiar feature that distinguishes ToppGene from the other approaches is the use of mouse phenotype for candidate gene prioritization. Among model organisms used in genetic research, the mouse is the most suitable animal model for the study of human diseases, as 99% of mouse genes have human orthologs. Thus, the use of mouse phenotype data could improve the prioritization of human candidate genes.

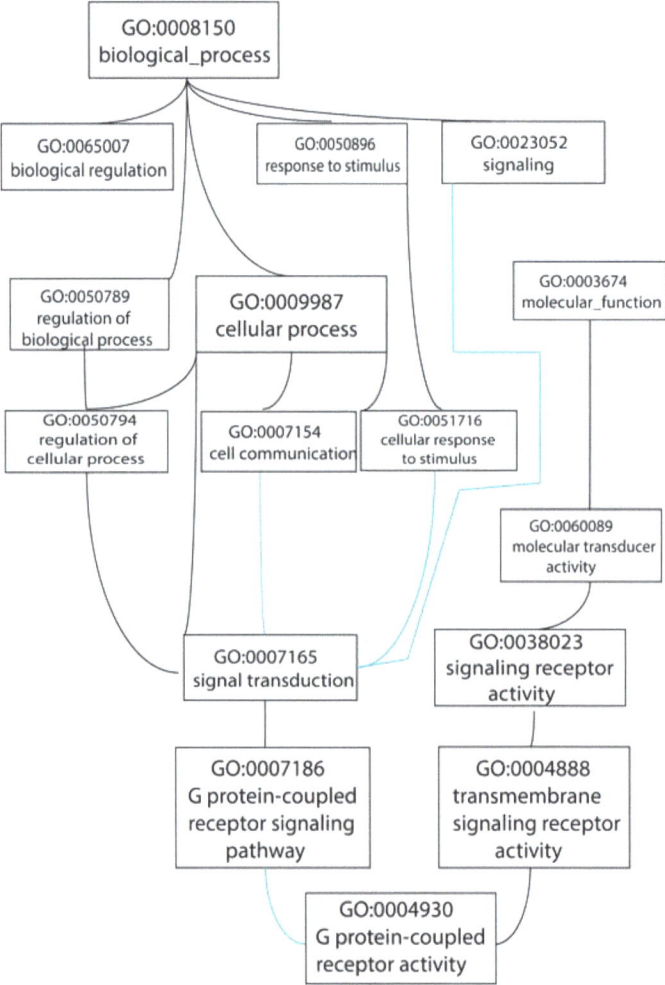

Fig. (2). Enrichment GO hierarchy of biological process. The figure shows an example of a node graph representing hierarchical categories of GO biological processes.

A limitation of this approach is that, to date, just a fraction of the human genome, exactly one fifth, presents pathway or phenotype annotations, and more than 40% of genes have yet to be annotated [10].

However, it is important to emphasize that the reliability of data obtained from the prioritization process also depends on the quality of the upstream NGS data analysis performed.

The prioritization process does not foresee a standard, rigid protocol to be followed. The researcher can choose number and type of filters to apply on the basis of the type of disease and, above all, on the basis of the final data to be obtained.

In this work, we prioritized the genes carrying variants, obtained from WES, of a patient affected by an orphan form of RP. This disease is particularly multigenic and multifactorial, so we used two software packages (CLC Genomics Workbench and DNASTAR Lasergene Suite) to perform data analysis with the aim of carrying out a comparative analysis by crossing the prioritized genes, and finally obtaining a more reliable, significant result. The ToppGene tool was used for the prioritization process since it is considered the most complete.

Filters were chosen with the aim of prioritizing the genes on the basis of variant frequency (polymorphisms or new mutations) and on the basis of the association between genes and pathology (genes "known" to be associated/causative or "unknown", never related genes).

Prioritization of Genes Carrying Variants Obtained From CLC Genomics Workbench

Before applying the selected filters, it is advisable to remove some information from the VCF file produced by CLC Genomics Workbench. Such variables, such as zygosity, coverage, frequency and others that are not necessary for the prioritization process, should be deleted to streamline the large amounts of available data and to simplify the method. At this point, it is possible to apply the first filters.

The first three variables by which we filtered were *"Gene biotype", "Qual"* and *"Non-synonymous"*. As far as Gene biotype is concerned, we filtered by protein-coding to select only the coding genes.

"Qual" is a measure of a called variant significance. It is expressed by a numeric value ranging from 0 to 200. This value is calculated as $-10\log_{10}(1-p)$, where p represents the probability that a particular variant exists in the sample. Thus, for p=1, "Qual" is 200. The higher the value, the more highly significant the correspondent variant. We selected all the variants with Qual>90. We chose a value that is not very high to avoid the risk of eliminating genes whose variants could play an important role.

The third filter concerns the type of coding variant: non-synonymous and synonymous. We selected all genes carrying *non-synonymous* variants and also genes lacking this information. All genes carrying synonymous variants were removed.

Then, it is important to distinguish known disease-associated/causative genes from genes that are not related. To realize this purpose, we applied the fourth filter. Known RP associated/causative genes, collected from RetNet (Retinal Information Network), were highlighted in the gene name column of Excel format.

Subsequently, the variable *"Coding region change in longest transcript"* was filtered (5°filter). Stop variants were filtered, and among the remaining non-synonymous variants, only those in known genes were selected (6°filter).

The seventh filter was applied for the variable *"dbSNPs"*. All polymorphisms in known and unknown genes were highlighted.

All known and unknown genes carrying stop variants and also all known genes carrying non-synonymous variants were copied into a new Excel sheet that was called *"STOP_ (KNO+UNK)_&_NONSYN_(KNOWN)* (8° filter).

The remaining unknown genes carrying non-synonymous variants were, then, transferred to another Excel sheet which was called *"NEW MUT&SNPs IN NEW GENES"*.

From this moment on, the filters were applied separately on the two sheets.

STOP_ (KNO+UNK) _&_NONSYN_(KNOWN)

After grouping the polymorphic variants, the filter for the collaborative consensus coding sequence (CCDS) variable was applied. The CCDS project tracks identical protein annotations on the reference mouse and human genomes with a stable identifier (CCDS ID) and ensures that they are consistently represented on the NCBI, Ensemble and UCSC Genome Browsers. Therefore, all genes lacking this information were removed.

The parameter *"Aminoacid change"* was also filtered. It describes change at the protein level. For example, in His334Arg, the Histidine at position 334 is changed into Arginine. Frameshift caused by nucleotide insertions and deletions are listed with the extension *fs*: e.g., Leu591fs denoting a frameshift at position 591 coding for Leucine. Therefore, all genes presenting a value in *"Aminoacid change"* were selected. However, among the known genes that had no value, those whose variants were found on Ensemble (protein-coding variant, coding sequence variant, frameshift variant, missense variant, stop coding variant, regulatory region variant, splicing variant) were selected and grouped. The unknown genes were eliminated.

At this point, it was necessary to perform the ToppGene analysis to further filter the unknown genes, obtained from the different filters, and remove all the genes with overall p-value > 0.05. Finally, all genes carrying polymorphic variants were checked on the Human Gene Mutation Database (HGMD). Only genes carrying polymorphic variants present on HGMD, evidencing an association with pathological phenotype, were filtered. These data were saved in a new Excel sheet called *"HGMD SNPs KNOWN GENES"*. The remaining known and unknown genes carrying new mutations were, instead, saved as "NON SYN NEW MUT KNOWN & UNKNOWN GENES".

NEW MUT & SNPS IN NEW GENES

In this case, it was necessary to apply several filters to obtain only new indel mutations. The variable *"SNPs"* was filtered and all genes carrying polymorphic variants were removed. Then we filtered for *"CCDS"*, eliminating all genes without CCDS value.

Moreover, only the genes presenting code *dup*, *ins* or *del* in *"coding region in longest transcript"* were filtered. All other genes were eliminated. Finally, only the genes whose variants showed a value in *"aminoacid changes"* were filtered. The genes which survived after all filtering procedures were prioritized by ToppGene and produced data were saved as *"NEW MUT IN NEW GENES"* datasheet.

Prioritization of Genes Obtained from DNASTAR Lasergene Suite

The first variable by which we filtered was *"Gene name"*. The genes known to be associated/causative of RP, collected from RetNet as already done during the CLC Genomics Workbench procedure, were selected in such a way as to be distinguished from the new putative genes. Thus, the known genes and the new candidate genes were filtered separately.

Known genes were filtered for the variables *"variant-LRT-pred"*, *"variant-mutationTaster"* and *"variant-sift-PRED"*.

These variables represent prediction algorithms based on different computational models. The "variant-LRT-pred" algorithm characterizes the variants based on the effect they have on the encoded protein. These variants could be classified as deleterious, neutral and unknown. The neutral variants correspond to the synonymous variants and have no impact on the encoded protein. We selected and grouped only genes carrying deleterious and unknown variants (1st filter).

The "variant-mutationTaster" algorithm predicts the likelihood that the variants could be causative of the disease of interest. It classifies variants in disease-causing and polymorphism. We selected only the genes carrying disease causing variant (2nd filter).

The "variant-sift-PRED" algorithm foresees the probability that a variant could damage the encoded protein, so all the genes carrying damaging variants were selected (3rd filter).

Subsequently, all genes carrying polymorphic variants were checked on HGMD. Only the genes carrying variants present on HGMD showing an associated pathological phenotype were filtered. These data were saved in a new Excel sheet called "KNOWN GENES HGMD SNPs". The remaining known genes carrying new variants were saved as "NEW MUTATIONS IN KNOWN GENES". Both polymorphism and new mutation carrying genes were filtered for "Depth" variable. All genes with a depth value < 75 were removed.

The same procedure was applied to the new candidate genes. The *"Depth"*, *"variant-LRT-pred"*, *"variant-mutationTaster"* and *"variant-sift-PRED"* variables were filtered in this order. Then, we filtered for *"variant classification"*, so only inframe, non sense and frameshift variants were highlighted.

Subsequently, selected genes were filtered for the parameter "dbSNPs" to distinguish new mutations from polymorphisms. Genes that had no value in the "dbSNPs" column were saved in a new sheet called "NEW MUTATIONS IN CANDIDATE GENES", and all genes carrying polymorphic variants were checked on HGMD. Only the genes carrying variants existing on HGMD that had presented an associated pathological phenotype were saved as "CANDIDATE GENES HGMD SNPs".

Lastly, both polymorphism and new mutation carrying genes were prioritized by ToppGene.

Prioritization by ToppGene

Once the gene filtering process was completed, the next step was to prioritize the unknown genes where association/causation towards the disease of interest is as yet undefined. The filtered genes were prioritized by the ToppGene suite using the Candidate Gene Prioritization application. This tool is free for use, and does not require a log-in or local installation (except for applications to visualize or analyze network). It prioritizes the genes included in a test list (test gene set), exploiting functional similarity to a list of training genes (training gene set) that is a reference list of genes, such as associated/known causative genes of a considered disease. The priority definition set on the functional annotations computes the similarity between two genes on the basis of gene-specific semantic annotations, calculating the Pearson correlation coefficient. The similarity scores for each calculated property are combined into a total score through statistical meta-analysis; each annotation is associated with a P-value derived from the probability that, within the genome, there are other genes with similar functional annotations. The P-value of similarity score S_i is defined as:

$$p(Si) = \frac{(\text{Count of genes having higher than G in the random sample})}{(\text{Count of genes in the random sample containing annotation})}$$

In our analysis, the training list included the genes already associated with RP, while the test list consisted of the genes resulting from the filtering of the exomic sequencing data. For the calculation of the similarity scores, several features were considered, such as: molecular function, biological process, cellular component, human phenotype, domain, interaction, gene family, co-expression, drug, pathway, PubMed and disease. P-values were corrected for multiple comparisons by the Bonferroni post-hoc test. As already mentioned, the ToppGene output was a list of genes ranked by statistical significance. We chose the genes considering a p-value threshold ≤ 0.05.

RESULTS

Results from CLC Genomics Workbench

From the WES of the RP patient, we obtained a large amount of raw data, that after alignment and variant calling by CLC Genomics Workbench, produced 89,395 variants in 16,377 genes. After the first three filters ("Gene biotype", "Qual" and "Non-synonymous") were applied, this huge amount of data shrunk considerably, with the number of variants decreased to 15,160 in 7,431 genes, as shown in Fig. (**3**).

Since these data included both new mutations and polymorphic variants in known and unknown genes, we chose to distinguish new indel mutations in unknown genes from all the other variants found in both known and unknown genes. We obtained 81 new variants in 67 unknown genes (Fig. **4**).

Several filters were applied to stop variants in known and unknown genes and to synonymous variants in known genes, with the purpose of separating polymorphisms in known genes from new non-synonymous mutations (including also stop variants) in known and unknown genes. Thus, we obtained 13 polymorphisms in 12 known genes and 44 new mutations in known and unknown genes (Figs. **5** and **6**).

Fig. (3). List of genes obtained after applying the first three prioritization filters. This figure shows the application of the first three prioritization filters based on the quality of variant calling (Qual), gene biotype and synonymy of considered variants. Chromosome: X,Y. Region: The region on the reference sequence at which the variant is located. Type: The type of variant. SNV (single-nucleotide variant), MNV (multi-nucleotide variant), insertion, deletion. Reference allele: Indicates if the variant is identical to the reference. Zigosity: Indicates whether the variant is homozygous or heterozygous. ccds (Consensus coding sequence): provides a dataset of protein-coding regions that are identically annotated on the human and mouse reference genome assembly in genome annotations. Aminoacid change in the longest transcript indicates the change of aminoacid in the longest transcript. Coding region change in the longest transcript: indicates the change of nucleotide in the longest transcript. dbSNP: each code identifies a unique polymorphism.

Fig. (4). List of unknown genes carrying only new indels mutations. This figure shows the list of unknown genes carrying new indels mutations obtained after the application of the "Coding region change in the longest transcript" filter, selecting only for indels mutations. The variables ccds and aminoacid change in longest transcript were also filtered; only genes with a value in these variables were chosen. Chromosome: X, Y. Region: The region on the reference sequence at which the variant is located. Type: The type of variant. SNV (single-nucleotide variant), MNV (multi-nucleotide variant), insertion, deletion. Reference allele: Indicates if the variant is identical to the reference. Zygosity: Indicates whether the variant is homozygous or heterozygous. ccds (Consensus coding sequence): provides a dataset of protein-coding regions that are identically annotated on the human and mouse reference genome assembly in genome annotations. Aminoacid change in longest transcript: indicates the change of aminoacid in the longest transcript. Coding region change in the longest transcript: indicates the change of nucleotide in the longest transcript.

Fig. (5). List of known genes carrying polymorphisms. The figure shows only genes carrying polymorphic variants existing on HGMD that had an associated phenotype. Chromosome: X, Y. Region: The region on the reference sequence at which the variant is located. Zygosity: Indicates whether the variant is homozygous or heterozygous. Qual: quality of variant calling. ccds (Consensus coding sequence): provides a dataset of protein-coding regions that are identically annotated on the human and mouse reference genome assembly in genome annotations. Aminoacid change: indicates the change of aminoacid in the coding region. Coding region change in longest transcript: indicates the change of nucleotide in the longest transcript. dbSNP: each code identifies a unique polymorphism.

Fig. (6). List of known and unknown genes carrying new mutations. The figure shows known genes (in green) and unknown genes (in white) carrying new mutations. All unknown genes carrying stop variants (value in red in coding region in the longest transcript). Chromosome: X, Y. Region: The region on the reference sequence at which the variant is located. Type: The type of variant. SNV (single-nucleotide variant), MNV (multi-nucleotide variant), insertion, deletion. Reference allele: Indicates if the variant is identical to the reference. Zygosity: Indicates whether the variant is homozygous or heterozygous. Qual: quality of variant calling. ccds (Consensus coding sequence): provides a dataset of protein-coding regions that are identically annotated on the human and mouse reference genome assembly in genome annotations. Aminoacid change: indicates the change of aminoacid in the coding region. Coding region change in longest transcript: indicates the change of nucleotide in the longest transcript.

Results from DNASTAR Lasergene Suite

62,109 variants in 58,321 genes were produced after alignment and variant calling by DNASTAR Lasergene Suite. These data included both known and unknown genes, so we chose to separate the known genes from the new candidate ones obtaining 173 variants in 90 known genes (Fig. **7**) and 12,015 variants in 6,690 new candidate genes (Fig. **8**).

1	Gene Name	dbSNP ID	RP32 Variant - Amino Acid Change	RP32 Variant - Classification	RP32 Variant - Genotype	RP32 Variant - LRT_pred	RP32 Variant - MutationTaster_pred	RP32 Variant - SIFT_pred
145	MYO7A	2276288	p.S1666C	Non-synonymous, targeted	Homo. Variant	Neutral (N)	Polymorphism - automatic (P)	Tolerated (T)
146	MYO7A	948962	p.L1954I, p.(=)	Non-synonymous, targeted	Hetero. Ref.	Neutral (N)	Polymorphism - automatic (P)	Tolerated (T)
147	CEP164	2305830	p.T988S, p.(=)	Non-synonymous, targeted	Hetero. Ref.	Neutral (N)	Polymorphism - automatic (P)	Tolerated (T)
148	CEP164	573455	p.Q1119R, p.(=)	Non-synonymous, targeted	Hetero. Ref.	Neutral (N)	Polymorphism - automatic (P)	Tolerated (T)
149	CEP164	756182128	p.T1311P, p.(=)	Non-synonymous, targeted	Hetero. Ref.	Neutral (N)	Polymorphism (N)	Tolerated (T)
150	CACNA2D4	10735005	p.I327V	Non-synonymous, targeted	Homo. Variant	Neutral (N)	Polymorphism - automatic (P)	Tolerated (T)
151	COL2A1	3803183	p.T9S	Non-synonymous, targeted	Homo. Variant	Neutral (N)	Polymorphism - automatic (P)	Tolerated (T)
152	TTLL5	2303345	p.A149V	Non-synonymous, targeted	Homo. Variant	Neutral (N)	Polymorphism - automatic (P)	Tolerated (T)
153	SPATA7	4904448	p.D2N	Non-synonymous, targeted	Homo. Variant	Neutral (N)	Polymorphism - automatic (P)	Tolerated (T)
154	TRPM1	2241493	p.S32N	Non-synonymous, targeted	Homo. Variant	Neutral (N)	Polymorphism - automatic (P)	Tolerated (T)
155	BBS4	2277598	p.I354T, p.(=)	Non-synonymous, targeted	Hetero. Ref.	Neutral (N)	Polymorphism - automatic (P)	
156	BBS2	4784677	p.S70N	Non-synonymous, targeted	Homo. Variant	Neutral (N)	Polymorphism - automatic (P)	Tolerated (T)
157	CNGB1	12927214	p.V535A, p.(=)	Non-synonymous, targeted	Hetero. Ref.	Neutral (N)	Polymorphism (N)	Tolerated (T)
158	CDH3	1126933	p.Q563H	Non-synonymous, targeted	Homo. Variant	Neutral (N)	Polymorphism - automatic (P)	Tolerated (T)
159	ADAMTS18	9930984	p.L769I, p.(=)	Non-synonymous, targeted	Hetero. Ref.	Neutral (N)	Polymorphism - automatic (P)	Tolerated (T)
160	GUCY2D	138836357	p.R365W, p.(=)	Non-synonymous, targeted	Hetero. Ref.	Neutral (N)	Polymorphism (N)	Damaging (D)
161	GPR179	369594894	p.R200P, p.(=)	Non-synonymous, targeted	Hetero. Ref.	Neutral (N)	Disease causing (D)	
162	LAMA1	607230	p.K2002E, p.(=)	Non-synonymous, targeted	Hetero. Ref.	Neutral (N)	Polymorphism - automatic (P)	Tolerated (T)
163	LAMA1	12607841	p.A1763V, p.(=)	Non-synonymous, targeted	Hetero. Ref.	Neutral (N)	Polymorphism - automatic (P)	Tolerated (T)
164	C3	2230199	p.R102G, p.(=)	Non-synonymous, targeted	Hetero. Ref.	Neutral (N)	Polymorphism - automatic (P)	Tolerated (T)
165	PNPLA6	17854645	p.A412P, p.(=)	Non-synonymous, targeted	Hetero. Ref.	Neutral (N)	Polymorphism - automatic (P)	Tolerated (T)
166	PANK2	3737084	p.G126A	Non-synonymous, targeted	Homo. Variant	Neutral (N)	Polymorphism - automatic (P)	Tolerated (T)
167	C21orf2	11552066	p.Q236R	Non-synonymous, targeted	Homo. Variant	Neutral (N)	Polymorphism - automatic (P)	Tolerated (T)
168	IFT27		p.A22E, p.(=)	Non-synonymous, targeted	Hetero. Ref.	Neutral (N)	Disease causing (D)	Damaging (D)
169	TUBGCP6	4838864	p.V1621L	Non-synonymous, targeted	Homo. Variant	Neutral (N)	Polymorphism - automatic (P)	Tolerated (T)
170	TUBGCP6	11703226	p.T1377A, p.(=)	Non-synonymous, targeted	Hetero. Ref.	Neutral (N)	Polymorphism - automatic (P)	Tolerated (T)
171	TUBGCP6	4838865	p.L567S, p.(=)	Non-synonymous, targeted	Hetero. Ref.	Neutral (N)	Polymorphism - automatic (P)	Tolerated (T)
172	CACNA1F	141159097	p.N746T	Non-synonymous, targeted	Variant	Neutral (N)	Disease causing (D)	Damaging (D)
173	OPN1MW		p.M153L	Non-synonymous, targeted	Variant	Neutral (N)	Polymorphism (N)	

Fig. (7). List of known genes carrying both polymorphic variants and new mutations. This figure shows known genes carrying both polymorphisms and new mutations. dbSNP ID: each code identifies a unique polymorphism. Variant aminoacid change: indicates the wild type aminoacid, the aminoacid change and the corresponding position. Variant classification: indicates the type of variant (non-synonymous, inframe, non-sense and frameshift). Variant-genotype: Indicates whether the variant is homozygous or heterozygous. Variant-depth: quality of variant calling. Variant-LRT_pred: pathogenicity prediction by LRT algorithm. Variant Mutation Taster_pred: pathogenicity prediction by Mutation taster algorithm. Variant - SIFT_pred: pathogenicity prediction by variant SIFT algorithm.

1	Gene Name	dbSNP ID	RP32 Variant - Amino Acid Change	RP32 Variant - Classification	RP32 Variant - Genotype	RP32 Variant - LRT_pred	RP32 Variant - MutationTaster_pred	RP32 Variant - SIFT_pred
11992	AF274856.1, MAGEA10	210585	p.R166K [MAGEA10]	Non-synonymous, targeted	Variant	Neutral (N)	Polymorphism - automatic (P)	Tolerated (T)
11993	GABRQ	3810651	p.I478F	Non-synonymous, targeted	Variant			
11994	CSAG1	2515848	p.R62K	Non-synonymous, targeted	Variant			
11995	PNMA5	146175766	p.A297T	Non-synonymous, targeted	Variant		Polymorphism (N)	Tolerated (T)
11996	PLXNB3	2266879	p.V598I	Non-synonymous, targeted	Variant	Neutral (N)	Polymorphism - automatic (P)	Tolerated (T)
11997	PLXNB3	6643791	p.E1156D	Non-synonymous, targeted	Variant	Neutral (N)	Polymorphism - automatic (P)	Tolerated (T)
11998	PLXNB3	5987155	p.M1535T	Non-synonymous, targeted	Variant	Neutral (N)	Polymorphism - automatic (P)	Tolerated (T)
11999	PLXNB3, SRPK3	146832392	p.V1596E [PLXNB3]	Non-synonymous, targeted	Variant	Neutral (N)	Polymorphism - automatic (P)	Tolerated (T)
12000	IRAK1	1059703	p.S532L	Non-synonymous, targeted	Variant	Neutral (N)	Polymorphism - automatic (P)	Tolerated (T)
12001	OPN1MW2	782285971	p.M153L	Non-synonymous, targeted	Variant	Neutral (N)	Polymorphism (N)	Tolerated (T)
12002	OPN1MW3		p.M153L	Non-synonymous, targeted	Variant	Neutral (N)	Polymorphism (N)	
12003	PLXNA3	5945430	p.E863D	Non-synonymous, targeted	Variant			
12004	UBL4A	7057286	p.H142R	Non-synonymous, targeted	Variant			
12005	CTAG2	17328091	p.E89Q	Non-synonymous, targeted	Variant			
12006	SLC25A6		p.Q50R	Non-synonymous, targeted	Variant			
12007	ASMTL		p.V458M	Non-synonymous, targeted	Variant			
12008	ASMTL		p.R113Q	Non-synonymous, splice, targeted	Variant			
12009	DHRSX		p.E297K	Non-synonymous, targeted	Variant			
12010	DHRSX		p.H292R	Non-synonymous, targeted	Variant			
12011	PCDH11Y	2524543	p.V917F	Non-synonymous, targeted	Variant			Tolerated (T)
12012	PCDH11Y	2563389	p.N1012K	Non-synonymous, targeted	Variant			Tolerated (T)
12013	TSPY8	410975	p.L239P	Non-synonymous, targeted	Variant			Tolerated (T)
12014	CDY2B		p.R57Q	Non-synonymous, targeted	Variant			Tolerated (T)
12015	CDY1		p.V497I	Non-synonymous, targeted	Variant			Tolerated (T)

Fig. (8). List of unknown genes carrying polymorphic variants but also new mutations. This figure shows unknown genes carrying both polymorphisms and new mutations. dbSNP ID: each code identifies a unique polymorphism. Variant aminoacid change: indicates the wild type aminoacid, the aminoacid change and the corresponding position. Variant classification: indicates the type of variant (non-synonymous, inframe, non-sense and frameshift). Variant-genotype: Indicates whether the variant is homozygous or heterozygous. Variant-depth: quality of variant calling. Variant-LRT_pred: pathogenicity prediction by LRT algorithm. Variant Mutation Taster_pred: pathogenicity prediction by Mutation taster algorithm. Variant - SIFT_pred: pathogenicity prediction by variant SIFT algorithm.

Gene Name	RP32 Variant - Called Seq	dbSNP ID	RP32 Variant - Amino Acid Change	RP32 Variant - Classification	RP32 Variant - Genotype	RP32 Variant - LRT_pred	RP32 Variant - MutationTaster_pred	RP32 Variant - SIFT_pred	RP32 Variant clinvar_clnsi	HGMD Phenotype
IQCB1	C>T|C	17849995	p.C434Y, p.(=)	Non-synonymous, targeted	Hetero. Ref.	Deleterious (D)	Polymorphism - automatic (P)	Tolerated (T)	Benign (2)	Sensorineural hearing loss
PDZD7	T>C|T	6584410	p.Q125R, p.(=)	Non-synonymous, targeted	Hetero. Ref.		Polymorphism - automatic (P)	Tolerated (T)		Macular degeneration, age-related, in smokers, association with
TTLL5	C>A	1981898	p.L262I	Non-synonymous, targeted	Homo. Variant		Polymorphism - automatic (P)	Tolerated (T)		Stationary night blindness, congenital
TRPM1	G>A|G	138886378	p.S157F, p.(=)	Non-synonymous, targeted	Hetero. Ref.	Deleterious (D)	Disease causing (D)	Damaging (D)		Leber congenital amaurosis
ADAMTS18	A>T|A	11640912	p.L626I, p.(=)	Non-synonymous, targeted	Hetero. Ref.	Deleterious (D)	Polymorphism - automatic (P)	Damaging (D)		Leber congenital amaurosis
ROM1	G>C	1799959	p.G118A	Non-synonymous, targeted	Homo. Variant	Neutral (N)	Polymorphism - automatic (P)	Tolerated (T)	Benign (2)	Usher syndrome 1b
MYO7A	T>C|T	1052030	p.L16S, p.(=)	Non-synonymous, targeted	Hetero. Ref.	Neutral (N)	Polymorphism - automatic (P)	Tolerated (T)		Deafness
TRPM1	A>G	4779816	p.M1?	No-start, targeted	Homo. Variant	Neutral (N)	Polymorphism - automatic (P)	Tolerated (T)		88Some (?)
ABCC6	T>C	6416668	p.M848V	Non-synonymous, targeted	Homo. Variant	Neutral (N)	Polymorphism - automatic (P)	Tolerated (T)		Bardet-Biedl syndrome
PITPNM3	C>T	3805835	p.A80T	Non-synonymous, targeted	Homo. Variant	Neutral (N)	Polymorphism - automatic (P)	Tolerated (T)	Benign (2)	Leber congenital amaurosis
LAMA1	T>C|T	662471	p.M1340V, p.(=)	Non-synonymous, targeted	Hetero. Ref.	Neutral (N)	Polymorphism - automatic (P)	Damaging (D)		Age-related macular degeneration, association with
C3	G>A|G	1047286	p.P314L, p.(=)	Non-synonymous, targeted	Hetero. Ref.	Neutral (N)	Polymorphism - automatic (P)	Damaging (D)	Benign (2)	Age-related macular degeneration, association with
DMD	C>T	1800280	p.R2937Q	Non-synonymous, targeted	Variant	Neutral (N)	Polymorphism - automatic (P)	Tolerated (T)	Benign (2)	Night blindness, congenital stationary 2

Fig. (9). List of known genes carrying polymorphic variants. This figure shows known genes carrying only polymorphisms existing on HGMD that have an associated phenotype. Variant call: indicates which nucleotide is changed. DbSNP ID: each code identifies a unique polymorphism. Variant aminoacid change: indicates the wild type aminoacid, the aminoacid change and the corresponding position. Variant classification: indicates the type of variant (non-synonymous, inframe, non-sense and frameshift). Variant-genotype: Indicates whether the variant is homozygous or heterozygous. Variant-depth: quality of variant calling. Variant-LRT_pred: pathogenicity prediction by LRT algorithm. Variant Mutation Taster_pred: pathogenicity prediction by Mutation taster algorithm. Variant - SIFT_pred: pathogenicity prediction by variant SIFT algorithm.

Gene Name	RP32 Variant - Called Seq	RP32 Variant - Amino Acid Change	RP32 Variant - Classification	RP32 Variant - Genotype	RP32 Variant - Depth	RP32 Variant - LRT_pred	2 Variant - MutationTaster_p	Variant - SIFT_pred
ALMS1	CTC > del 3	CTC	p.S524_P525delinsS	Inframe deletion, disruptive, targeted	Hetero. Ref.	136		
CEP250	A>C|A	p.K1714?, p.(=)	Non-synonymous, targeted	Hetero. Ref.	353	Deleterious (D)	Polymorphism (N)	Damaging (D)
USH2A	A>G|A	p.L3606?, p.(=)	Non-synonymous, targeted	Hetero. Ref.	315	Neutral (N)	Disease causing (D)	Damaging (D)
IFT27	G>T|G	p.A22E, p.(=)	Non-synonymous, targeted	Hetero. Ref.	145	Neutral (N)	Disease causing (D)	Damaging (D)
OPN1MW	A>C	p.M153L	Non-synonymous, targeted	Variant	180	Neutral (N)	Polymorphism (N)	

Fig. (10). List of known genes carrying new mutations. This figure shows known genes carrying only new mutations. Variant call: indicates which nucleotide is changed. dbSNP ID: each code identifies a unique polymorphism. Variant aminoacid change: indicates the wild type aminoacid, the aminoacid change and the corresponding position. Variant classification: indicates the type of variant (non-synonymous, inframe, non sense and frameshift). Variant-genotype: Indicates whether the variant is homozygous or heterozygous. Variant-depth: quality of variant calling. Variant-LRT_pred: pathogenicity prediction by LRT algorithm. Variant Mutation Taster_pred: pathogenicity prediction by Mutation taster algorithm. Variant - SIFT_pred: pathogenicity prediction by variant SIFT algorithm.

Gene Name	RP32 Variant - Called Seq	dbSNP ID	RP32 Variant - Amino Acid Change	RP32 Variant - Classification	RP32 Variant - Genotype	RP32 Variant - Depth	RP32 Variant - MutationTaster_pred
COL6A2	- > ins C	-	149954350	p.T160fs, p.(=)	Frameshift, targeted	Hetero. Ref.	293	
CCHCR1	C>T|C	3130453	p.W78, p.(=)	Nonsense, targeted	Hetero. Ref.	100	Polymorphism - automatic (P)
GPSM1	C>A|C	59873903	p.S428., p.(=)	Nonsense, targeted	Homo. Variant	181	Polymorphism - automatic (P)
OR4X1	T>A	10838851	p.Y273.	Nonsense, targeted	Homo. Variant	117	Polymorphism - automatic (P)
HELB	G > del 1	G	148126992	p.E522fs, p.(=)	Frameshift, targeted	Hetero. Ref.	95	
GPR33	G>A	17097921	p.R140.	Nonsense, targeted	Homo. Variant	177	
OR2J1	C>T|C	2394517	p.Q194., p.(=)	Nonsense, targeted	Hetero. Ref.	316	
TAAR9	A>T|A	2842899	p.K61., p.(=)	Nonsense, targeted	Hetero. Ref.	272	
SETBP1	> ins TCTT	-	3085861	p.T228fs, p.(=)	Frameshift, targeted	Hetero. Ref.	164	
OR52N4, TRIM5	A>T|A	4910844	p.R172., p.(=) [OR52N4], Change, genic, targeted [TRIM5]	Nonsense, targeted [OR52N4]	Hetero. Ref.	199	Polymorphism - automatic (P)
SERPINB11	G>T	4940595	p.E90.	Nonsense, targeted	Homo. Variant	157	
SLC3A1	T > del 1	T	766198611	p.L380fs, p.(=)	Frameshift, targeted	Hetero. Ref.	271	
OR10X1	C>T|C	863362	p.W66., p.(=)	Nonsense, targeted	Hetero. Ref.	172	Polymorphism - automatic (P)

Fig. (11). List of unknown genes carrying polymorphic variants. This figure shows unknown genes carrying polymorphisms that existing on HGMD and had an associated phenotype. The genes highlighted in green have an overall p-value ≤ 0.05. Variant call: indicates which nucleotide is changed. dbSNP ID: each code identifies a unique polymorphism. Variant aminoacid change: indicates the wild type aminoacid, the aminoacid change and the corresponding position. Variant classification: indicates the type of variant (non-synonymous, inframe, non-sense and frameshift). Variant-genotype: Indicates whether the variant is homozygous or heterozygous. Variant-depth: quality of variant calling. Variant-LRT_pred: pathogenicity prediction by LRT algorithm. Variant Mutation Taster_pred: pathogenicity prediction by Mutation taster algorithm. Variant - SIFT_pred: pathogenicity prediction by variant SIFT algorithm.

Among known genes, we have selected polymorphic variants found on HGMD that showed an associated pathological phenotype. Also, new mutations were selected. We obtained 14 polymorphism variants in 14 different known genes

(Fig. **9**) and 6 new mutations in 6 different known genes (Fig. **10**).

As already mentioned, we filtered both new mutations and polymorphisms in new genes obtaining 14 polymorphism variants (Fig. **11**) and 267 new mutations (Fig. **12**). However, among these variants, only those that, after being prioritized by ToppGene, showed an overall p-value ≤ 0.05, were chosen.

	Gene Name	RP32 Variant - Called Seq	RP32 Variant - Amino Acid Change	RP32 Variant - Classification	RP32 Variant Genotype	RP32 Variant - Depth	RP32 Variant - LRT_pred	RP32 Variant - MutationTaster_pred	RP32 Variant - SIFT_pred
236	DCCX8	C>G|C	p.W916C, p.(=)	Non-synonymous, targeted	Hetero. Ref	186	Deleterious (D)	Disease causing (D)	Damaging (D)
237	FCGBP	TG>CT|TG	p.P1827Q, p.(=)	Non-synonymous, targeted	Hetero. Ref	539			
238	FCGBP	CA>TG|CA	p.L1624P, p.(=)	Non-synonymous, targeted	Hetero. Ref	540			
239	FCGBP	T>G|T	p.T1501P, p.(=)	Non-synonymous, targeted	Hetero. Ref	463			
240	FCGBP	GC>TG|GC	p.P1500T, p.(=)	Non-synonymous, targeted	Hetero. Ref	472		Polymorphism (N)	
241	FCGBP	G>A|G	p.P828S, p.(=)	Non-synonymous, targeted	Hetero. Ref	825		Polymorphism (N)	
242	FCGBP	GG>AT|GG	p.P750S, p.(=)	Non-synonymous, targeted	Hetero. Ref	722			
243	FCGBP	CA>TG|CA	p.L423P, p.(=)	Non-synonymous, targeted	Hetero. Ref	683			
244	FCGBP	T>C	p.H133R	Non-synonymous, targeted	Homo. Variant	236			
245	MAP3K10	T>G|T	p.S779P, p.(=)	Non-synonymous, targeted	Hetero. Ref	84	Neutral (N)	Polymorphism (N)	Tolerated (T)
246	IZUMO1	C>A|C	p.E215, p.(=)	Nonsense, targeted	Hetero. Ref	290	Neutral (N)	Disease causing - automatic (A)	
247	LILRA2	G>A|G	p.G16D, p.(=)	Non-synonymous, targeted	Hetero. Ref	93	Neutral (N)	Polymorphism (N)	Tolerated (T)
248	LILRA2	C>A|C	p.L141I, p.(=)	Non-synonymous, targeted	Hetero. Ref	594	Deleterious (D)	Polymorphism (N)	Damaging (D)
249	LILRA1	T>A|T	p.W48R, p.(=)	Non-synonymous, targeted	Hetero. Ref	341	Neutral (N)	Polymorphism (N)	
250	LILRB1	C>G|C	p.Q6E, p.(=)	Non-synonymous, targeted	Hetero. Ref	465		Polymorphism (N)	Damaging (D)
251	LILRB1	G>T|G	p.G10V, p.(=)	Non-synonymous, targeted	Hetero. Ref	541		Polymorphism (N)	Tolerated (T)
252	LILRB1	T > del 1	T	p.S16fs, p.(=)	Frameshift, targeted	Hetero. Ref	420			
253	ZNF444	CCCGGCAG > del 9	CCCGGCAG	p.H229_S232delinsH	Inframe deletion, disruptive, targeted	Hetero. Ref	134			
254	ZNF311	G > del 1	p.V106fs	Frameshift, targeted	Homo. Variant	183			
255	DEFB132	TGGTCT > del 6	TGGTCT	p.L8_L8delinsL	Inframe deletion, disruptive, targeted	Hetero. Ref	176			
256	PP565260.3	G>A|G	p.V128?, p.(=)	Non-synonymous, targeted	Hetero. Ref	121			
257	DDT	A>C|A	p.M48R, p.(=)	Non-synonymous, targeted	Hetero. Ref	293	Deleterious (D)	Disease causing (D)	Damaging (D)
258	KIAA1671	G>C|G	p.A183P, p.(=)	Non-synonymous, targeted	Hetero. Ref	144	Neutral (N)	Polymorphism (N)	Damaging (D)
259	SEZ6L	A>C|A	p.K888T, p.(=)	Non-synonymous, targeted	Hetero. Ref	997	Deleterious (D)	Disease causing (D)	Damaging (D)
260	SLC5A4, SLC5A4-AS1	C > del 1	p.V143fs [SLC5A4]	frameshift, targeted [SLC5A4], Change, genic, targeted [SLC5A4-AS...	Homo. Variant	91			
261	APOL4	CT > del 2	CT	p.E111fs	Frameshift, targeted	Hetero. Ref	110			
262	MKL1	A>C|A	p.F304V, p.(=)	Non-synonymous, targeted	Hetero. Ref	299	Deleterious (D)	Disease causing (D)	Tolerated (T)
263	GPR50	CACCACTGGCCA > del 12	p.P501_M505delinsP	Inframe deletion, disruptive, targeted	Variant	136			
264	SLC25A6	T>C	p.Q50R	Non-synonymous, targeted	Variant	195			
265	ASMTL	C>T	p.V458M	Non-synonymous, targeted	Variant	88			
266	DHRSX	T>C	p.H292R	Non-synonymous, targeted	Variant	84			
267	CD1	G>A	p.V497I	Non-synonymous, targeted	Variant	94			Tolerated (T)

Fig. (12). List of unknown genes carrying new mutations. This figure shows unknown genes carrying new mutations. Only 31 genes have an overall p-value ≤ 0.05 (data not shown). Variant call: indicates which nucleotide is changed. dbSNP ID: each code identifies a unique polymorphism. Variant aminoacid change: indicates the wild type aminoacid, the aminoacid change and the corresponding position. Variant classification: indicates the type of variant (non-synonymous, inframe, non-sense and frameshift). Variant-genotype: Indicates whether the variant is homozygous or heterozygous. Variant-depth: quality of variant calling. Variant-LRT_pred: pathogenicity prediction by LRT algorithm. Variant Mutation Taster_pred: pathogenicity prediction by Mutation taster algorithm. Variant - SIFT_pred: pathogenicity prediction by variant SIFT algorithm.

Results from ToppGene

The last step consisted of the indirect prioritization of yet unknown RP associated/causative genes. In general, ToppGene generates two types of output: the training results and the test results.

The training results show the results of each annotation used for the prioritization analysis. A sub-ranking is created for each annotation. The most relevant notations are those associated with the highest number of genes. Our obtained training results are shown in Fig. (**13**).

The test results, instead, show a prioritization ranking of candidate genes based on the calculation of similarity with the annotations. Genes are arranged in ascending order based on the value of the overall p-value. Genes that present an overall p-value < 0.05 are statistically more significant. Our obtained training results are shown in Fig. (**14**).

Fig. (13). ToppGene representation of training results. The figure shows the results produced by ToppGene after filtering process. These results represent the outputs of the semantic correlation between the input genes and the annotations. Molecular Function: describes the biochemical activity of gene product. Biological process: describes all the molecular activities carried out by a gene product. Cellular component: refers only to cellular anatomy. Human Phenotype: gives phenotype information on product genes. Pathway: network between genes. PubMed: related genes linked in the same paper. Interaction: indicates genes interaction. Coexpression: correlation between genes that are coexpressed.

Test Results [Hide Detail] [Download] [Show Network]

Rank (r=1)	Gene Symbol	Gene ID	Average score	Overall P-value
1	COL18A1	80781	5.456E-1	7.907E-4
2	DHFR	1719	5.673E-1	1.253E-3
3	CFAP251	144406	3.998E-1	4.529E-3
4	KRT10	3858	4.407E-1	1.013E-2
5	COL27A1	85301	4.179E-1	1.123E-2
6	ANLN	54443	4.826E-1	1.134E-2
7	NEFH	4744	4.357E-1	1.467E-2
8	SMPD1	6609	4.270E-1	1.550E-2
9	MUC4	4585	4.482E-1	1.757E-2
10	RUNX2	860	4.311E-1	1.766E-2
11	CASP3	836	3.232E-1	2.647E-2
12	FMN2	56776	4.080E-1	2.966E-2
13	TOP2B	7155	3.335E-1	4.594E-2
14	HLA-B	3106	3.094E-1	5.225E-2
15	MPRIP	23164	3.213E-1	5.643E-2
16	WDR47	22911	2.892E-1	7.672E-2
17	MUC20	200958	2.530E-1	7.809E-2
18	IST1	9750	3.254E-1	9.316E-2
19	MUC6	4588	2.988E-1	1.131E-1
20	MSH3	4437	2.649E-1	1.166E-1
21	NOTCH4	4855	2.760E-1	1.279E-1
22	HLA-A	3105	2.503E-1	1.291E-1
23	HLA-DRB1	3123	2.502E-1	1.309E-1
24	ECD	11319	2.841E-1	1.328E-1
25	HLA-DQB1	3119	2.502E-1	1.364E-1
26	PCSK9	255738	2.962E-1	1.424E-1
27	LFNG	3955	2.895E-1	1.437E-1
28	LURAP1L-AS1	101929467	4.991E-1	1.445E-1
29	ZFPM1	161882	2.872E-1	1.462E-1
30	MUC12	10071	1.278E-1	1.526E-1
31	TPSAB1	7177	2.147E-1	1.848E-1
32	ARID1B	57492	2.910E-1	1.904E-1
33	BPTF	2186	2.699E-1	2.039E-1

Fig. (14). Toppgene representation of test results. The figure shows the results obtained by ToppGene after filtering process. This is a list of genes ordered according to a decreasing statistical significance value.

Unknown genes carrying both polymorphisms and new mutations obtained from CLC Genomics Workbench and DNASTAR Lasergene Suite were prioritized by ToppGene after being filtered. We obtained 69 genes carrying new mutations from CLC Genomics Workbench, but only the first 17 genes were considered reliable (overall p-value < 0.05) (Fig. **15**).

	GeneSymbolO:	Molecular Function pValu	GO: Biological Process pValue	GO: Cellular Component pValue	Human Phenotype pValue	Overall pValue
2	CASP3	0.09256390395042603	0.010069713400464756	0.05635166537567777	0.0	7,00E+11
3	COL18A1	0.047250193648334625	0.028272656855151047	0.052672347017815646	0.014910921766072812	0.0011011154939315482
4	HLA-A	0.09256390395042603	0.13439194422927964	0.05635166537567777	0.014910921766072812	0.0035744517176515833
5	DHFR	0.022269558481797055	0.05867544539116964	0.1795120061967467	0.030015491866769946	0.011132693551697382
6	RUNX2	0.0029047250193648335	0.021688613477924088	0.07939581719597212	0.022269558481797055	0.013775608068991807
7	NEFH	0.042602633617350893	0.013361735089078234	0.017234701781154668	0.020333075135553835	0.014123964182042315
8	SMPD1	0.05015491866769946	0.09256390395042603	0.11463981409759876	0.017041053446940357	0.014364571246918034
9	KRT10	0.04240898528272657	0.06022463206816421	0.030983733539891558	0.037180480247869865	0.015376682047432921
10	WDR66	0.5666150271107668	0.1386522075910147	0.0029047250193648335	0.0	0.01943303328258028
11	HLA-B	0.09256390395042603	0.13439194422927964	0.05635166537567777	0.014910921766072812	0.022238759696324717
12	HLA-DRB1	0.5666150271107668	0.13439194422927964	0.05635166537567777	0.014910921766072812	0.02762505073335486
13	NOTCH4	0.09256390395042603	0.032532920216886134	0.061967467079783116	0.0	0.02827548211014219
14	MPRIP	0.06177381874515879	0.133423702556158	0.022850503485670023	0.0	0.02849118964377262
15	PCSK9	0.06525948876839659	0.0245493338497288925	0.05635166537567777	0.014910921766072812	0.029000019483872208
16	ANLN	0.06177381874515879	0.03756777691711851	0.027885360185902403	0.03111738187451588	0.045065469485283005
17	HLA-DQB1	0.06525948876839659	0.13439194422927964	0.05635166537567777	0.014910921766072812	0.046154062611940994
18	ECD	0.09256390395042603	0.1690549961270333	0.14136328427575523	0.0	0.04628944465751206

Fig. (15). Toppgene rank of significant "unknown" gene from CLC Genomics Workbench. The figure shows a list of "unkown" mutated genes obtained from ToppGene and CLC Genomics Workbench results. Only genes with an overall pvalue < 0.05 are shown.

220 genes carrying new mutations were obtained from the ToppGene prioritization process of data generated after all filtering procedures on DNASTAR Lasergene Suite dataset, but only the first 28 genes were selected (Fig. **16**). Regarding polymorphic variants, we obtained 14 genes carrying SNPs, of which only 3 were relevant (Fig. **17**).

1	GeneSymbol	GO: Molecular Function pValue	GO: Biological Process pValue	GO: Cellular Component pValue	Human Phenotype pValue	Overall pValue
2	OPN1MW3	0.0017428350116189002	0.012006196746707979	0.009295120061967466	0.0	5,34E+10
3	GFAP	0.039504260263361735	0.039504260263361735	0.027498063516653758	0.017041053446940357	1,05E+11
4	WDR60	0.09101471727343145	0.007552285050348567	0.0021301316808675446	0.016266460108443067	4,16E+12
5	TUBA4A	0.0034856700232378003	0.007552285050348567	0.015104570100697134	0.06254841208365608	5,70E+10
6	KIF17	0.012393493415956624	0.007939581719597211	5,81E+11	0.0	9,77E+11
7	CEP295	0.05325329202168862	0.10670023237800155	0.012199845081332301	0.0	0.001013368275499249
8	CCDC103	0.06564678543764524	0.007552285050348567	0.0036793183578621223	0.0	0.005522888486688027
9	RTBDN	0.03640588690937258	0.2352827265685515	0.047250193648334625	0.0	0.005565559568035505
10	MDK	0.08597986057319908	0.014136328427575524	0.2546475600309837	0.0	0.006709700847849831
11	GPSM1	0.006777691711851278	0.12296669248644462	0.08249419054996127	0.0	0.007607244468867402
12	DNAAF5	0.09101471727343145	0.007939581719597211	0.044151820294345466	0.04686289697908598	0.008995399898863332
13	NOTCH3	0.0687451587916344	0.0313710302091402	0.08094500387296669	0.016266460108443067	0.011944328897440792
14	PTGES3	0.09101471727343145	0.05460883036405887	0.017041053446940357	0.0	0.013377713661589796
15	NEFH	0.038536018590240126	0.015491866769945779	0.02536793183578621	0.020333075135553835	0.015289999122305331
16	MAP3K1	0.012393493415956624	0.021107668474051124	0.03679318357862122	0.016266460108443067	0.015529034975175549
17	VWF	0.03582494190549961	0.12645236250968242	0.22618125484120838	0.03969790859798606	0.01897535095556757
18	ALPK2	0.026529821843532145	0.06080557707203718	0.23412083656080557	0.0	0.022073874314664232
19	AMBRA1	0.09101471727343145	0.0687451587916344	0.005422153369481022	0.0	0.02324573402963881
20	TSPEAR	0.5675832687838884	0.061967467079783116	0.0023237800154918666	0.049573973663826494	0.02324962917595297
21	ACTN2	0.0017428350116189002	0.018590240123934933	0.009876065065840434	0.048218435321456234	0.024752284747917797
22	NLRP3	0.015298218435321457	0.06797056545313711	0.13226181254841207	0.016266460108443067	0.025467853263363982
23	TBX6	0.02072037180480248	0.0085205267234070178	0.2410921766072812	0.03756777691711851	0.02979122193379935
24	SOBP	0.09101471727343145	0.020526723470178157	0.2546475600309837	0.04240898528272657	0.031184212508603926
25	MPRIP	0.061192873741285826	0.16208365608055772	0.029821843532145623	0.0	0.03229005634420179
26	TNIP2	0.09101471727343145	0.11328427575522851	0.2410921766072812	0.0	0.0414168245859301
27	ERBB3	0.010263361735089079	0.06371030209140201	0.1979085979860573	0.032339271882261815	0.047805232736798375
28	HMCN2	0.04279628195197521	0.6200619764670798	0.05615801704105345	0.0	0.04873806042784323
29	EML3	0.05325329202168862	0.13303640588690938	0.0261425251742835	0.0	0.04890083529584144

Fig. (16). Toppgene rank of significant "unknown" gene carrying new mutation from DNASTAR Lasergene Suite. The figure shows a list of "unknown" genes carrying new mutations obtained from Toppgene and DNASTAR Lasergene Suite results. Only genes with an overall p-value < 0.05 are shown.

1	GeneSymbol	GO: Molecular Function pValue	GO: Biological Process pValue	GO: Cellular Component pValue	Human Phenotype pValue	Overall pValue
2	GPSM1	0.009488768396591789	0.09430673896204493	0.05247869868319133	0.0	0.00472041913709087
3	CCHCR1	0.06835786212238575	0.09082106893880712	0.028272656855151047	0.0	0.016083869886416524
4	COL6A2	0.04783113865220759	0.08733539891556932	0.09450038729666925	0.03446940356312936	0.04984762804099763

Fig. (17). Toppgene rank of significant "unknown" gene carrying SNPs from DNASTAR Lasergene Suite. The figure shows a list of genes carrying polymorphic variants obtained from Toppgene and DNASTAR Lasergene Suite results. Only genes with an overall p-value < 0.05 are shown.

DISCUSSION

In this work, genes from the exome analysis of a patient with an orphan form of retinitis pigmentosa were prioritized. Generally, one tool only is sufficient for a complete NGS data analysis, but we chose to use two different software packages (CLC Genomics Workbench and DNASTAR Lasergene Suite) with the aim of making a comparison between both output data sets, trying to obtain a more statistically significant result. ToppGene was then selected as the tool for the prioritization process, as it is considered the most powerful and reliable. Like initial NGS data analysis phases, also downstream prioritization is usually performed using more than one tool, to narrow down selection to the genes most statistically associated with the disease of interest [11, 12]. Actually, if the number of input genes to compare is very high, there is the risk of obtaining an unreliable result because the statistical bias is higher. Therefore, our proposed strategy could allow this drawback to be overcome, helping researchers to carry out more accurate and reliable analyses. The data we obtained from WES was filtered before being prioritized by ToppGene. This approach made it possible to work with significantly fewer genes, producing more truthful and statistically reliable data at the end of analytic processes. We used Excel software to perform the filtering process, exploiting many advantages coming from its use [13]. It is universal software, available to everyone, easy to use and with the "conditional formatting" option that offers an immediate visual impact of filtered data, given the large amount of data to analyze. Once the initial wide quantity of data was reduced, ToppGene prioritization could be performed. We chose this tool over others as it is the most complete, no log-in is required, nothing need be installed, is free of charge and, above all, is reliable. Furthermore, it offers better performance if compared to the other available tools, and the output results from the combination of 6 different data sources. Another unique feature is the use of mouse phenotype for candidate gene prioritization [14].

In conclusion, we proposed a complex analytic pipeline for gene prioritization analysis, based on a mixed approach of initial filtering and powerful downstream tools. This approach could offer more reliable results that could help data analysts to perform better and more significant downstream analysis.

REFERENCES

[1] Guala D, Sonnhammer ELL. A large-scale benchmark of gene prioritization methods. Sci Rep 2017; 7: 46598.
     [http://dx.doi.org/10.1038/srep46598] [PMID: 28429739]

[2] Adie EA, Adams RR, Evans KL, Porteous DJ, Pickard BS. SUSPECTS: enabling fast and effective prioritization of positional candidates. Bioinformatics 2006; 22(6): 773-4.
     [http://dx.doi.org/10.1093/bioinformatics/btk031] [PMID: 16423925]

[3] Seelow D, Schwarz JM, Schuelke M. GeneDistiller--distilling candidate genes from linkage intervals. PLoS One 2008; 3(12): e3874.
     [http://dx.doi.org/10.1371/journal.pone.0003874] [PMID: 19057649]

[4] Hutz JE, Kraja AT, McLeod HL, Province MA. CANDID: a flexible method for prioritizing candidate genes for complex human traits. Genet Epidemiol 2008; 32(8): 779-90.
     [http://dx.doi.org/10.1002/gepi.20346] [PMID: 18613097]

[5] Pesquita C, Faria D, Falcão AO, Lord P, Couto FM. Semantic similarity in biomedical ontologies. PLOS Comput Biol 2009; 5(7): e1000443.
     [http://dx.doi.org/10.1371/journal.pcbi.1000443] [PMID: 19649320]

[6] Ashburner M, Ball CA, Blake JA, *et al.* Gene ontology: tool for the unification of biology. Nat Genet 2000; 25(1): 25-9.
     [http://dx.doi.org/10.1038/75556] [PMID: 10802651]

[7]   Schriml LM, Mitraka E, Munro J, *et al.* Human Disease Ontology 2018 update: classification, content and workflow expansion. Nucleic Acids Res 2019; 47(D1): D955-62.
[http://dx.doi.org/10.1093/nar/gky1032] [PMID: 30407550]

[8]   Osborne JD, Flatow J, Holko M, *et al.* Annotating the human genome with Disease Ontology. BMC Genomics 2009; 10 (Suppl. 1): S6.
[http://dx.doi.org/10.1186/1471-2164-10-S1-S6] [PMID: 19594883]

[9]   Chen J, Bardes EE, Aronow BJ, Jegga AG. ToppGene Suite for gene list enrichment analysis and candidate gene prioritization. Nucleic Acids Res 2009; 37: W305-11.
[http://dx.doi.org/10.1093/nar/gkp427] [PMID: 19465376]

[10]   Rosenfeld JA, Mason CE, Smith TM. Limitations of the human reference genome for personalized genomics. PLoS One 2012; 7(7): e40294.
[http://dx.doi.org/10.1371/journal.pone.0040294] [PMID: 22811759]

[11]   Köhler S, Bauer S, Horn D, Robinson PN. Walking the interactome for prioritization of candidate disease genes. Am J Hum Genet 2008; 82(4): 949-58.
[http://dx.doi.org/10.1016/j.ajhg.2008.02.013] [PMID: 18371930]

[12]   Aerts S, Lambrechts D, Maity S, *et al.* Gene prioritization through genomic data fusion. Nat Biotechnol 2006; 24(5): 537-44.
[http://dx.doi.org/10.1038/nbt1203] [PMID: 16680138]

[13]   Nitsch D, Gonçalves JP, Ojeda F, de Moor B, Moreau Y. Candidate gene prioritization by network analysis of differential expression using machine learning approaches. BMC Bioinformatics 2010; 11: 460.
[http://dx.doi.org/10.1186/1471-2105-11-460] [PMID: 20840752]

[14]   Chen J, Xu H, Aronow B, Jegga A. Improved human disease candidate gene prioritization using mouse phenotype. BMC Inform 2007; 8: 392.

CHAPTER 4

New Integrated Differential Expression Approach for RNA-Seq Data Analysis

Abstract: The correct identification of differentially expressed genes is a key concept of many areas of genetic studies. Since 1990s, many different approaches, methods, algorithms and statistics tools have been developed to analyze gene expression levels of thousands of genes.

However, due to the growing complexity of managing, processing and interpreting sequencing data in order to obtain reliable results, there is no consensus about the most appropriate protocols and tools for the identification of differentially expressed genes, starting from RNA-Seq data.

Thus, we propose an integrated and comprehensive approach that combines the most used algorithms for DEG analysis, starting from the raw count data table. The proposed method consists of three main steps: 1) preliminary data analysis and visualization; 2) differential gene expression analysis, using Bioconductor packages (DESeq2, edgeR, Limma, SAMSeq, TweeDESeq) and standard ANOVA (ez and afex packages); 3) integration of results, using two main graphical outputs, through SuperExactTest, UpSetR plots and ComplexHeatmaps packages.

In this way, a more robust output could be obtained in a simple manner, and with no previous bioinformatic knowledge.

Keywords: Clustering comparison, Combination-based procedure, Concordance analysis, Differential Expression Analysis, Intersections, Integration of results, Normalization, Overlap proportion, Parametric and non- parametric, Performance evaluation, p-values and Π score, RNA-Seq Data, ROC, Sensitivity, Simulations, Specificity, SuperExactTest, Tools comparison, UpSetR and ComplexHeatmaps, Validity of DEG tools.

INTRODUCTION

For most of the past decades, DNA microarrays were the predominant technology for expression profiling, but in the past few years, RNA sequencing has emerged as a new tool for transcriptomics. Since its introduction, RNA sequencing protocols have been improved, and nowadays, it is used for many applications.

Luigi Donato, Simona Alibrandi, Rosalia D'Angelo, Concetta Scimone, Antonina Sidoti and Alessandra Costa

RNA-Seq data are represented by counts for each gene so that a count table, with features as rows and samples as columns, is the starting point for all the analysis. Moreover, for RNA-Seq protocol, the negative binomial (NB) distribution, sometimes called overdispersed Poisson distribution, is assumed as the gold standard, because of its ability to accurately model RNA-Seq data both with a low number of replicates and with higher variance with respect to the classical Poisson distribution. However, RNA-Seq data often suffers from many zero counts, that make it harder to fit a standard negative binomial distribution, so that a more recent paper [1] introduced the possibility to use a more general family of distribution, the Poisson Tweedie family. It can automatically adapt to highly skewed count data with excessive zeros, without the need to introduce some zero-inflated components or without dropping those zero counts from the sample of analysis, but through the estimation of the correspondent Tweedie power parameters.

Moreover, the methods for differential gene expression analysis can be grouped into two subsets: parametric and non-parametric. Parametric algorithms are able to capture all the information about the data, within the set parameters, because they map each expression value for gene into a particular distribution chosen by the researcher, while non-parametric methods are based on ranking and they do not assume a prior distribution form for the data, so that they are able to capture and analyze more details about distribution.

Regarding the RNA-Seq DEG analysis, some tools, such as edgeR and DESEq2, assume a negative binomial distribution, while others, such as NOISeq and SAMSeq, adopt a non-parametric method, but there is no agreement about the best tool to use. In bioinformatics, there are no standard methods available to detect DE genes based on such data, and this topic is still developing, even if some past researches focus on the evaluation and comparison of the available tools. In particular, Kvam *et al.* [2] offered a systematic review of statistical methods for detecting differentially expressed genes by distinguishing among methods based on Poisson distribution and those based on negative binomial. Rappaport *et al.* [3] evaluated a set of the most commonly used packages (Cuffdiff, edgeR, PoissonSeq, baySeq and limma) by focusing on normalization methods, accuracy metrics and sequencing depth. Zhang *et al.* [4], comparing the performances of three tools of DEG analysis (Cutfflinks-Cuffdiff2, DESeq and edgeR), founded that edgeR performs slightly better in terms of ability to uncover true positive and suggested to use the intersection of differentially expressed genes individuated by each method, if the number of false-positive is the main focus of the analysis.

More recently, Spies *et al.* [5] compared existing TC RNA-Seq tools on a simulation dataset and validated the best performing tool using a published dataset. Finally, Assefa *et al.* [6] evaluated the performances of DEG analysis, by focusing on long non-coding RNA sequencing data and low expressed mRNAs, showing the superior ability of controlling the false discovery rate (FDR) for Limma and SAMSeq.

Therefore, in order to perform an accurate DEG analysis, we propose an integrated pipeline, that starts from row count data table and results in a unique set of differentially expressed genes, by combining different Bioconductor tools (DESeq2, edgeR, limma, SAMSeq and TweeDESeq) and standard R packages (ez and afex) for performing ANOVA and various pipelines.

A schematic workflow of the whole pipeline is reported in Fig. (**1**).

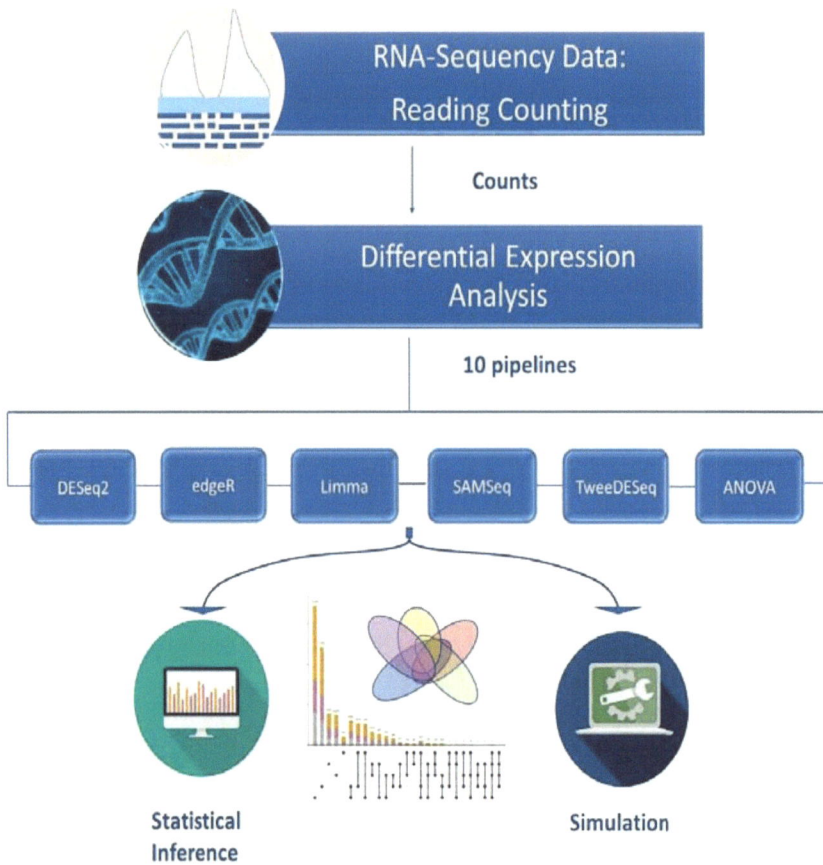

Fig. (1). Diagram of DEG analysis proposed pipeline. Here, it is summarized the whole pipeline used throughout the entire chapter.

MATERIAL AND METHODS

Software Packages for Detecting Differentially Expressed Genes

Here, we briefly introduce the R packages used for defining the new combined pipeline for the differential gene expression analysis between two groups of samples. For each package, we follow the instructions and the recommendations provided in the software manuals so that for more detailed descriptions, one could refer to the original publications (see Table **1**).

Table 1. List of DE tools. List of DE tools used in this chapter with software information (version of each tool) and statistical characteristics.

Pipeline		Version	Ref.	Family Distrib.	Norm.	Correction for Multiple Testing
DESEq2	Default GLM	1.24.0	Love *et al.* (2014)	Negative Binomial	DESEq2 Median of ratios	Benjamini Hockberg
DESeq2_NoFiltering	GLM with independent filtering disabled					
edgeR	Default with common and tagwise dispersion factor	3.26.8	Robinson *et al.* (2010)	Negative Binomial	TMM	Benjamini Hockberg
edgeR_robust	Robust GLM		Zhou *et al.* (2014)			
LimmaVoom	Gaussian distribution on log-transformed counts, with mean-variance trend incorporated into the precision weights	3.40.6	Law *et al.* (2014)	Linear model	TMM	Benjamini Hockberg
LimmaVoom_robust	Robust fit					
Limma_trend	Gaussian distribution on log-transformed counts, with the trend incorporated into the empirical Bayes moderation.					

(Table 1) contd.....

SAMSeq	Non parametric default method based on Wilcoxon rank statistic	3.0	Li and Tibshirani (2011)	None	Poisson Sampling	Permutation
TweeDESeq	Default	1.34.0	Esnaola *et al.* (2013)	Tweedie distr. family	edgeR TMM	Benjamini Hockberg
ANOVA	Default	ez:: 4.0-0 afex::0.27-2	-	Linear Model	Log2	Benjamini Hockberg

DESEeq2

DESeq2 is the natural successor of DESeq package. It relies on count data and tests for differences among expression gene levels in different conditions on the basis of a negative binomial distribution. As a normalization method, DESeq2 proposes the median of ratio method, combined with the gene-wise normalization factor, while the dispersion parameter is fitted through a three- steps procedure. First, a dispersion value is estimated with a maximum likelihood approach for each gene; second, a smooth curve is fitted for obtaining a reliable estimate for the expected dispersion value for each gene and finally, the dispersion parameter is estimated through a Bayes approach, that allows the shrinkage of the estimated gene-wise dispersion parameter toward the value predicted by the curve. Finally, for each gene, after a GLM fit, DESeq2 tests whether each model coefficient is different from zero, by adopting a Wald test on the shrunken estimate of LFC. Moreover, when testing for differences in the expression levels, DESeq2 automatically provides an independent filter that allows to increase the power of the multiple testing procedure by fixing a threshold to maximize the number of significant genes, at a given level of false discovery rate (FDR). Obviously, this filter could be disabled [7].

edgeR

edgeR is based on a negative binomial distribution, but differently from DESeq2, the normalization uses the Trimmed Mean of M-values (TMM) approach. Moreover, it moderates the degree of overdispersion through a Bayes procedure. For testing the differences among expression gene levels, the procedure varies among the existing pipelines because edgeR classic (or, simply, edgeR) uses a Fisher's exact test while edgeR robust, less sensitive to outliers and more powerful, tests for differences through the GLM likelihood ratio test, by incorporating weights computed from residuals. Finally, for both edgeR variants, the p-values are corrected with Benjamini-Hockeberg [8].

Limma

Limma-based methods were originally proposed for microarray data, but they are commonly used for RNA-Seq data. With respect to other methods, Limma-based approaches rely on linear modeling, and they do not work on raw count data, but they require a transformation of the data before entering into the limma pipeline. Instead of focusing on the specification of the exact probabilistic distribution of the counts, Limma concentrates on the estimation of the mean-variance relationship, and the estimation process differs among pipelines. In particular, Limma Voom uses precision weights while Limma trend enters the normalize log-counts and associated precision weights into any statistical pipeline. Moreover, while Limma trend estimates the mean-variance relationship at gene level, Limma voom applies it at observation levels. Finally, all the variants apply Benjamini-Hockeberg correction for multicomparisons [9].

SAMSeq

SAMSeq is a more recent R tool for the analysis of RNA-Seq data, and it is the only one parametric approach we describe in more detail and we include in the analysis. Since it is a non-parametric method, it does not make any assumption about the distribution of data counts so that it is able to capture more details about real data. Moreover, it could be applied to different classes of outcomes (quantitative, survival, two-class or multiple class outcomes), guaranteeing more flexibility in the analysis to be conducted with respect to other methods (to our knowledge, only PoissonSeq could be applied for quantitative and multiclass outcomes, but no for survival data, while other parametric approaches are limited to the two-class outcomes). SAMSeq tests for differences in gene expression levels with an average Wilcoxon ran-sum statistic, based on a resampling Poisson strategy, for overcoming variability in sequencing depth of counts. Finally, since the distribution of the averaged Wilcoxon statistic is unknown, SAMSeq applies a permutation plug-in to generate the null distribution and to estimate FDR [10].

TweeDESeq

TweeDESeq R package allows for taking into account zero values in raw count data, through a Tweedy family distribution. The latter includes a series of distributions with variance modeled through a multiplicative structure between the mean and the dispersion parameter, respectively M and φ, so that $var(x)=\varphi M p$, with p a shape parameter whose values range from zero of a normal distribution to infinite of extreme stable distributions. Through Tweedy distributions, TweeDESeq package is able to directly fit heavy-tails and zero inflation. From a technical point of view, TweeDESeq relies on TMM and quantile to quantile count normalization procedures of edgeR package, and tests for differences in expression levels with a Poisson-Tweedie (PT) statistic, leading to more accurate p-values. The correction for multiple testing is based on Benjamini-Hockeberg's FDR [1].

ANOVA

The Analysis of variance (ANOVA) is a more general and powerful tool, that provides an integrated approach to normalization, estimation of expression level and testing for differential expression (ez and afex R-packages) [11].

Other Methods

Many other DE methods are available, such as DESeq [12], NOISeq [13], NBPSeq [14], PoissonSeq [15] and NBAMSeq (this is the most recent tool that allows for considering multiple covariates in variance estimation, with an additive linear structure, but the corresponding manual has not been published yet) [16], for which we refer to the relative papers.

Datasets and Methods

For the practical comparison and for the concordance analysis, this work adopts a real dataset under publication, that analyzes two biological samples about cerebral cavernous malformations (the control and the treated groups), each of them with three biological replicates.

Previously described six DE tools were evaluated, through 10 pipelines, obtained with various settings of the tools.

For DESeq2, we used two pipelines: (1) default that applies independent filtering and flags outliers through Cook distance; (2) default, but with independent filtering disabled. Similarly, two edgeR pipelines were considered: (1) classic edgeR, based on an exact test on negative binomial distribution; (2) edgeR_robust, based on a robust generalized linear model with the default prior degrees of freedom (pDF=10) to estimate robust gene-wise dispersion parameter. For limma DE tool, we run the analysis using three variants: (1) limma_voom; (2) limmaVoom_robust; (3) limma-trended (limma_trend), in which the mean-variance relationship is incorporated into the Bayes procedure.

For SAMSeq tool, we did not use the R Shiny package, but we relied on samr package, by using the function SAMseq, specifically designed for count data.

TweeDESeq was run with the default parameters, by using edgeR TMM as normalization approach.

Finally, for ANOVA, in our approach, we introduced log2 transformation of raw count data and tested for differences of expression levels among conditions with a t-test with Benjamini-Hockberg's FDR correction.

DE Tools and Normalization Methods

Proposing a new integrated approach for DE analysis require careful attention to normalization methods used by the selected tools [17], which could affect the DE results. Even if is out of the scope of this chapter to compare normalization methods, we adopted three different normalization approaches, together with DE tools:

1. DESeq2 median of ratios, introduced with the DESeq that is simply based on a DESeq2 scaling factor computed as a median ratio, for each gene, of its counts over its geometric mean. In particular, even if every statistic software easily computes a DESeq2 normalization, the procedure requires some steps: 1) the creation, for each gene, of a pseudo-reference sample; 2) the calculation of the geometric mean for all the samples; 3) the computation of each sample/reference ratio; 4) the determination of the normalization factor for each sample and, finally 5) the computation of normalized counts, obtained by dividing each raw count value by the sample normalized factor.
2. Trimmed Mean of M-values (TMM), computed as a log expression ratio between the test and the reference, after excluding the most expressed genes. Since TMM approach assumes that most genes are not differently expressed, one could reasonably expect that this log ratio is closed to 1 and, otherwise, this statistic provides the correction factor that must be applied to the library sizes.
3. SAMSeq normalization, that is based on a resampling strategy, under the assumption that counts follow a Poisson distribution.

In particular, DESeq2 median of ratios is implemented in DESeq2 tool, SAMSeq Poisson resampling- based normalization is adopted only for SAMSeq tool, while TMM approach is the base of the others DE pipelines (edgeR, limma, TweeDESeq). Finally, for ANOVA procedure, we adopted a classical log2 normalization of raw cunt data.

Fig. (**2**) presents the boxplots, that provide an easy way to visualize the count distribution in each sample. In panel **A** the boxplot shows the raw counts, whose distribution is highly skewed, so that successive panels show the effect of normalization procedures: the DESeq2 median of ratios, in panel **B**; the TMM normalized counts in panel **C**; SAMSeq normalized counts, in panel **D**; ANOVA normalized counts or pseudo-counts, in panel **E**.

All the normalization approaches adjust the data according to the sequencing depth of each sample. DESeq2 and TMM methods show a certain degree of similarity, for all samples and replicates, while SAMSeq normalization procedure is able to better reduce differences per sample due to the sequencing and differently from other methods, it better preserves the positive skewness of counts, for all groups, characterized by lower medians. Finally, ANOVA pseudo-counts (log2(count+1)) normalization approach evidences more symmetry of the distribution.

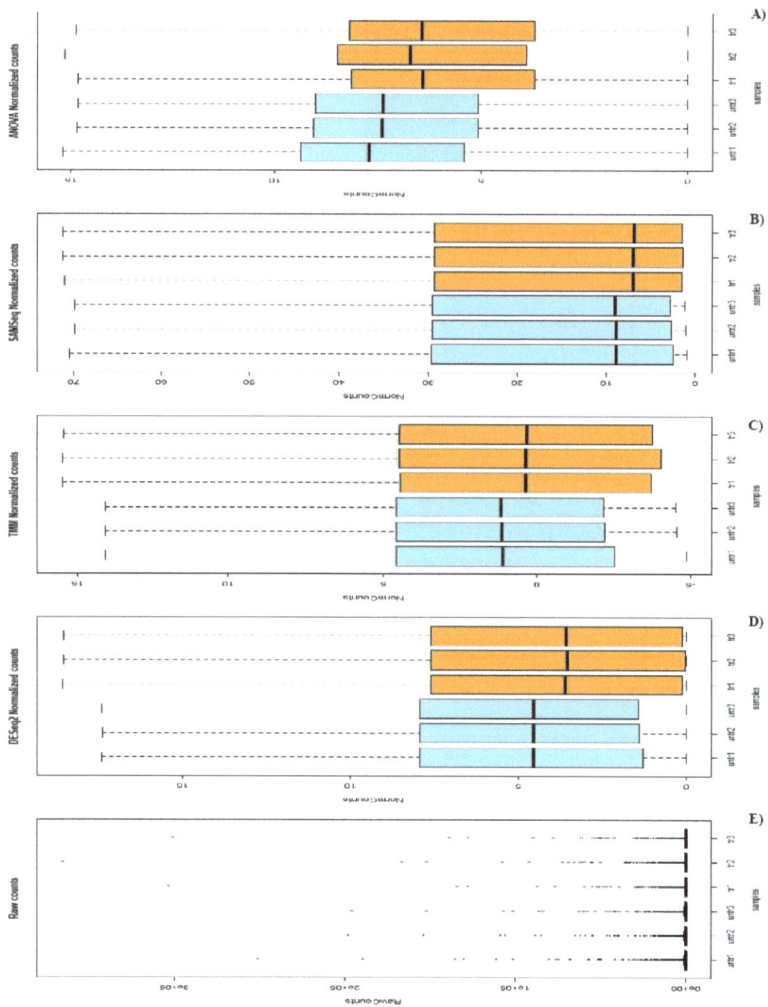

Fig. (2). Boxplots of different normalization methods on raw count data. Boxplots showing expression distributions for unnormalized (raw) data and normalized counts, with different approaches (DESeq2 median of ratios, TMM, SAMSeq and ANOVA log-2). The two colors represent the conditions (control replicates in light blue and treated replicates in orange) and the title of each plot refers to the type of normalization applied.

Moreover, boxplots of the relative log expression (RLE) in Fig. (**3**) show that all normalization methods succeeded in removing unwanted variation related to technical factors and not of biologic interest. All the boxplots are centered near zero and show a small spread; ideally, they should be of the same size (this is especially true for SAMSeq method) [18]. Thus, there are no noticeable library size effects after normalization.

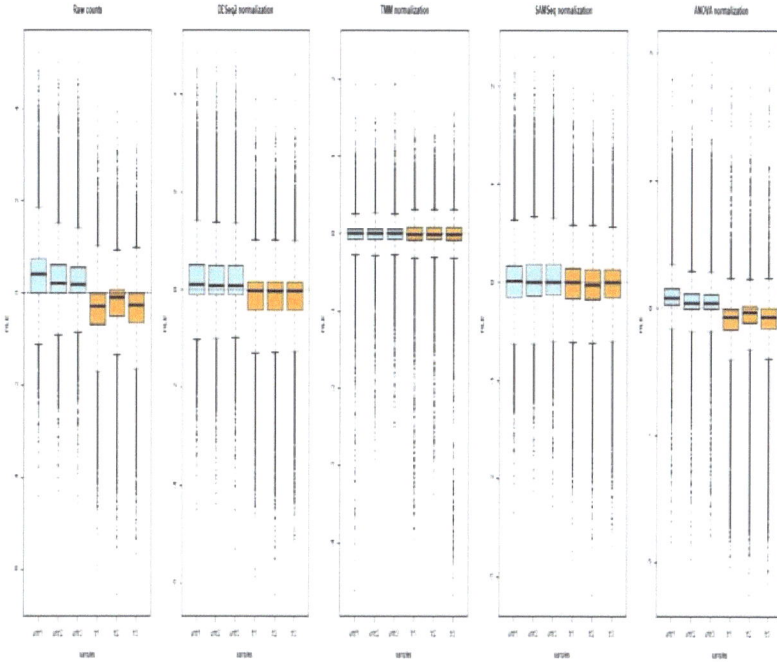

Fig. (3). RLE plots of different normalization methods on raw count data. RLE plots of normalization approaches. The two colors represent the conditions (control replicates in light blue and treated replicates in orange) and the title of each plot refers to the type of normalization applied. All the methods success in removing unwanted variations.

ANALYSIS

Before turning into the DE analysis, the output was checked by multi-dimensional scaling (MDS) plot, for the visualization of similarities/dissimilarities among samples. As shown in Fig. (**4**), the conditions of the replicates correctly cluster among all samples and there were no batch effects [19]. Moreover, the replicates of control group were very close to each other, while a wider dispersion was detected among tr1 replicate and other treated replicates (tr2 and tr3).

MDS Plot for Count Data

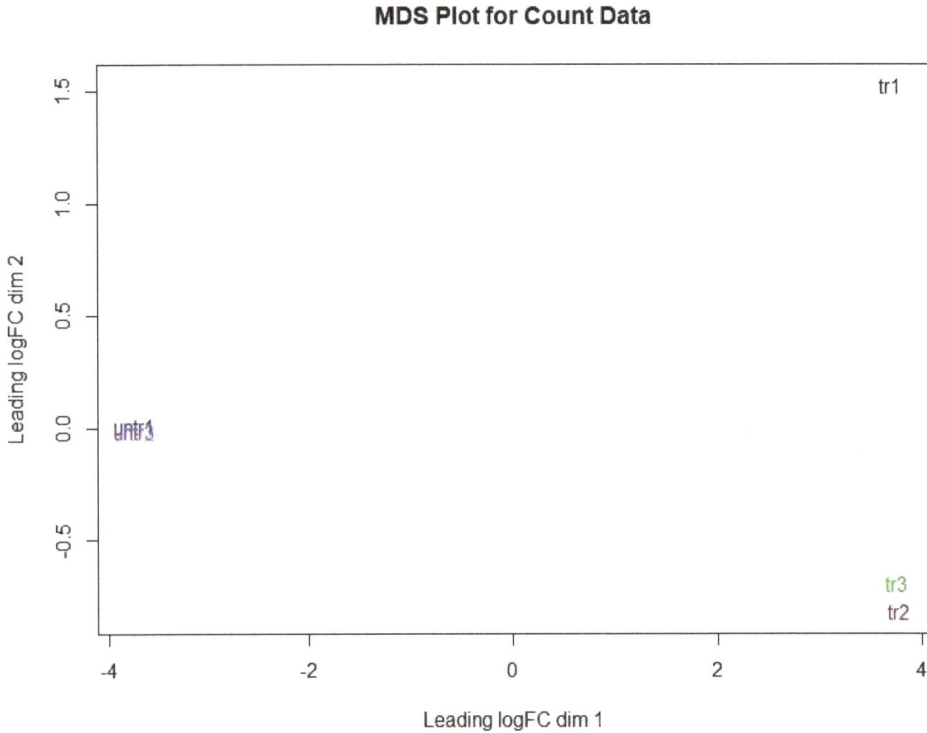

Fig. (4). MDS Plot of raw count data. MDS plots of log-CPM values over dimensions 1 and 2 for both samples (treated and untreated) and all replicates. Distances on the plot correspond to the leading fold-change. No batch effects are present.

Once MDS plot has been analyzed, the differential expression analysis was run, following the 10 pipelined described above.

In particular, for differentially expressed genes, we used the raw count data of expression genes levels, represented by a large matrix of 28491 rows and six columns, where each row is a gene, each column is a sample, so that each entry at each location represents the expression level of that gene in that particular sample, so that:

$$
C = \begin{bmatrix} c_{1,1} & c_{1,2} & \cdots & c_{1,j} \\ c_{2,1} & c_{2,2} & \cdots & 0 \\ \vdots & \vdots & \ddots & \vdots \\ c_{i,1} & c_{i,2} & \cdots & c_{i,j} \end{bmatrix}
$$

Even if ideally one could directly compare the expression levels between any group of samples, there are many factors that could skew the original data, so that before running DE analysis, data requires some transformations depending on the specific tool.

DESeq2 and DESeq2_NoFilt pipelines were run through DESeq2 package. It required as input a matrix incorporating raw counts and a design formula, indicating the condition for modelling the samples. Since our dataset included only two sample groups (control and treatment), our design matrix relied on those two conditions. Afterwards, the analysis was performed through DESeq function, that incorporate all the default steps of estimation of size factor and dispersion measures (for median ratio normalization), and of hypothesis testing with Wald test. DESeq2 resulted in a table with log2 fold-changes, p-values and adjusted p-values with FDR correction (we used a threshold of 0.05).

For edgeR pipelines [20], we defined a DGElist, with row counts and a data frame with information about the samples. Before running DGE list, we filtered our genes, by excluding all with zero counts in both samples. As suggested in the reference manual, we did not pass through the estimation of a linear model, but we directly verified the differences between gene expression levels in the sample with an exact test similar to Fisher's exact test. Additionally, edgeR required a normalization of the library sizes (calcNormFactors) and the estimation of dispersion measures (estimateCommonDisp). Even though edgeR allows for two different measures, in our analysis, we employed the common dispersion parameter, instead of tagwise dispersion coefficient, because of the low number of replicates for each sample group. The estimation of the dispersion coefficient resulted in a matrix of pseudo-counts, internally used by edgeR to speed up the computation of the conditional likelihood. To facilitate the user, it is necessary to specify that edgeR refers to pseudo-counts as normalized counts, while Scommonly, they refer to starting values added to zero counts for avoiding missing or infinite values, when computing logarithms. Since we additionally consider the robust version of edgeR, we also estimated a robust dispersion parameter, in order to lower the sensitivity to outliers and to improve the detection of differentially expressed genes, also reducing the false positives (with estimateGLMRobustDisp and glmLRT functions).

Limma package [9] integrates a number of features useful for large-scale experiment studies. In our analysis, we preliminary created a DGE list object using the edgeR package, and then we removed that genes with zero or very low counts, based on counts per million (cpm). Afterwards, we created a voom transformation object, through the definition of a specific design matrix (since we relied on two samples, each with three replicates, the resulting matrix had dimensions (6, 2), with one if the sample belongs to a specific condition, and zero otherwise). Finally, limma pipelines fitted a linear model and extract differentially expressed genes list, after making contrasts, based on an eBayes function. Moreover, from a computational point of view, the robust approach only required a modification of the linear model to be fitted (in R script, the corresponding command raw becomes *fit.voom.robust <- lmFit(y, mm,method = "robust")*, while Limma-trended pipeline needed a preliminary conversion of raw counts into logCPM values before the linear fit (in this case, logCPM values are then inserted in the standard Limma pipeline, using the trend=TRUE argument).

SAMSeq approach was run on the basis of the *samr* package. As required by the traditional approach, we defined a *sam* object, by choosing as resp.type variable "two-class unpaired", by setting 100 as number of permutations for computing delta table and by fixing the FDR threshold at nominal rate of 0.05.

TweeDESeq estimation required two additional R packages, *TeeDESeq* and *tweeDEseqCountData,* but the estimation was made following the steps defined in the reference manual. Before doing the estimation, we normalized raw counts through TMM approach, filtered low count data and finally tested for differential expression between conditions using *tweeDE* function, that resulted in a data frame containing the overall mean of each gene across sample, the sample means, the log2FC, the p-values and the corrected p-values.

Finally, for ANOVA pipeline, we firstly filtered counts by deleting all the unexpressed genes and then transposed the original count data matrix. We introduced a vector, codified with a dichotomous variable, to identify the group to which each expression gene level belonged to, and afterward we run a standard ANOVA (with *ez* and *afex* packages). The latter resulted in a list of differentially expressed genes, with associated p-values and FDR corrections. Finally, post-hoc comparisons were made with *multicomp* package.

After running all pipelines, the results were integrated by intersecting the different DEGs list obtained. The results have been further exploited with a concordance analysis based on the number of differentially expressed genes and two other ranking metrics (the p-value and the Π score).

While the proportion of differently expressed genes and the p-values allowed for a complete statistical comparison among methods, the Π score, obtained by the combination of p-values and logFC allowed to take into account the biological importance of significance. Finally, in order to individuate the best-integrated approach for DE analysis, the performance evaluation was made on a simulated RNA-Seq data (from *QuasiSeq-* R package) through a combination-based approach together with ROC standard pattern of analysis.

RESULTS

By comparing the output of DE methods, we tried to understand which DE methods were more similar to others in terms of proportion of DE genes. Looking at the barplot in Fig. (**5**), representing the number of DE methods at a nominal FDR of 5%, we can immediately see that the largest number of detections were obtained through the non-parametric SAMseq procedure, while DESeq2, DESeq2_NoFilt (with independent filtering disabled), TweeDESeq and classical ANOVA were more conservative. However, there was no a marked spread along all pipelines (the ratio of the number of DE genes between the most liberal SAMSeq and the most conservative ANOVA is about 1.66). To figure out why the non-parametric approach gave such different results, we took a closer look at the differentially expressed gene detected. We observed that genes detected by SAMSeq tended to have some large values in one class respect to the other or, sometimes, it individuated genes that had larger raw counts in the treated group but the differences were not large enough to be detected as differentially expressed, by parametric methods. Additionally, SAMSeq identified many genes that presented lower expression levels in the treated group, not identified as DEGs by parametric approaches, because of the group means were almost the same.

Moreover, when comparing the number of DE genes detected by each approach, we had to consider that ANOVA was the unique pipeline that required an additional filtering procedure before starting, by deleting all genes unexpressed through all samples or unexpressed in one of the condition, but not in another, reducing the number of genes in the analysis (from 28491 for each replicate to 18080).

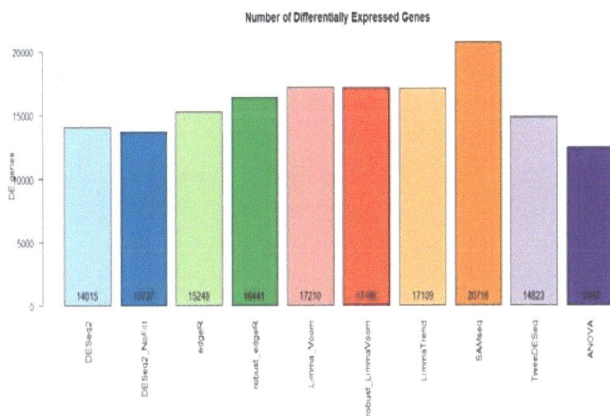

Fig. (5). Barplot of DE genes. Number of genes detected as DE by each pipeline at a nominal FDR of 5% for the RNA-Seq dataset.

Afterwards, we examined the consistency of the detections between pipelines by calculating their overlaps. More specifically, we determined the lists of differentially expressed genes obtained with each tool package and then calculated their overlaps.

From the pairwise overlaps in Table **2**, it was easily to see that there was agreement among DE pipelines, because the vast majority of genes that were included in DE set of one method was also included in the DE set of other methods. Moreover, SAMSeq and ANOVA showed less concordance with all other pipelines and for the non-parametric procedure, this was driven by the fact that it in general classified more genes as DE compared to other approaches. Moreover, the MDS plot of DE overlap between methods in Fig. (**6**) showed different clusters.

Table 2. Overlap table of DE genes detected by each pipeline. Overlap DE genes between pipelines at nominal FDR of 5%. The elements on the main diagonal (highlighted in grey boxes) represent the number of DE genes found by each method, while the number off-diagonals show the number of DEGs shared by each pairs of methods.

	DESeq2	DESeq2NoFilt	edgeR	robust_edgeR	LimmaVoom	robust_LimmaVoom	LimmaTrend	SAMSeq	TweeDESeq	ANOVA
DESeq2	**14015**	13737	13966	13154	13466	13310	12778	14002	13644	10069
DESeq2NoFilt	13737	**13737**	13704	12938	13278	13151	12614	13727	13435	9939
edgeR	13966	13704	**15248**	14261	13957	13768	13241	15131	14253	10413
robust_edgeR	13154	12938	14261	**16441**	13169	13248	13678	15742	13730	11335
LimmaVoom	13466	13278	13957	13169	**14126**	13793	13280	14101	13852	10384
robust_LimmaVoom	13310	13151	13768	13248	13793	**14343**	13448	14226	13864	10555
LimmaTrend	12778	12614	13241	13678	13280	13448	**16296**	14659	13453	11721
SAMSeq	14002	13727	15131	15742	14101	14226	14659	**20716**	14787	11476
TweeDESeq	13644	13435	14253	13730	13852	13864	13453	14787	**14823**	10718
ANOVA	10069	9939	10413	11335	10384	10555	11721	11476	10718	**12442**

SAMSeq and ANOVA were still completely separated from other methods, while edgeR_robust and LimaTrend tended to cluster together. This was due to the way of assigning weights to each observation of the samples. In particular, both procedures were set up in a negative binomial GLM framework, even if the two approaches involved different steps. Limma trend computed standard deviation for each gene on the basis of a gene-wise linear model fitted to the log count per million (cpm) values, fitted a robust trend to the residual standard deviations and, finally, computed the weights for each observation as the inverse squared predicted standard deviations obtained from the interpolation of standard deviation trend. edgeR_robust computed weights for each observation through the Hubert function based on Pearson residuals coming from the maximization of the adjusted profile likelihood (APL) of Cox and Reid. Despite differences in the step procedures, both approaches produced the same effect of attributing lower weights to observations that strongly deviated from the model fit.

Finally, the other methods were grouped together with some subgrouping by family of methods, such as DESeq2 and DESeq2NoFilt, but there was also a more heterogeneous group of four pipelines (robust_LimmaVoom, classic edgeR, TweeDESeq and LimmaVoom) due to their common TMM normalization approach.

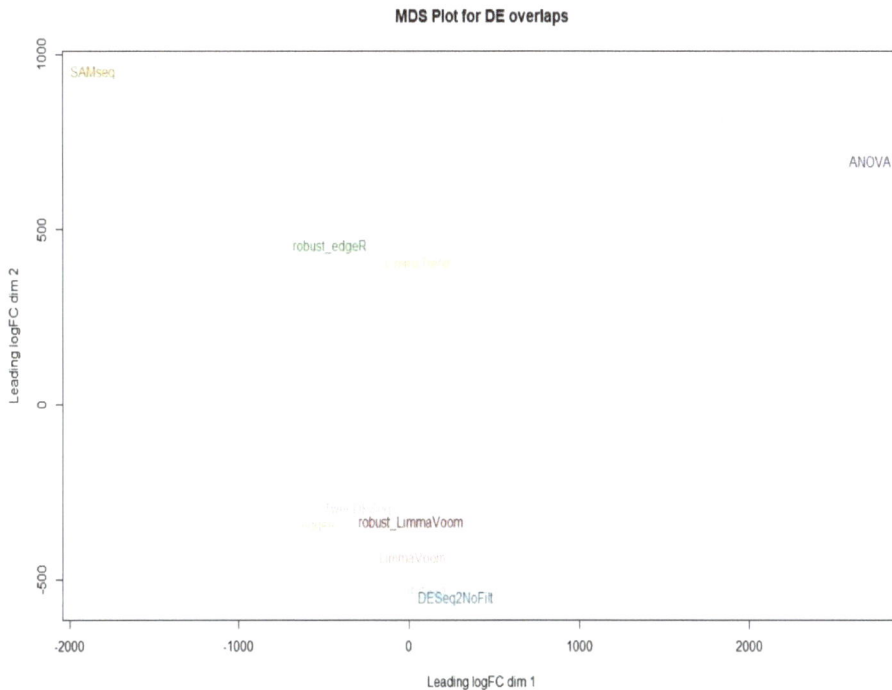

Fig. (6). MDS Plot of DE overlaps. MDS plot DE overlap between methods. Construction of the MDS-plot is based on the chi-square distance.

Validity of DEG Analysis Tools and Concordance Analysis

After run the selected DE pipelines, the results were integrated in order to obtain a unique list of genes. After Benjamini-Hochberg false discovery correction, genes with adjusted p-values less than 0.05 were considered as differentially expressed for all methods.

8997 DEGs were identified in total, even if the user could work with either the intersection or the union of some of all the methods (increasing the number of DE genes up to 23191).

The results of the integration are plotted in Fig. (**7**), through the SuperExactTest R package [21], that provides useful tools for testing and visualizing multi-intersections. Fig. (**7**) presents a circular plot showing intersections between differentially expressed gene lists from all the 10 pipelines. The 10 tracks of the circle represent the DE genes detected by each pipeline, with the individual blocks showing the presence (green) or the absence (grey) of the corresponding DE tools in each intersection. By considering all the selected approach, the plot shows 1023 combinations among the 10 pipelines. The height of the outermost track of the graph is proportional to the intersection size and the color of the bar represents the statistical significance of each intersection (from yellow implying lower significance to red implying the highest achieved significance of the intersection), in terms of -log10 transformed adjusted p-values. Moreover, in our plot, the combinations were ordered by set (even if the R package allows different ordering options, by p-value, size or degree).

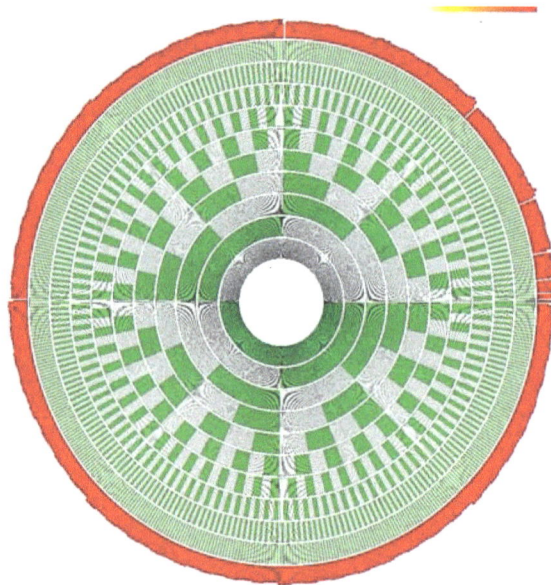

Fig. (7). Multi-Set intersection plot of DEGs lists. Multi-Set intersection plot of the 1023 combinations of differentially expressed genes lists obtained from the 10 pipelines, where green blocks indicate the presence of pipeline in each intersection, otherwise the blocks are white. The color intensity of the external bars is a representation of the significance of the intersections (−log10(PV)).

Since we relied on a large matrix, to facilitate the efficient visualization of relations among pipelines and to focus on the integrated results of the different pipelines, the UpSet [22] barplot in Fig. (**8**) specifically displays the intersections across more than seven pipelines.

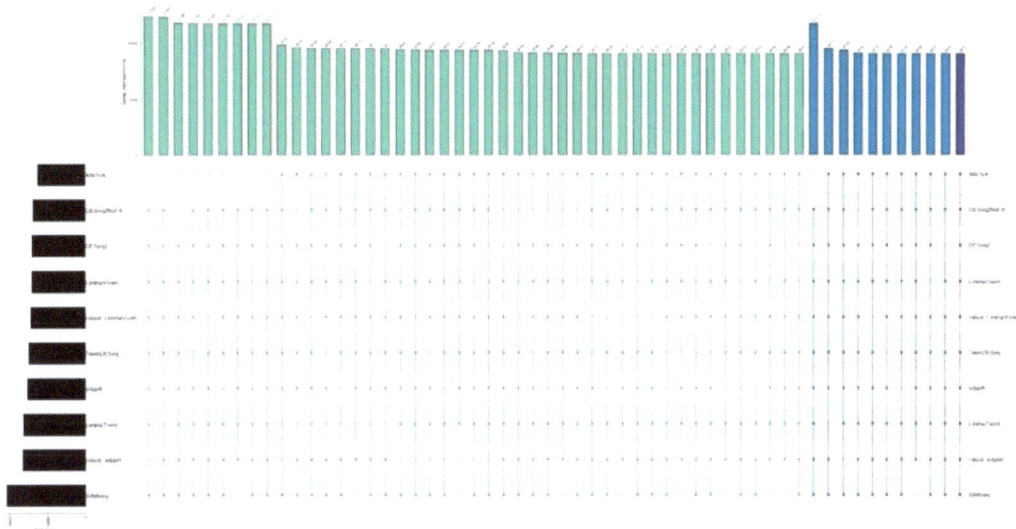

Fig. (8). UpSet barplot of intersected DE gene lists. UpSet plot of differentially expressed genes across ten R pipelines for DEG analysis (DESeq2, DESeq2NoFilt, edgeR, robust_edgeR, Limma_Voom, robust_LimmaVoom,LimmaTrend, SAMSeq, TweeDESeq, ANOVA), illustrating all the possible combinations of intersections of more than 7 DE genes lists (at a nominal FDR of 5%). The nature of a given intersection is indicated by the dots below the bar plot. For instance, the 8997 genes in the last column are detected as DE for all the pipelines and represent the integrated unique DE genes list.

The degree of agreement among the DE tools has been further exploited using two other metrics of gene ranking: the p-value and the Π score.

Looking at the p-values is one way of analyzing whether the different methods have a similar ranking of the genes by significance. When plotting the estimated p-values for each method versus others (Fig. **9**), using gclus package, the pipelines with the highest correlations were closed to the diagonal and the corresponding box were highlighted in pink. The strongest correlations were founded among different specifications of the same pipelines: edgeR and robust_edgeR (corr. 0.99), LimmaTrend and robust_LimmaVoom (corr. 0.953), robust_LimmaVoom and LimmaVoom (0.993). Moreover, it is important to note that the correlations are still high among edgeR and Limma different specifications, and across ANOVA and other pipelines (TweeDESeq, SAMSeq, DESeqNoFilt).

Kendall correlation coefficients between the logarithmic fold changes estimated by each method ranged from -0.95 (between DESEq2_NoFilt and ANOVA) to 0.98 (of TweeDESeq and DESEq2_NoFilt); moreover, the range of estimated log fold changes varied, especially for the genes that were expressed only in one group. In particular, TweeDESeq assigned infinite values (either positive and negative) for the log fold changes expressed only in one group, while other methods estimated log fold changes, ranging from -14.1229 to 14.7689.

P-values correlations

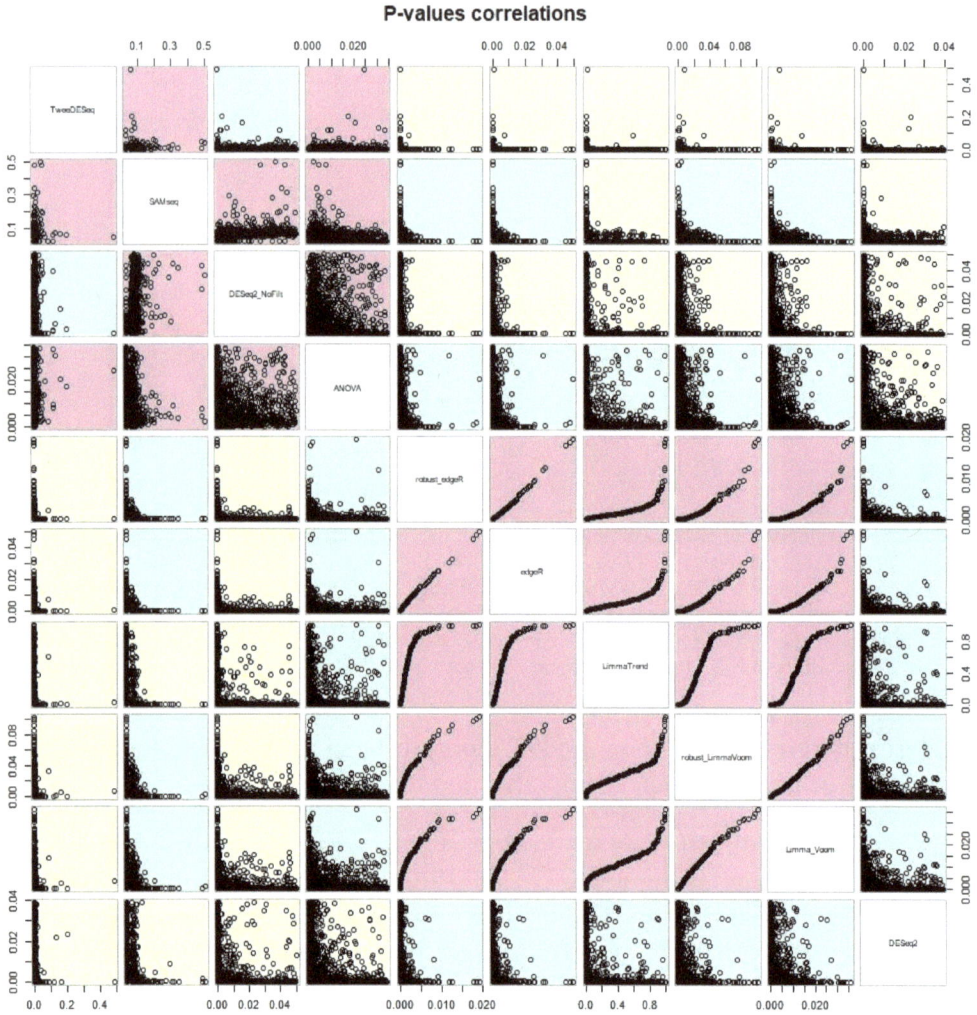

Fig. (9). Scatterplot of p-values. Spearman correlation between p-values of pairs of DE pipelines. Pink indicates a strong correlation, green a weak correlation and yellow indicates the data are uncorrelated.

In order to gain in comparability, we relied on the Π, highlighting both the magnitude and the significance of differential expression. The Đi value, computed for each gene is obtained as:

$$\Pi_i = I \cdot \phi_i$$

$$\text{where } I = \begin{cases} 1, & logFC \geq 0 \\ -1, & logFC < 0 \end{cases}$$

I is an indicator variable able to capture the sign of logFC while ɸi is the estimated adjusted p-value, generated from t-statistics, except for SAMSeq, for which ɸi is estimated through delta table (with n=100 permutations).

The results were combined in a hierarchical clustering analysis of DE pipelines, resulting into 4 clusters, with a good agreement among pipelines. Fig. (**10**) compares hierarchical clustering based on correlation distance measure and Ward distance approach [23]. The dendrogram on the left evidences how correlation among tools varies between 0.2 of the first cluster (LimmaVoom and robust_LimmaVoom) to almost 1.0 of some pipelines of the fourth cluster. LimmaVoom and robust_LimmaVoom cluster together because of their highly correlated Đi values and their quasi-perfect overlap, while ANOVA (with the lowest number of significant differentially expressed genes) and, surprisingly, robust_edgeR are completely separated from other pipelines. Finally, the fourth cluster includes edgeR, DESeq2, LimmaTrend, TweeDESeq, DESeq2NoFilt and SAMSeq, generally showing the highest number of SDE genes and greater overlaps with other pipelines. Moreover, the right dendrogram shows the relationship of the 10 pipelines, hierarchically clustered by using ward method, that allows minimizing the total within-cluster variance and it is the best suitable approach for gene expression analysis[1]. The results are slightly different than before, but they better reflect the normalization differences across the procedures. The first cluster includes six pipelines (robust_edgeR, edgeR, LimmaVoom, DESeq2, robust_LimmaVoom, and ANOVA), most of them based on TMM normalization approach. The second cluster includes TweeDESeq and DESeq2NoFilt, while the third and the fourth clusters comprise a single pipeline, respectively SAMSeq and LimmaTrend, highlighting the different nature of the parametric SAMSeq approach.

Moreover, the graphical comparison of dendrograms allows to immediately note the similitudes and the differences among clusters, because "unique" nodes, with a combination of labels/items not present in the other tree, are highlighted with dashed lines.

Results obtained with previous analysis (p-value and Π score), were not markedly different (especially for Ward dendrogram): in both cases, edgeR and Limma pipelines show better concordance, while results of ANOVA and DESeq2 are less stable, showing variable correlations. To come to an overall conclusion, we evaluated the performances of the different techniques for the detection of DEGs, through the receiver operating characteristic (ROC) curve (AUC) [24, 25].

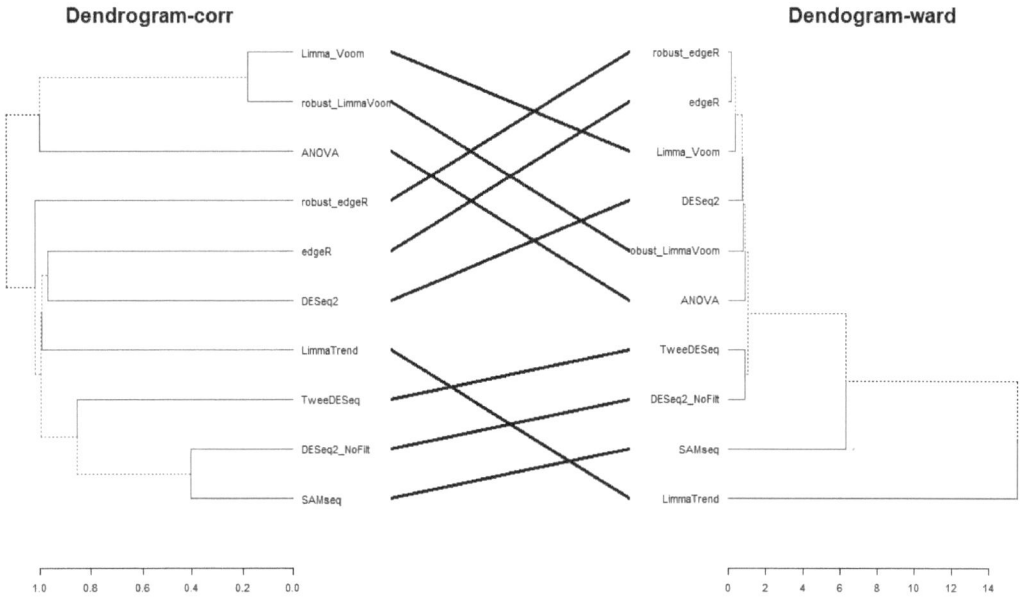

Fig. (10). Comparison of clustering of SDE genes. Comparison of hierarchical clustering based on correlation distance (left dendrogram) and on Ward method (right dendrogram), showing the relationship among pipelines. The hierarchical clustering was computed on the Ði=I·φi values, obtained from the combination of the adjusted p-values (FDR correction) and the sign of logFC of the common significant differentially expressed 8997 genes.

Despite previous studies tried to assess the performances of each approach by using as benchmark the results obtained through qRT-PCR [26], we tried to assess the overall performance of our approach, through pairwise comparisons of each DEGs list versus the unique common genes list of 8997 genes. Thus, performance measures were calculated based on the comparison results between each DGEs list and the reference dataset, represented by the intersected genes set list, assuming that those genes are truly differentially expressed. Fig. (**11**) shows ROC curves for each pipeline and Table **3** presents the performance of each adopted method.

It is possible to notice that SAMSeq presents the lowest TPR (True Positive Rate) and the lowest ACC (Accuracy), but it has been shown that its results are strictly dependent on the data and are influenced by the sample size and the number of replicates and, moreover, it suffers from low power [27]. ANOVA performs better than other pipelines, with the highest performance measures, but also DESeq2_NoFilt and DESeq2, Limma_Voom and robust_LimmaVoom and TweeDESeq perform well, showing consistent results in experiments with a low number of samples.

Table 3. Performances of DEGs software tools. Performance measures adopted: TPR (True Positive Rate), SPC (Specificity), ACC (Accuracy), PPV (Positive Predictive Value), Detection Rate, Fvalue[2].

Tool	TPR	SPC	ACC	PPV	Det.Rate	Fvalue
DESeq2	**0,762**	**1,000**	**0,842**	**1,000**	**0,508**	**0,865**
DESeq2_NoFilt	**0,777**	**1,000**	**0,851**	**1,000**	**0,518**	**0,875**
edgeR	0,698	1,000	0,798	1,000	0,465	0,822
robust_edgeR	0,635	1,000	0,757	1,000	0,429	0,777
Limma_Voom	**0,757**	**1,000**	**0,885**	**1,000**	**0,504**	**0,861**
robust_LimmaVoom	**0,744**	**0,997**	**0,828**	**0,998**	**0,496**	**0,853**
LimmaTrend	0,617	0,949	0,728	0,960	0,411	0,751
SAMSeq	0,410	1,000	0,607	1,000	0,273	0,581
TweeDESeq	**0,719**	**0,999**	**0,813**	**0,999**	**0,480**	**0,836**
ANOVA	**0,845**	**1,000**	**0,897**	**1,000**	**0,563**	**0,916**

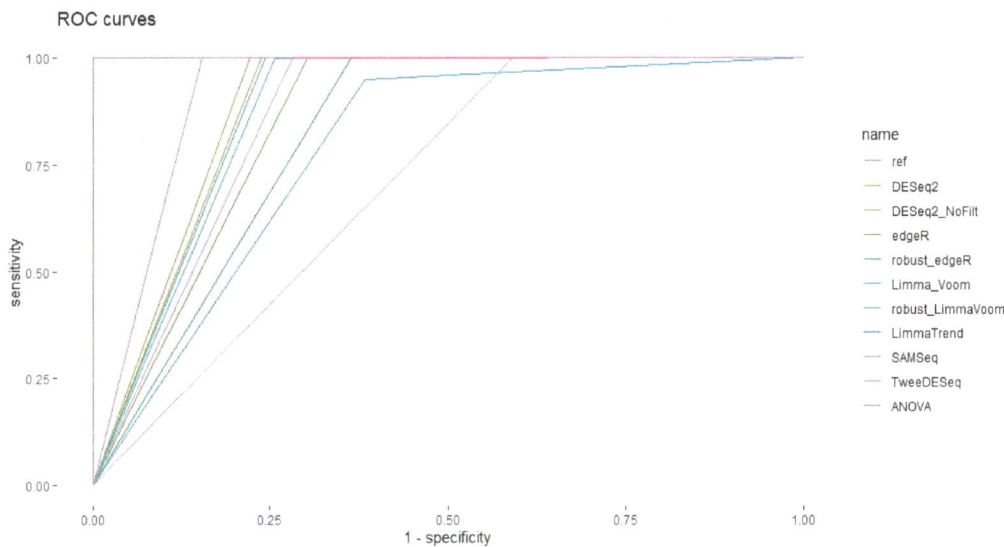

Fig. (11). ROC curves for DEGs software tools. ROC curves for DEGs software tools, through pairwise comparisons of each tools with the reference set of DEGs, obtained from the intersection of all the lists of differentially expressed genes.

Integration of DEG Methods and Performances Evaluation

Previous analysis indicates that each DEG method led to different results. In order to identify the possible improvement in performance, we evaluated the results of the integration of the different pipelines analyzed before, through a simulated RNA seq dataset. The dataset comes from *QuasiSeq* (Analyzing RNA Sequencing Count Tables Using Quasi-Likelihood) R package. It creates a matrix of RNA-

Seq reads using a negative binomial distribution with 10000 genes and 8 experimental units with a balanced two -treatment comparison design (two samples, each of them with four replicates) and with 3500 truly differentially expressed genes (with the corresponding true logFC). In order to evaluate the performance of the DEG integration methods, we verified the combination of methods that perform better, by presenting (Table **4**) the result for each subset of methods: ten, nine, eight, seven, six, five, four, three, two and one, without a specific selection criterion. For each combination of methods, we adopted the ROC curve. In particular, it is possible to notice that the inclusion of different pipelines in DE analysis allows for gains in specificity when moving from six methods up to 9 pipelines, while the consensus among 10 methods led to a slightly improvement in the sensitivity and detection rate, however presenting a decline in specificity, ACC and PPV measures. Moreover, the combinations of nine methods presents the most efficient solutions among all the pipelines, obtaining the best balance between the performance measures of specificity and sensitivity and also maximizing PPV and Det.Rate[3].

Table 4. Performances of each subset of DEG pipelines. Performance measures adopted: TPR (True Positive Rate), SPC (Specificity), ACC (Accuracy), PPV (Positive Predictive Value), Detection Rate, Fvalue. Each subset does not have a specific selection criterion, but only the frequency of indications is observed.

N. of pipelines	TPR	SPC	ACC	PPV	Det.Rate	Fvalue
1	0,985	0,629	0,861	0,831	0,640	0,902
2	0,985	0,629	0,861	0,831	0,640	0,902
3	0,985	0,625	0,859	0,830	0,640	0,901
4	0,982	0,634	0,861	0,833	0,639	0,902
5	0,984	0,623	0,858	0,829	0,640	0,899
6	0,981	0,625	0,856	0,893	0,637	0,899
7	0,841	0,679	0,784	0,829	0,546	0,835
8	0,844	0,694	0,792	0,837	0,549	0,841
9	**0,855**	**0,695**	**0,799**	**0,838**	**0,556**	**0,847**
10	0,870	0,645	0,791	0,820	0,565	0,844

In order to individuate which group of methods has the best consensus, it is important to verify how much each pipeline contributes to the aggregate results, especially for the group of consensus, with nine pipelines. For this purpose, after individuating the list of differentially expressed genes for each pipeline, we defined a binary matrix where, for each gene and for each DEGs list, 0 means not differentially expressed and 1 differentially expressed. We then compute all the possible intersections of all the combinations of different DE tools, resulting in a large matrix of 1023 combinations.

For each of them we computed the ROC curve and the corresponding performance measures (TPR, SPC, ACC, PPV, Det.Rate and Fvalue).

In particular, regarding the consensus of nine methods (reported in Table **5**) it is possible to note that the subset able to identify DEGs with more accuracy is the one that includes DESeq2 and DESeq2NoFilt, edgeR and robust_edgeR, LimmaVomm, robust_LimmaVoom and LimmaTrend, the non-parametric SAMSeq and TweeDESeq, by excluding ANOVA approach from the best subset of methods (TPR=1, SPC= 0.971703, ACC= 0.9944, PPV= 0.993067, Det.Rate=0.8021, Fvalue= 0.996521). The selected aggregate group of pipelines is the only one in the subset of 9 pipelines (10 combinations) able to reduce the number of false positive.

Table 5. ROC performances of the consensus subset of 9 pipelines. ROC performance measures of the consensus group (9 pipelines), for each combination of pipelines. Combination group highlighted in bold represents the best set of methods to use for gaining in accuracy in the DE analysis.

DE tools' Combinations		TPR	SPC	ACC	PPV	Det.Rate	Fvalue
DESeq2 DESeq2NoFilt edgeR robust_edgeR LimmaVoom	**robust_LimmaVoom LimmaTrend SAMseq TweeDESeq**	**1**	**0,9717028**	**0,9944**	**0,9930667**	**0,8021**	**0,99652131**
DESeq2 DESeq2NoFilt edgeR robust_edgeR LimmaVoom	robust_LimmaVoom LimmaTrend SAMseq ANOVA	1	0,3799898	0,8773	0,8673226	0,8021	0,92894783
DESeq2 DESeq2NoFilt edgeR robust_edgeR LimmaVoom	robust_LimmaVoom LimmaTrend TweeDESeq ANOVA	1	0,3774633	0,8768	0,8668539	0,8021	0,92867894
DESeq2 DESeq2NoFilt edgeR robust_edgeR LimmaVoom	robust_LimmaVoom SAMseq TweeDESeq ANOVA	1	0,3774633	0,8768	0,8668539	0,8021	0,92867894
DESeq2 DESeq2NoFilt edgeR robust_edgeR LimmaVoom	LimmaTrend SAMseq TweeDESeq ANOVA	0,99987	0,3774633	0,8767	0,866839	0,8021	0,92861692
DESeq2 DESeq2NoFilt edgeR robust_edgeR robust_LimmaVoom	LimmaTrend SAMseq TweeDESeq ANOVA	0,99987533	0,3774633	0,8767	0,866839	0,8020	0,92861692

(Table 5) contd.....

DESeq2 DESeq2NoFilt edgeR LimmaVoom robust_LimmaVoom	LimmaTrend SAMseq TweeDESeq ANOVA	1	0,3774633	0,8768	0,8668539	0,8021	0,92867894
DESeq2 DESeq2NoFilt robust_edgeR LimmaVoom robust_LimmaVoom	LimmaTrend SAMseq TweeDESeq ANOVA	0,99987533	0,3774633	0,8767	0,866839	0,8020	0,92861692
DESeq2 edgeR robust_edgeR LimmaVoom robust_LimmaVoom	LimmaTrend SAMseq TweeDESeq ANOVA	1	0,3774633	0,8768	0,8668539	0,8021	0,92867894
DESeq2NoFilt edgeR robust_edgeR LimmaVoom robust_LimmaVoom	LimmaTrend SAMseq TweeDESeq ANOVA	1	0,3774633	0,8768	0,8668539	0,8021	0,92867894

DISCUSSION

In this manuscript, we preliminary present and extended review of the most used R-tools for the identification of differentially expressed genes (DEG) for RNA-Seq data, by considering different pipelines and by taking into account the corresponding effect of the different normalization approaches (median of ratios, Trimmed Mean of M-values, Poisson resampling strategy and log2 scaling).

We then compared and evaluated DGE analysis methods, through a two steps analysis:

1. The concordance analysis, for understanding similarities and dissimilarities among DE pipelines;
2. The integration of results and the performance evaluation, for assessing the performances of the integration process.

For the concordance analysis, we used a real RNA-Seq dataset (with 28491 genes and 2 samples, each of them with three biological replicates), and we run 10 different pipelines (DESeq2, DESeq2NoFilt, edgeR, robust_edgeR, LimmaVoom, robust_LimmaVoom, LimmaTrend, SAMSeq, TweeDESeq and ANOVA). After obtaining lists of differentially expressed genes (at nominal FDR of 5%) for each method, we compared them by considering the number of overlaps between each pair of pipelines [28], the Spearman correlation among p-values and the Π score (obtained combining the p-values and the signs of log fold changes). Whatever is the metric used, the results were not markedly different. Different versions of the same pipelines were strongly related and tend to detect the same genes as differentially expressed (for example, edgeR and robust_edgeR, LimmaVoom, robust_LimmaVoom and LimmaTrend, *etc.*). Moreover, the only one non-parametric procedure (SAMSeq) tends to individuate a large number of DEGs respect to other methods, but it was able to better exploit all the possible information from the data and, consequently, to identify as DE many genes that present small, but significant, expression levels differences (not large enough to be detected by parametric approaches). ANOVA was the most conservative pipeline, able to detect only a small number of DEGs but it had the best performance measures among all the pipelines, when we considered ROC curves. For the latter, without resorting the qRT-PCR, we assessed the performances of each methods by using as benchmark the unique genes set list of the common DEGs detected by all pipelines (8997 genes). There was no concordance among all the analyzed pipelines and it could not be possible to assess the absolute superiority of one method for differential expression analysis, since each of them had particular strengths useful for specific RNA-Seq data. This suggested us to define a useful approach for the correct integration of the results obtained from each pipeline. In particular, despite previous studies suggested to integrate the highest number of available pipelines or to select one method, we suggested to integrate the available tools, by combining the different DGEs lists obtained, through a combination approach. We preliminary individuate the combination of methods that perform better and then identify which specific combination of methods had the best consensus in the aggregate result group. For evaluating the performance of each cardinality (from one to ten pipelines), we adopted the ROC (Receiver Operating Characteristic) curve by reporting many performance measures (TPR, SPC, ACC, PPV, Det.Rate, Fvalue). Considering the specificity rate (SPC), it has been possible to notice that the combination of nine methods presented the most efficient solution among other combinations, since it was able to better balance false positive rate and accuracy of the DE analysis. Finally, with an overlap function, we computed all the possible combinations of intersection among DEGs lists, by obtaining 1023 combinations, and for each of them we computed the ROC curves. Focusing on the aggregate results group of consensus (nine pipelines), we chose the one with the highest SPC (0.97) and TPR (1).

CONCLUDING REMARKS

Since NGS technologies provide high throughput dataset with precision and accuracy, appropriate statistical analysis is essential to the research. Moreover, the emergence of different algorithms and tools for RNA-Seq data has led to the need of a more accurate approach to be followed for generating an accurate list of differentially expressed genes. Among all the approaches that have been proposed, the integration of different available pipelines, as suggested here, allows for a better DE statistical analysis and inference.

NOTES

[1] See Md. Bipul Hossen* and Md. Siraj-Ud-Doulah, "Identification of Robust Clustering Methods in Gene Expression Data Analysis", Current Bioinformatics (2017) 12: 558. https://doi.org/10.2174/1574893611666160610103926

[2] For further details see Zhang E., Zhang Y. (2009) F-Measure. In: LIU L., ÖZSU M.T. (eds) Encyclopedia of Database Systems. Springer, Boston, MA. https://doi.org/10.1007/978-0-387-39940-9

[3] When adopting this approach, the user could refer to the qRT-PCR data for validation of DE analysis on RNA-Seq data, and it could arbitrarily change the number of methods to consider, by considering the cost of the change for the other performance measure, or could decide to use only one of the methods for DE analysis, by concentrating on the one with maximize the desired performance measure. Moreover, the user could use other performance measures (Brier score, Log loss, Average precision) as criteria for ROC selection.

REFERENCES

[1]   Esnaola M, Puig P, Gonzalez D, Castelo R, Gonzalez JR. A flexible count data model to fit the wide diversity of expression profiles arising from extensively replicated RNA-seq experiments. BMC Bioinformatics 2013; 14: 254.
       [http://dx.doi.org/10.1186/1471-2105-14-254] [PMID: 23965047]

[2]   Kvam VM, Liu P, Si Y. A comparison of statistical methods for detecting differentially expressed genes from RNA-seq data. Am J Bot 2012; 99(2): 248-56.
       [http://dx.doi.org/10.3732/ajb.1100340] [PMID: 22268221]

[3]   Rapaport F, Khanin R, Liang Y, *et al.* Comprehensive evaluation of differential gene expression analysis methods for RNA-seq data. Genome Biol 2013; 14(9): R95.
       [http://dx.doi.org/10.1186/gb-2013-14-9-r95] [PMID: 24020486]

[4]   Zhang ZH, Jhaveri DJ, Marshall VM, *et al.* A comparative study of techniques for differential expression analysis on RNA-Seq data. PLoS One 2014; 9(8): e103207.
       [http://dx.doi.org/10.1371/journal.pone.0103207] [PMID: 25119138]

[5]   Spies D, Renz PF, Beyer TA, Ciaudo C. Comparative analysis of differential gene expression tools for RNA sequencing time course data. Brief Bioinform 2019; 20(1): 288-98.
       [http://dx.doi.org/10.1093/bib/bbx115] [PMID: 29028903]

[6]   Assefa AT, De Paepe K, Everaert C, Mestdagh P, Thas O, Vandesompele J. Differential gene expression analysis tools exhibit substandard performance for long non-coding RNA-sequencing data. Genome Biol 2018; 19(1): 96.
       [http://dx.doi.org/10.1186/s13059-018-1466-5] [PMID: 30041657]

[7]   Love MI, Huber W, Anders S. Moderated estimation of fold change and dispersion for RNA-seq data with DESeq2. Genome Biol 2014; 15(12): 550.
       [http://dx.doi.org/10.1186/s13059-014-0550-8] [PMID: 25516281]

[8]   McCarthy DJ, Chen Y, Smyth GK. Differential expression analysis of multifactor RNA-Seq experiments with respect to biological variation. Nucleic Acids Res 2012; 40(10): 4288-97.

[http://dx.doi.org/10.1093/nar/gks042] [PMID: 22287627]

[9]   Ritchie ME, Phipson B, Wu D, *et al.* limma powers differential expression analyses for RNA-sequencing and microarray studies. Nucleic Acids Res 2015; 43(7): e47.
[http://dx.doi.org/10.1093/nar/gkv007] [PMID: 25605792]

[10] Li J, Tibshirani R. Finding consistent patterns: A nonparametric approach for identifying differential expression in RNA-Seq data. Stat Methods Med Res 2013; 22(5): 519-36.
[http://dx.doi.org/10.1177/0962280211428386] [PMID: 22127579]

[11] Rouder JN, Engelhardt CR, McCabe S, Morey RD. Model comparison in ANOVA. Psychon Bull Rev 2016; 23(6): 1779-86.
[http://dx.doi.org/10.3758/s13423-016-1026-5] [PMID: 27068543]

[12] Della Corte M, Malzone A, Palomba M, Attanasio G. Dens invaginatus. Arch Stomatol (Napoli) 1990; 31(3): 441-9.
[PMID: 2097962]

[13] Tarazona S, García-Alcalde F, Dopazo J, Ferrer A, Conesa A. Differential expression in RNA-seq: a matter of depth. Genome Res 2011; 21(12): 2213-23.
[http://dx.doi.org/10.1101/gr.124321.111] [PMID: 21903743]

[14] Cumbie JS, Kimbrel JA, Di Y, *et al.* GENE-counter: A computational pipeline for the analysis of RNA-Seq data for gene expression differences. PLoS One 2011; 6(10): e25279.
[http://dx.doi.org/10.1371/journal.pone.0025279] [PMID: 21998647]

[15] Li J, Witten DM, Johnstone IM, Tibshirani R. Normalization, testing, and false discovery rate estimation for RNA-sequencing data. Biostatistics 2012; 13(3): 523-38.
[http://dx.doi.org/10.1093/biostatistics/kxr031] [PMID: 22003245]

[16] Ren X, Kuan PF. Negative binomial additive model for RNA-Seq data analysis. BMC Bioinformatics 2020; 21(1): 171.
[http://dx.doi.org/10.1186/s12859-020-3506-x] [PMID: 32357831]

[17] Bullard JH, Purdom E, Hansen KD, Dudoit S. Evaluation of statistical methods for normalization and differential expression in mRNA-Seq experiments. BMC Bioinformatics 2010; 11: 94.
[http://dx.doi.org/10.1186/1471-2105-11-94] [PMID: 20167110]

[18] Gandolfo LC, Speed TP. RLE plots: Visualizing unwanted variation in high dimensional data. PLoS One 2018; 13(2): e0191629.
[http://dx.doi.org/10.1371/journal.pone.0191629] [PMID: 29401521]

[19] Goh WWB, Wang W, Wong L. Why batch effects matter in omics data, and how to avoid them. Trends Biotechnol 2017; 35(6): 498-507.
[http://dx.doi.org/10.1016/j.tibtech.2017.02.012] [PMID: 28351613]

[20] Robinson MD, McCarthy DJ, Smyth GK. edgeR: A bioconductor package for differential expression analysis of digital gene expression data. Bioinformatics 2010; 26(1): 139-40.
[http://dx.doi.org/10.1093/bioinformatics/btp616] [PMID: 19910308]

[21] Wang M, Zhao Y, Zhang B. Efficient test and visualization of multi-set intersections. Sci Rep 2015; 5: 16923.
[http://dx.doi.org/10.1038/srep16923] [PMID: 26603754]

[22] Lex A, Gehlenborg N, Strobelt H, Vuillemot R, Pfister H. UpSet: visualization of intersecting sets. IEEE Trans Vis Comput Graph 2014; 20(12): 1983-92.
[http://dx.doi.org/10.1109/TVCG.2014.2346248] [PMID: 26356912]

[23] Strauss T, von Maltitz MJ. Generalising ward's method for use with manhattan distances. PLoS One 2017; 12(1): e0168288.
[http://dx.doi.org/10.1371/journal.pone.0168288] [PMID: 28085891]

[24] Hajian-Tilaki K. Receiver operating characteristic (roc) curve analysis for medical diagnostic test

evaluation. Caspian J Intern Med 2013; 4(2): 627-35.
[PMID: 24009950]

[25]   Wan L, Sun F. CEDER: accurate detection of differentially expressed genes by combining significance of exons using RNA-Seq. IEEE/ACM Trans Comput Biol Bioinform. 2012;9(5):1281-92.

[26]   Rajkumar AP, Qvist P, Lazarus R, *et al.* Experimental validation of methods for differential gene expression analysis and sample pooling in RNA-seq. BMC Genomics 2015; 16: 548.
[http://dx.doi.org/10.1186/s12864-015-1767-y] [PMID: 26208977]

[27]   Seyednasrollah F, Laiho A, Elo LL. Comparison of software packages for detecting differential expression in RNA-seq studies. Brief Bioinform 2015; 16(1): 59-70.
[http://dx.doi.org/10.1093/bib/bbt086] [PMID: 24300110]

[28]   Plaisier SB, Taschereau R, Wong JA, Graeber TG. Rank-rank hypergeometric overlap: identification of statistically significant overlap between gene-expression signatures. Nucleic Acids Res 2010; 38(17): e169.
[http://dx.doi.org/10.1093/nar/gkq636] [PMID: 20660011]

CHAPTER 5

Innovations in Data Visualization for Straightforward Interpretation of Nucleic Acid Omics Outcomes

Abstract: With the increasing availability of big data in every field of science, the development of visual collecting tools able to simplify the interpretation of such quantity of data is essential. However, many scientists do not have a specific concept of data visualization, manifesting serious problems in implementing it, especially for omics data. Thus, bioinformatics specialists continuously develop new algorithms and tools to perform the deepest analysis of these data, along with innovative methods to simplify their output representation.

In this work, we evaluated a set of free tools that we considered highly suitable for enhancing the interpretation of next-generation sequencing analysis outcomes, above all regarding exomic and transcriptomic experiments.

Visualization of both kinds of omics data is frequently employed in biomedical research to access knowledge within a genomic context, to communicate, and to explore datasets to elaborate well-defined hypotheses. To realize this purpose, it is necessary to adopt dedicated algorithms and tools specific for each kind of analysis.

Circos and VIsualization of VAriants (VIVA) tools allowed us a straightforward, summarized representation of exomic outcomes, while the Omics Playground platform produced powerful results from RNA-Seq analyses. Finally, both omics sources represented the input of pathway analysis by ClueGO and CluePedia tools, which produced enriched network maps useful to discover novel insights from obtained data.

Today, a huge variety of visualization tools is available to data scientists and it can be difficult to select the right one. Data visualization users should, thus, mainly focus their choice on ease of use and whether a tool has the features they need.

Keywords: Bioinformatics, Circos, ClueGO, CluePedia, Data analysis, Data visualization, dbSNP, Enrichment, HeatMap, NGS, Omics Playground, Pathway analysis, Plot, RNA-Seq, RP, Terms, Variants, VIVA, WES, WGS.

INTRODUCTION

Following the continuous growth of data science fields, data visualization has cer-

Luigi Donato, Simona Alibrandi, Rosalia D'Angelo, Concetta Scimone, Antonina Sidoti and Alessandra Costa

tainly become one of the buzz words of today. Analyzing large sets of data is not always straightforward. Sometimes, data sets are so big that it is quite impossible to discern anything useful from them. No matter what data you want to analyze, performing data visualization appears to be a necessary step. However, many people do not have a specific concept of data visualization, manifesting serious problems in implementing it [1].

Generalized data visualization involves several disciplines such as information technology, graphics, natural science, statistical analysis, interaction, and geographic information. However, data visualization can be summarized as a combination of three branches: information visualization, scientific visualization, and visual analytics [2].

Information visualization analyzes interactive visual representations of abstract data to improve human cognition. Such data includes both digital and non-digital data such as geographic information and text. Graphics such as trend graphs, histograms, Jow flowcharts and tree diagrams also belong to this group of visualization, and the design of these graphics transforms abstract concepts into visual information [3].

Scientific visualization represents an interdisciplinary research and application field which focuses on the visualization of three-dimensional phenomena, such as meteorology, architecture, medicine or biological systems. Its purpose is to graphically depict scientific data, allowing scientists to understand, explain, and collect patterns from the data [4].

Visual analytics is the most recently developed field that has arisen from the combination of two previously described branches of visualization, with an emphasis on analytical reasoning through an interactive visual interface [5].

Thus, it is clear that data visualization represents a very important emerging field, also supported by a biological and physiological basis. The quantity of information that humans acquire through vision is considerably higher than that of other organs. Visualization can help people to deal with more complex information and enhance memory [6]. Moreover, most people do not own complete statistical skills, and basic statistical indicators (mean, median, variance, *etc.*) are not in line with human cognitive nature [7]. One of the most curious examples is Anscombe's quartet, consisting of four data sets that show almost identical simple descriptive statistics but very different distributions, as appear when plotted [8]. So, data visualization is the use of human natural skills to enhance data processing and organization efficiency.

Theoretically, the easiest understanding of data visualization foresees the mapping from data space to graphic space. A typical visual implementation pipeline consists of data processing and filtering, transforming it into an expressible visual form, and then rendering it into a user-friendly version.

Generally, experts in data visualization have to master several skills regarding the main technology stacks, such as basic mathematics (trigonometric function, linear algebra, geometric algorithm), engineering algorithms (from basic to common layout ones), graphics (graph theory, computer graphics, SVG, WebGL, *etc.*), data analysis (data cleaning and modeling, statistical analyses), design aesthetics (from basic principles to cognition), visual basis (coding, analysis and graphic interaction) and visualization solutions (proper application of charts, *etc.*) [9].

To achieve this goal, data visualization tools can be an easier way to create visual representations of large data sets, which can include hundreds or thousands or millions of data points, automating the process of creating a visualization that can be interpreted immediately.

The most powerful data visualization tools on the market show common features: handle huge sets of data in a single visualization, are easy to use and feel intuitive to the user, output an array of different chart and graph types, and are affordable [10].

Among the most famous tools adopted for data visualization, we cite Tableau, D3.js, InfoGram, ChartBlocks, Leaflet, Datawrapper, Google Charts, Vega, FusionCharts, Chart.js, HighCharts, Grafana, Power BI, Chartist.js, Sigmajs, FineReport, Polymaps, Echarts and deck.gl [11].

Even if all previously listed tools could be suitable for every necessity of data visualization, they require a lot of settings before they can be used in omics sciences applications [12]. It is well known that big data coming from genomics, transcriptomics and proteomics analyses represent the largest amount of information [13]. Thus, bioinformatics experts develop new algorithms and tools every day to perform the deepest analysis of such data, along with innovative methods to simplify their output representation. In this work, we selected a set of free tools that we consider highly suitable for enhancing the interpretation of next generation sequencing (NGS) analysis outcomes, above all regarding nucleic acid experiments.

MATERIALS AND METHODS

Visualization of transcriptomic and genomic data is frequently employed in biomedical research to access knowledge within a genomic context, to communicate, and to explore datasets to elaborate hypotheses. Due to the continuously increasing amount of biomedical research produced data and due to the frequent lack of well-defined hypotheses, it is a key challenge to discover unexpected patterns and to formulate questions in an unbiased manner amongst vast amounts of genomic and other associated data [14]. To realize this purpose, it is necessary to adopt dedicated algorithms and tools specific for each kind of analysis.

DNA-Sequencing: Circos and VIVA tools

The principal DNA-Sequencing output consists of a genomic variant list, used down-stream to identify putative genes involved in a specific disease or related to a particular biological condition. A relevant quantity of information also comes from intermediate steps of DNA-Seq analysis and linking it to final outcomes helps users to improve the general quality of any study. The best way to summarize the connections between all main outcomes of DNA-Seq data is probably the circular plot.

The most complete tool which permits to create powerful and informative circular plots is Circos, a visualization tool born to simplify the identification and analysis of similarities and differences from comparisons of genomes [15]. It is effective in displaying variations in genome structure and, usually, any other kind of positional relationships between genomic intervals. These data are regularly produced by sequence alignments, genome mapping, hybridization arrays and genotyping studies. Circos applies a circular ideogram layout to facilitate the representation of relationships between pairs of positions by the use of ribbons, which encode the position, size, and orientation of related genomic elements. Moreover, Circos can show data such as heat maps, tiles, scatter, line and histogram plots, connectors and text. Even if Circos is wide-ranging and useable in any data domain, features have been added to mitigate in-built difficulties in visualizing large-scale multi-sample genomic data. In particular, to resolve the issue of sparseness, the scale on each ideogram can be independently adjusted (both locally and globally) to focus on regions of interest. To achieve this objective, axis breaks can be used to map chromosomes onto any number of ideograms drawn in any order or orientation. Furthermore, data points can present their value and format characteristics altered by flexible rules to clarify patterns in the data. Lastly, the tool is set by flat-text configuration files which can be generated and adjusted automatically to create visualizations as part of an analysis workflow, helping to integrate Circos into analysis pipelines. Circos is licensed under GPL and available at http://mkweb.bcgsc.ca/circos.

Interestingly, another tool was developed to particularly analyze data present in Variant Calling Format (VCF) files, produced during the variant calling process and containing genomic information and locations of variants in a group of sequenced samples. This tool is VIVA (VIsualization of VAriants), a command line tool for evaluating and sharing genomic data for variant analysis and quality control of sequencing experiments from VCF files [16]. The standard workflow for visualization of genomic variant data from VCF files generally requires the application of a combination of existing tools. VIVA mixes the main features of current tools into a single command to interactively evaluate and share genomic data, also creating publication-quality graphics. Plotting functions are based on PlotlyJS.jl library, producing heatmaps for plotting read depth and genotype data, as well as scatter plots to generate summary plots of average read depth values. Numerical arrays of genotype values are translated into a graph producing a multi-sample categorical heatmap, highlighting the Viridis color palette of Python Matplotlib 2.0. These plots show genotype values: homozygous variant, heterozygous variant, homozygous reference, or no call for all selected samples and variants. Read depth values, instead, are plotted in a continuous value heatmap using shades of blue and, for both heatmaps, x-axes are labeled with sample IDs, while y-axes are labeled with chromosome positions.

Thus, we performed the graphical representation by both tools on a VCF file produced by whole exome sequencing (WES) of a patient affected by an orphan form of retinitis pigmentosa (RP), a genetic degenerative disease targeting the retina, which frequently leads to blindness. Data outputted from the whole analysis is under publication.

RNA-Sequencing: Omics Playground Suite

While DNA-Sequencing represents a challenge for data scientists, RNA-Seq probably overcomes such limits. Transcriptomics analyses could produce a huge amount of data, from coding to non-coding RNA expression quantification, from transcript isoform identification to reverse variant discovery.

Today, numerous tools able to manage this data are available, but due to the wide output of each analysis, the correct interpretation of results can be very complex or incorrect. Thus, one major necessity of data analysts is to perform the whole analysis pipeline with a subsequent outcome able to combine all results. Our research group has used several algorithms and tools throughout the last few years, but none was as complete as the Omics Playground platform [17].

The Omics Playground platform presents important distinguishing features in handling RNA-seq (with particular details for single cell data), LC-MS/MS proteomics data and gene expression microarray, also supporting human and mouse species. The platform takes advantage of seven differential expression algorithms, such as DEseq 2 and edgeR, and of enrichment multiple methods including Fisher's exact test and Spearman correlation. Then a meta-analysis combines all applied statistical methods, producing a complete list of highly reliable hits detected across algorithms. Additionally, Omics Playground provides a graphical representation of individual gene expression profiles on KEGG pathway schemes, along with barcode plots and drug connectivity maps (CMap). Another particular feature of the platform is the special modules for immune cell profiling and both biomarker selection and survival analysis.

We loaded a dataset into the Omics Playground made of 3 transcriptome data coming from our previous experiment of RNA-Sequencing on retinal pigment epithelium (RPE) cells, treated with the oxidant agent N-retinylidene-N-retinylethanolamine (A2E), and evaluated during a follow-up of 3h and 6h [18 - 20]. Each transcriptome data used was the result of the mean of 3 biological replicates for each considered condition. After plotting descriptive statistics of input datasets, we proceeded with a holistic clustering analysis, producing a heatmap of samples performed on a gene level expression, along with a PCA/tSNE plot of samples, obtained by principal components analysis or t-distributed stochastic embedding algorithms. Then, after differential expression analysis and related plots, we performed a gene set enrichment analysis using seven different methods, including GSVA, ssGSEA, Spearman rank correlation, GSEA, Fisher's exact test, camera and fry. The next step foresaw functional analysis, a higher level functional and visual examination of the contrast space using the KEGG and GO graph structures. Finally, we performed advanced evaluation of transcriptome data realizing intersection, signature and biomarker analyses. The first allowed us to compare multiple contrasts by intersecting the genes of profiles, with the purpose of detecting contrasts showing similar profiles. Signature analysis tested gene signatures by calculating an enrichment score, then comparing the input gene list with all the gene sets and pathways in the platform through several statistical approaches. The last advanced analysis consisted of biomarker selection for classification or prediction purposes. This was reached by computation of a variable importance score for each feature using state-of-the-art machine learning algorithms, helping to find which genes, mutations, or gene sets most influence the final phenotype.

Pathway Analysis: ClueGO and CluePedia Cytoscape plug-ins

All previously described tools can compute and plot pathways analysis data, one of the major purposes of down-stream analysis of nucleic acid omics experiments. However, none of them is characterized by the high flexibility and customization of Cytoscape. Cytoscape is a major computational platform to visualize and analyze networks [21]. One of its greatest strengths is the continuously developed set of plug-ins, which widen the elaboration possibility of the software. Two of the most popular and richest plug-ins of Cytoscape are ClueGO and CluePedia, which significantly improve biological interpretation of large lists of genes.

ClueGO integrates Gene Ontology (GO) terms (Biological Process, Cellular Component, Molecular Function and Immune System Process), as well as CLINVAR, INTERPRO, KEGG, REACTOME (Pathways and Reactions), WIKIPATHWAYS and CORUM 3.0 ontologies, creating a functionally organized GO/pathway term network [22]. After the upload of gene identifiers, ClueGO performs single cluster analysis and comparison of clusters, starting from the ontology sources used, and with terms filtered by various set criteria. Correlated terms sharing similar associated genes are fused to reduce redundancy. The produced network is based on kappa statistics and shows the relationships between the terms based on the similarity of their associated genes, and the significance of the terms and groups is automatically calculated. ClueGO first creates a binary gene-term matrix with chosen terms and their associated genes. Based on this matrix, a term-term similarity matrix is computed using chance corrected kappa statistics to evaluate the association strength between the terms. Finally, the generated network shows the terms as nodes which are connected based on a kappa score threshold, which can be initially adjusted on a positive scale from 0 to 1 to restrict network connectivity in a customized way. The dimensions of the nodes reflect the enrichment significance of the terms. The functional groups, created by iterative merging of initially defined groups based on the predefined kappa score threshold, highlight their leading term in the network and provide an insightful view of their interrelations. Network node color can be switched between functional groups and cluster distributions. ClueGO plots highlight the specificity and common aspects of the biological role. Very usefully, ClueGO permits to compute enrichment/depletion tests for terms and groups as left-sided (Enrichment), right-sided (Depletion) or two-sided (Enrichment/Depletion) tests based on hypergeometric distribution, and outputted p-values can be corrected for multiple testing by several methods (Bonferroni, Bonferroni step-down, and Benjamini-Hochberg). To build the annotations network, ClueGO provides customizable functional analysis settings, ranging from general to very specific ones, based on one's needs. Interestingly, Cytoscape offers users the GO hierarchy as an alternative to the kappa score grouping, using parent-child relationships to produce functional groups. Additionally, ClueGO provides overview charts presenting the groups and their leading terms as well as detailed term histograms for both cluster specific and common terms. ClueGO options have been set as follows: CLINVAR, GO, INTERPRO, KEGG, REACTOME, WIKIPATHWAYS and CORUM 3.0 as selected ontologies; GO Tree Interval Min Level = 3 and Max Level = 8; GO Term/Pathway Selection

Min # Genes = 3 and % Genes = 4.000; GO Term/Pathway Network Connectivity (Kappa Score) = 0.4; Statistics Options set on Enrichment/Depletion (Two-Sided hypergeometric test), with pV correction = Bonferroni step-down. CluePedia was used following default settings. Finally, only GO terms with p < 0.01 were selected.

CluePedia, the second adopted plug-in, offers a widespread view on a pathway or process by investigating experimental and in silico data from different viewpoints: protein–protein interactions, gene interrelations, miRNAs regulatory features, functional context, in conjunction with ClueGO [23]. CluePedia computes statistical linear and non-linear correlation for markers of interest from experimental data, implementing Spearman's rank, Pearson correlation, distance correlation and maximal information coefficient (MIC). Finally, CluePedia plots custom correlation weights along with known interaction and miRNA-binding scores as edges on the network, which can be enriched with markers showing the highest interaction score for all or each of the selected nodes. In our analysis, CluePedia was run with standard settings.

As input file, we used a list of genes outputted from WES analyses of five patients affected by orphan forms of RP, with the final purpose to discover new candidate causative genes and new potential involved pathways (data under publication).

RESULTS

WES Circular Plot by Circos and Heat Maps by VIVA Provide a Strength Summary of Variant Data

Variant analysis of RP patient WES detected about 48,800 different variants, distributed through all human chromosomes. All variants found were classified by gene biotype in protein coding, antisense RNA, lincRNA, processed transcript, sense overlapping, TEC (To be Experimentally Confirmed), transcribed processed pseudogene, transcribed unitary pseudogene, transcribed unprocessed pseudogene and unprocessed pseudogene. Each variant shows a condition of heterozygosity or homozygosity, was determined as synonymous or not, if present in dbSNP database or not and if a known 3D model of a mutated protein in consequence of the presence of one of the detected variants exists. Furthermore, each variant was characterized by a specific frequency in the general population, computed by CLC Genomics Workbench analysis by exploring dedicated databases such as 1000 Genomes or gnomAD. Very important, each variant calling reliability was assessed by calculating several quality scores, such as original read depth and quality score of variant calling, ensuring the goodness of output data. All these outcomes were summarized by a single graph, the circular plot produced by Circos, available in Fig. (**1**). As can be seen, it simplified the initial evaluation of the whole produced big data incredibly, providing an overview of the entire output before proceeding with subsequent analytic steps.

While Circos provided different data type representation, VIVA maximized its usefulness plotting a single kind of information for each heat map but handling a huge quantity of data for that info. In Fig. (**2**), both genotype and read depth data for the considered WES sample are represented.

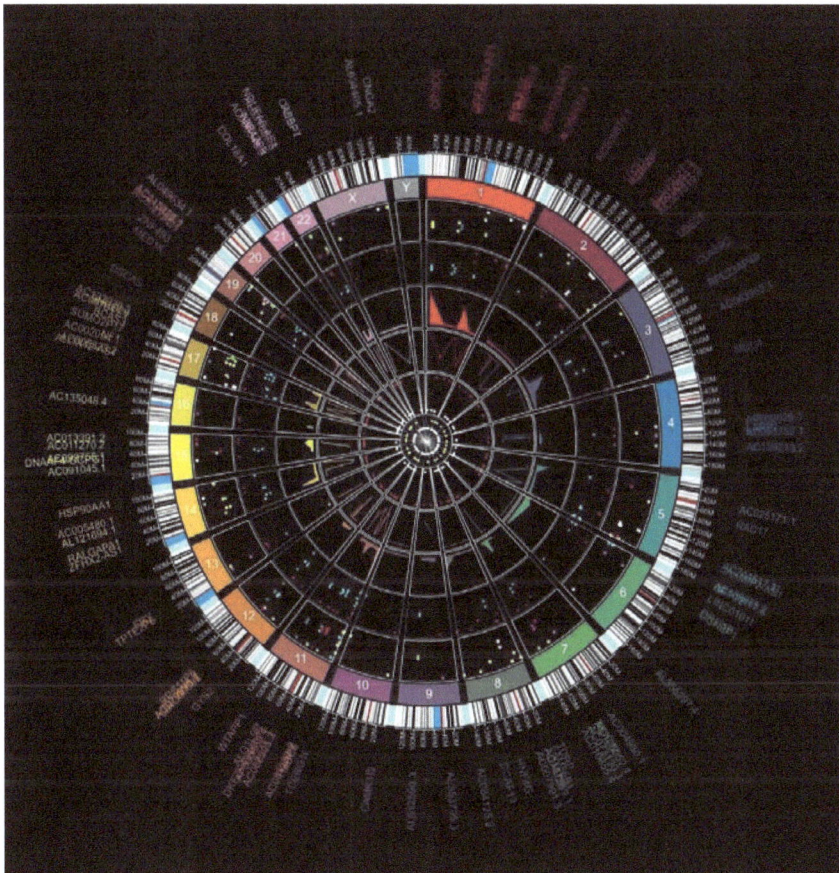

Fig. (1). Circular plot of WES variants by Circos. Represented circular plot summarizes the whole variant calling and annotation output of WES analysis. From the outer to the inner circle: Track 1 = Gene names. Track 2 = Hg38 cytobands numeric positions. Track 3 = Hg38 cytobands. Track 4 = Chromosome. Track 5 = Scatterplot of variant frequency in relationship with gene biotype (yellow = protein coding, white = antisense RNA, turquoise = lincRNA, light green = processed transcript, red = sense overlapping, light purple = TEC, petrol green = transcribed processed pseudogene, olive green = transcribed unitary pseudogene, purple = transcribed unprocessed pseudogene, pink = unprocessed pseudogene). Track 6 = Scatter plot of variant frequency in relation with heterozygosity (light blue) or homozygosity (red). Track 7 = Area Plot of Read Depth. Track 8 = Line Plot of variant calling quality score. Track 9 = Scatter plot of variant presence in dbSNP database (red = present, white = absent). Track 10 = Scatter plot of availability of 3D protein structure modified by presence of identified variants (yellow = variant misfolds protein, white = variant does not influence protein folding).

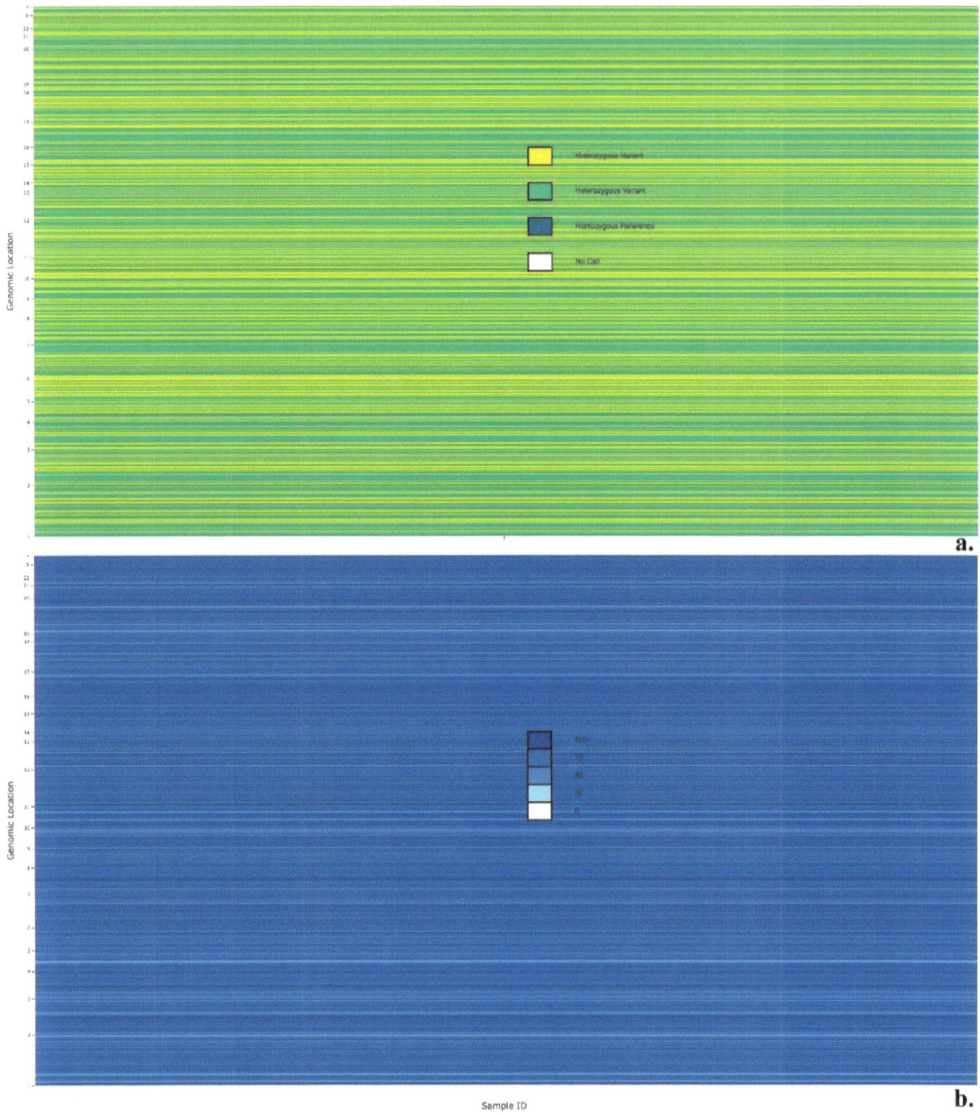

Fig. (2). VIVA heatmaps. In both heatmaps, unique variant positions are stored in rows and individual samples are stored in columns. **(a)** differential weight of putative disease associated variants in a heatmap of genotype values. **(b)** read depth information.

Omics Playground Provided a Straightforward Full-featured Output of RNA-Seq Samples

While the main advantage of circular plots lies in summarizing possibilities, the major benefit of the Omics Playground platform is its impressive, rich outputs. For example, the alpha-1-B-glycoprotein (*A1BG*) gene was abundantly expressed in liver, and expression increased over time (maximum at 6h), showing an almost uniform distribution among biological replicates (Fig. **3**). Interestingly, a global up-regulation among best differentially expressed genes was outputted. In detail, four clusters showed particular trends: the S3 (led by genes involved in "Early Estrogen response") was over-expressed throughout the whole treatment with oxidative stress inducing A2E, with the exactly opposite situation involving cluster S2 (led by genes involved in "Protein Secretion"); mixed scenarios, instead, emerged from S1 and S2 clusters, led by genes involved in "WNT-Bet--catenin signaling" and "KRAS signaling up-regulation", respectively. The main feature-set regarded ribosomal proteins, also mitochondrial ones (Fig. **4**). Moreover, between most differentially expressed genes we found the one encoding for tubulin tyrosine ligase like 7 (*TTLL7*), absolutely among best down-regulated genes, especially after 3h of treatment. Generally, the highest number of over- and down-expressed genes (2528 and 2811, respectively) was seen at 6h from A2E exposition, with the most statistically reliable shown by DESeq2 modelling and Wald's test (Fig. **5**). Returning to the example of *A1BG*, it evidenced a strong correlation with the ARV1 homolog fatty acid homeostasis modulator gene (*ARV1*), with Tudor domain containing 3 gene (*TDRD3*) and with Golgi brefeldin A resistant guanine nucleotide exchange factor 1 gene (*GBF1*). Additionally, an *A1BG* over-expression was correlated to interactions with several ligands, such as insulin-like growth factor (IGF-I) and transforming growth factor beta (TGF-β) (Fig. **6**). Curiously, among the most significantly enriched pathways, "Cholesterol biosynthesis" emerged as the most dysregulated at 3h, mainly showing over-expressed genes, like 3-Hydroxy-3-Methylglutaryl-CoA Synthase 1 (*HMGCS1*). Regarding this enrichment step, the best statistical significance was reached by Fisher methods (Fig. **7**). After KEGG database exploration, one of the most deregulated and characterized pathways was "Protein export", exerting prominent effects by down-regulation of several signal recognition particles (SRPs), such as B, 19 and 54. Analyzing data in GO database, instead, the most deregulated pathways found were the already cited "Cholesterol biosynthesis", along with "Inflammatory response", with possible induced changes in DNA geometry when up-regulated (Fig. **8**). Then, the aesthetically-pleasing word cloud confirmed previous outcomes highlighting, among the most represented words, "cholesterol", "cycle" and "mitotic". Some other very useful information came from drugs able to act on most dysregulated identified gene targets, which were importazole and chlorpromazine (Fig. **9**). Evaluating common features between the two considered time-points, positive correlations emerged between them, and about 1751 common genes were differentially expressed (Fig. **10**). Furthermore, over-expression is dominant over down-expression, especially at 6h. Best common significant pathways in both time-points were "Immune checkpoint", "Regulation of homotypic cell-cell adhesion", "Interleukin-12 complex" and "Cell differentiation markers" (Fig. **11**).

Finally, after biomarker selection analysis, major candidate biomarkers were Nudix Hydrolase 6 (*NUDT6*) and TMX2-CTNND1 readthrough (*TMX2-CTNND1*), NMD candidate coding for a long non-coding RNA (lncRNA) (Fig. **12**).

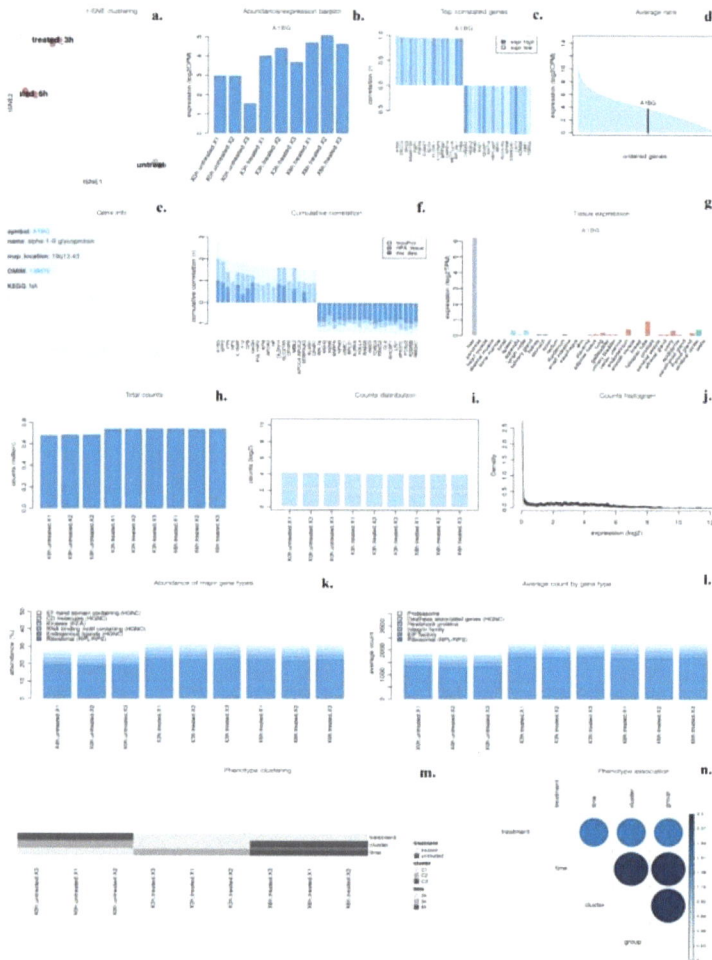

Fig. (3). DataView plots summarizing information and descriptive statistics. Gene plots. **(a)** t-SNE of samples colored in function of selected gene expression. **(b)** Considered gene expression/abundance across groups. **(c)** Top correlated genes, with shades of grey correlated to gene absolute expression. **(d)** Average rank of the considered gene in comparison to other genes. **(e)** Additional information about the considered gene from public databases. **(f)** Barplot exhibiting cumulative correlation in other datasets. **(g)** Tissue expression of considered gene. **(h)** Total counts per sample or average per group. **(i)** Distribution of total counts per sample/group. **(j)** Histograms of total counts distribution per sample/group. **(k)** Abundance of major gene types per sample/group. **(l)** Average count by gene type per sample/group. **(m)** Clustered heatmap of phenotype data. **(n)** Clustered heatmap of phenotype association. The values correspond to the -log$_{10}$(p) value of the corresponding statistical test between two phenotype variables. A higher value corresponds to higher significant "correlation".

Fig. (4). Cluster Analysis of similar genes/samples by unsupervised machine learning approaches. **(a)** Heatmap highlighting gene expression sorted by 2-way hierarchical clustering (Red = overexpression, blue = underexpression). **(b)** Clustered heatmap, showing gene expression on the basis of different groupong criteria. **(c)** Top ranked annotation features correlated to each gene cluster as represented in the heatmap. **(d)** Plots showing the distribution of the phenotypes superposed on the t-SNE clustering, hypothesizing that t-SNE distribution might be driven by the particular phenotype that is regulated by the experimental condition or unwanted batch effects. **(e)** PCA/tSNE plot shows the similarity in expression of samples as a scatterplot in 3D. Similar samples are clustered near to each other, while differentially expressed samples are positioned farther away. Groups of samples with analogous profiles will appear as clusters in the plot. **(f)** The plot ranks the discriminative power of feature sets (or gene sets) as the cumulative discriminant score for all phenotype variables. **(g)** The Parallel Coordinates plot evidences the expression levels of considered genes across all conditions. The x-axis represents the experimental conditions, while the y-axis shows the expression level of the genes grouped by condition. The colors correspond to the gene groups as defined by the hierarchical clustered heatmap.

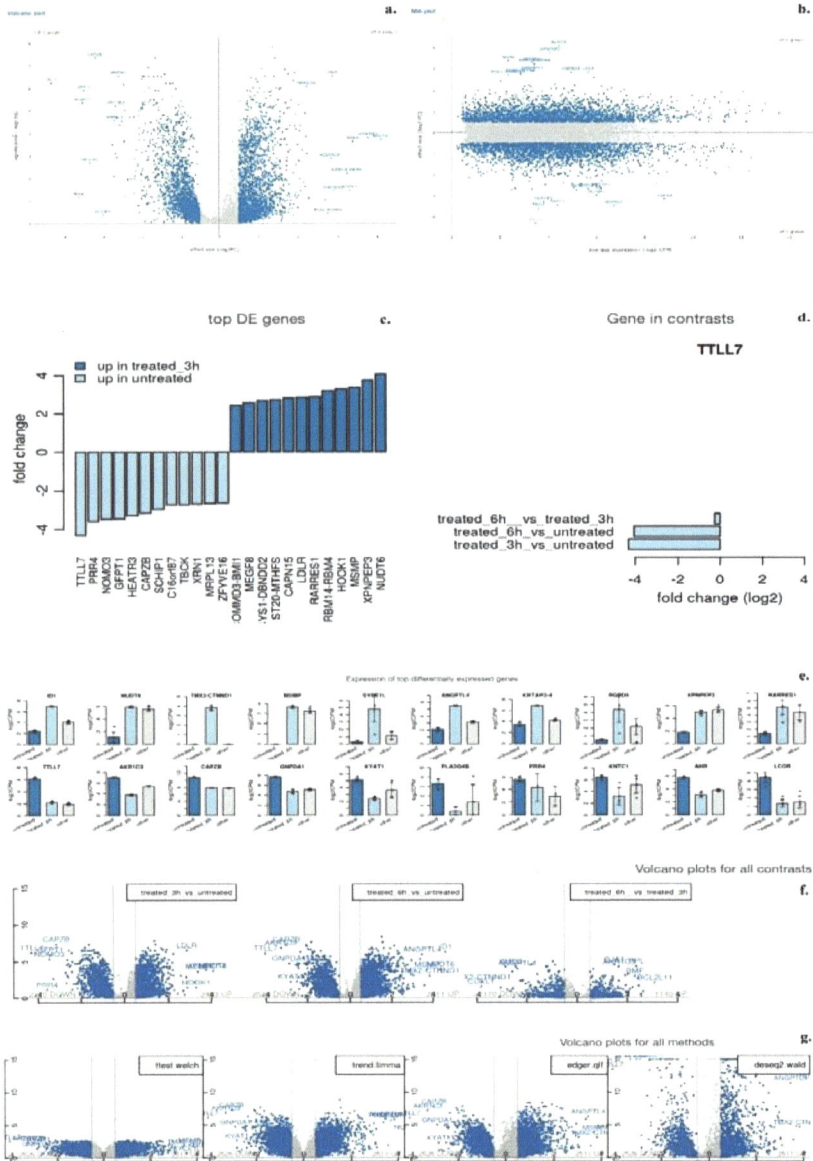

Fig. (5). Differential expression plots associated with the considered contrast groups. **(a)** Volcano-plot representing significance (y-axis) vs fold-change (x-axis). **(b)** MA-plot visualizing fold-change (y-axis) vs signal intensity (x-axis). **(c)** Sorted barplot of the top diffentially expressed genes with widest (absolute) fold-change for selected contrast. **(d)** Sorted barplot of the differential expression of the considered gene across all contrasts. **(e)** Barplots of the top differentially expressed genes (both positively and negatively) for the selected contrast. **(f)** Volcano plot for all contrasts. Experimental contrasts with better statistical significance will show volcano plots with "higher" wings. **(g)** Volcano plot for all statistical methods. Methods showing better statistical significance will show volcano plots with "higher" wings.

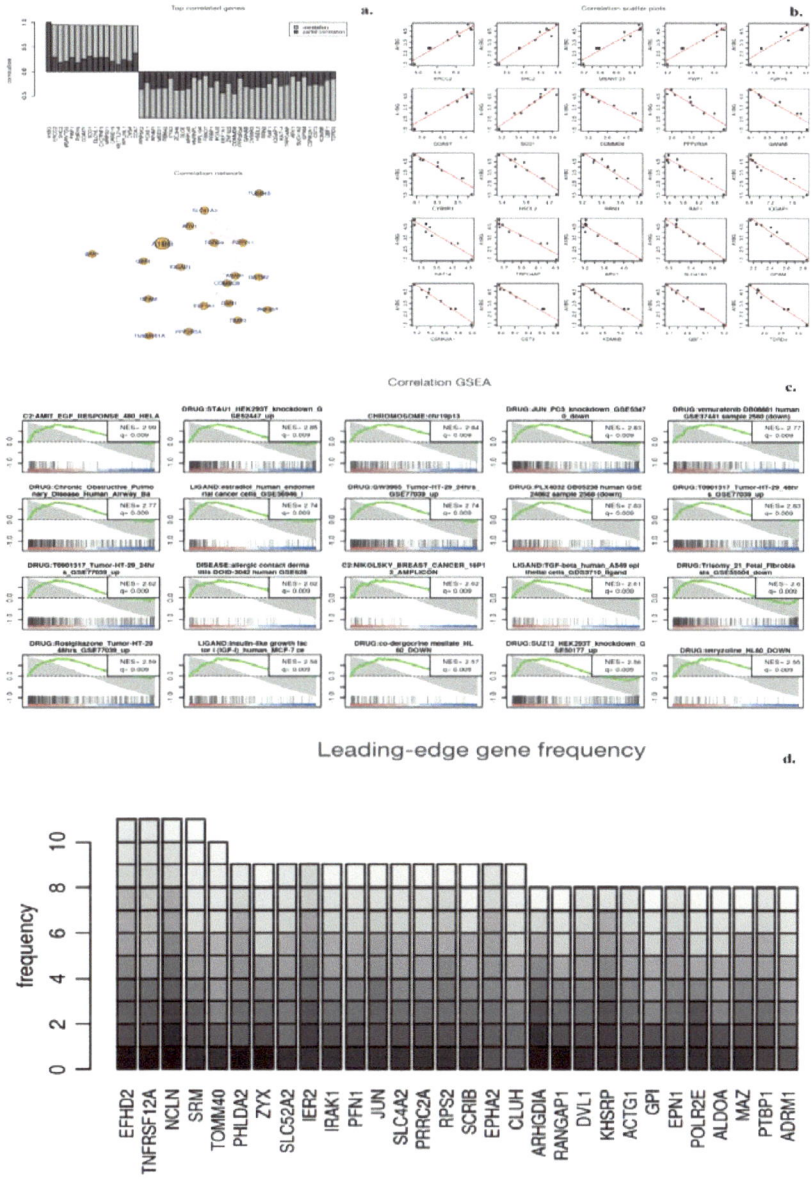

Fig. (6). Statistical correlation analysis between genes to find coregulated modules. **(a)** Top-ranked correlation of features in relationship to selected gene and correlation network around the selected gene. **(b)** Scatter plots of gene expression of top correlated genes. **(c)** Top enriched gene sets using the GSEA correlation as rank metric. The black bars indicate the genes in the gene set and their position in the sorted rank metric. **(d)** Frequency of leading edge genes in top correlated genesets.

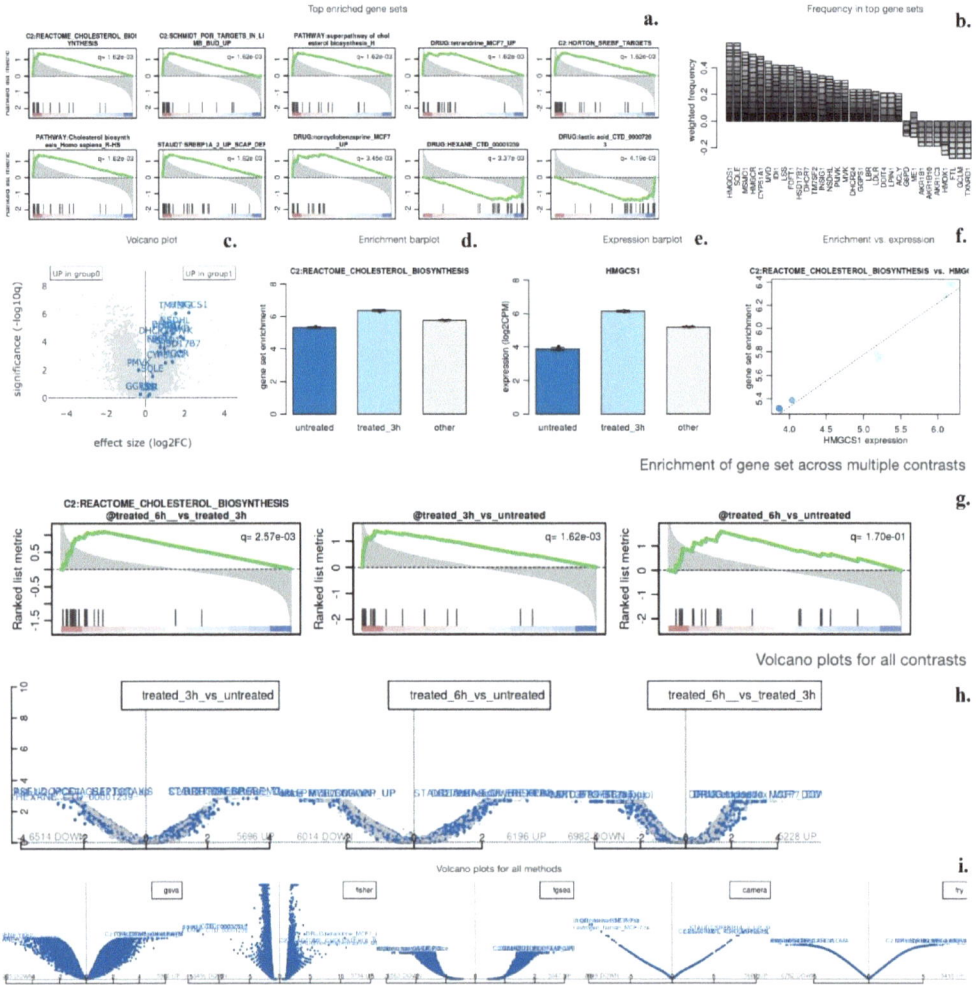

Fig. (7). Geneset enrichment analysis.**(a)** Enrichment plots of the top differentially enriched gene sets. Black vertical bars represent the rank of genes in the gene set in the sorted list metric, while the green curve indicates the "running statistics" of the enrichment score. **(b)** Plot showing the number of times a gene is present in the top-N genesets sorted by frequency. **(c)** Volcano-plot highlighting significance (y-axis) vs fold-change (x-axis). Genes in the gene set are highlighted in blue. **(d)** Barplot of the gene set enrichment in the groups. **(e)** Barplot of the gene expression of the gene. **(f)** Scatter plot of the enrichment versus the expression of the selected geneset and gene, on the y and x axes, respectively. **(g)** Enrichment plots for the considered gene set across multiple contrasts. **(h)** Volcano plots showing enrichment score (x-axis) vs significance (y-axis). Experimental contrasts showing better statistical significance will show volcano plots with "higher" wings. **(i)** Volcano plots of gene sets for different enrichment methods. The ones showing better statistical significance will show volcano plots with "higher" wings.

Fig. (8). Specific functional analysis.**(a)** KEGG pathway map, with upregulated genes in red and downregulated in blue. **(b)** Activation matrix showing the activation levels of pathways across contrasts. **(c)** Gene ontology graph visualizing the enrichment of the GO terms as a tree structure. **(d)** Activation matrix showing the enrichment of GO terms across multiple contrast profiles.

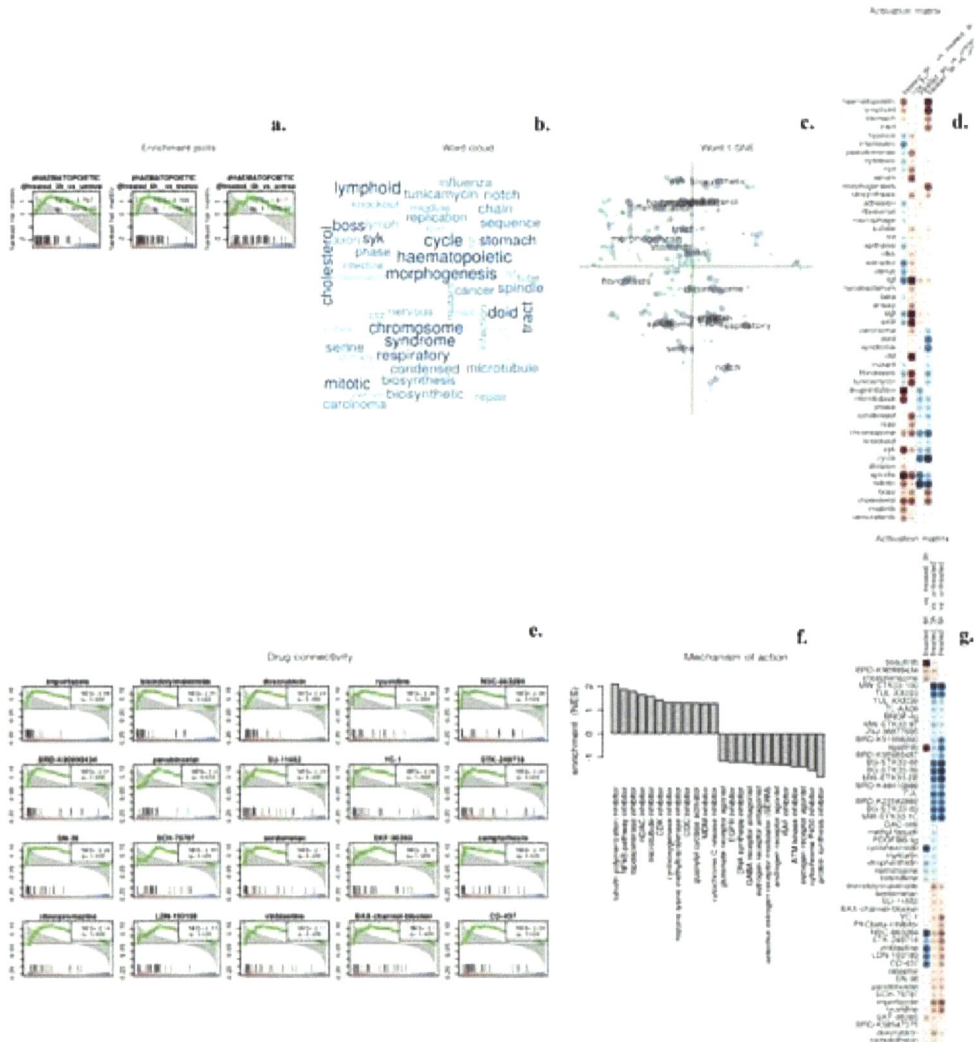

Fig. (9). WordCloud analysis for the enrichment of keywords for the contrasts and Drug Connectivity analysis to see if certain drug activity or drug sensitivity signatures match experimental signatures. **(a)** Word enrichment plots for the top most significant contrasts. Black vertical bars depict the position of gene sets, in the ranked enrichment scores, which contains the "keyword", while the green curve highlights the "running statistics" of the keyword enrichment score. **(b)** Word cloud, with word size related to the normalized enrichment score (NES) from the GSEA computation. **(c)** Word t-SNE of keywords extracted from the titles/descriptions of the genesets. **(d)** Activation matrix visualizing keyword enrichment across contrasts. **(e)** Drug connectivity relating considered signature with drug perturbation profiles from the L1000 database. The figures highlight the most similar (or opposite) profiles by running the GSEA algorithm on the profile correlation space. **(f)** Mechanism-of-action plot evidencing the top most frequent drug class (or target genes) having similar or opposite enrichment compared to the query signature. **(g)** Activation matrix showing enrichment levels of drug signatures across multiple contrast profiles.

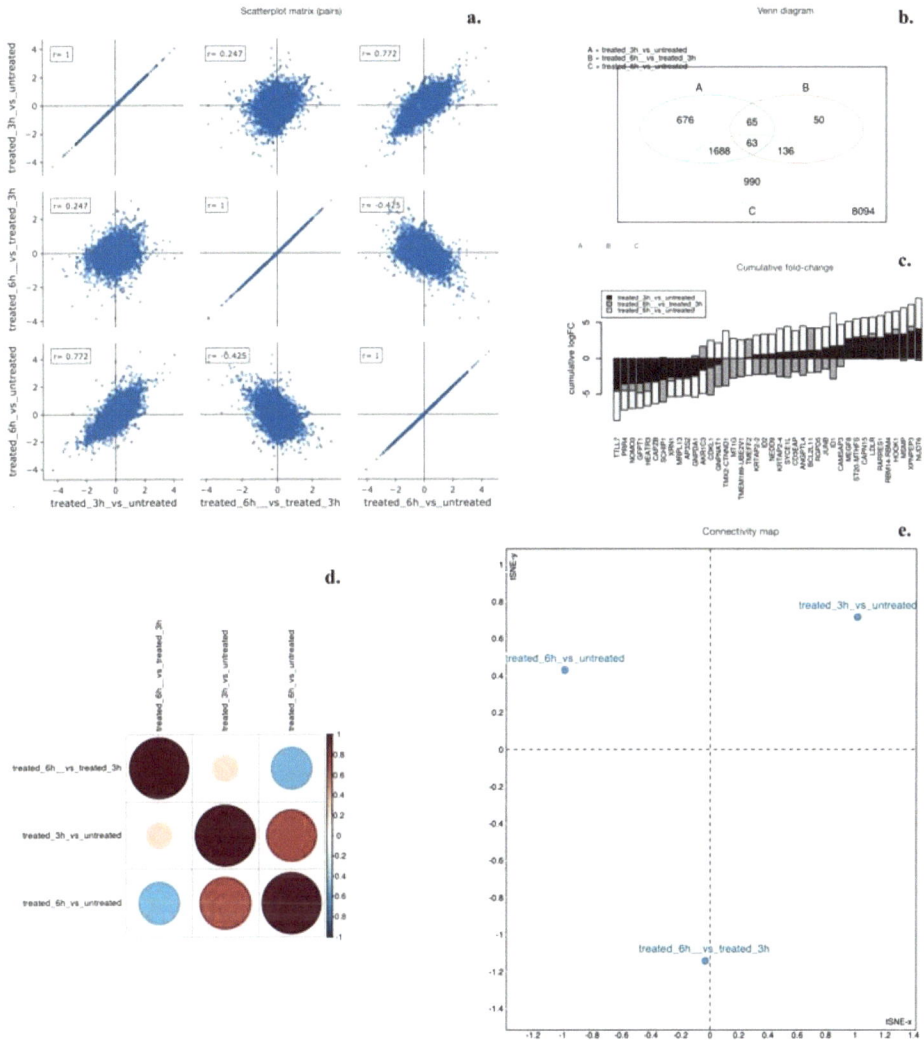

Fig. (10). Intersection analysis to identify contrasts showing similar profiles and genes which are commonly up/down regulated between two contrasts. **(a)** Pairwise scatterplots for two or more differential expression profiles for multiple selected contrasts. Similar profiles show points close to the diagonal. **(b)** Venn diagram showing the number of overlapping genes for multiple contrasts. **(c)** Cumulative fold-change plot of genes in the selected overlap region. **(d)** Constrast heatmap, in which the numeric value in the cells corresponds to the Pearson correlation coefficient (Red = positive correlation, blue = negative correlation). **(e)** Connectivity Map that shows the similarity of the contrasts as a t-SNE plot. Similar contrasts are clustered close together, while different contrasts are positioned farther away.

Fig. (11). Signature analysis of contrasts which take the top differentially expressed genes as signature. **(a)** Enrichment plots of the query signature in all contrasts. Positive enrichment means that this particular contrast evidences similar expression changes as the query signature. **(b)** Overlap/Similarity table. The vertical axis shows the overlap score of the gene set which combines the odds ratio and significance (q-value) of the Fisher's test. **(c)** T-SNE plot for each gene, where the dots (corresponding to samples) are colored depending on the upregulation (in red) or downregulation (in blue) of that particular gene.

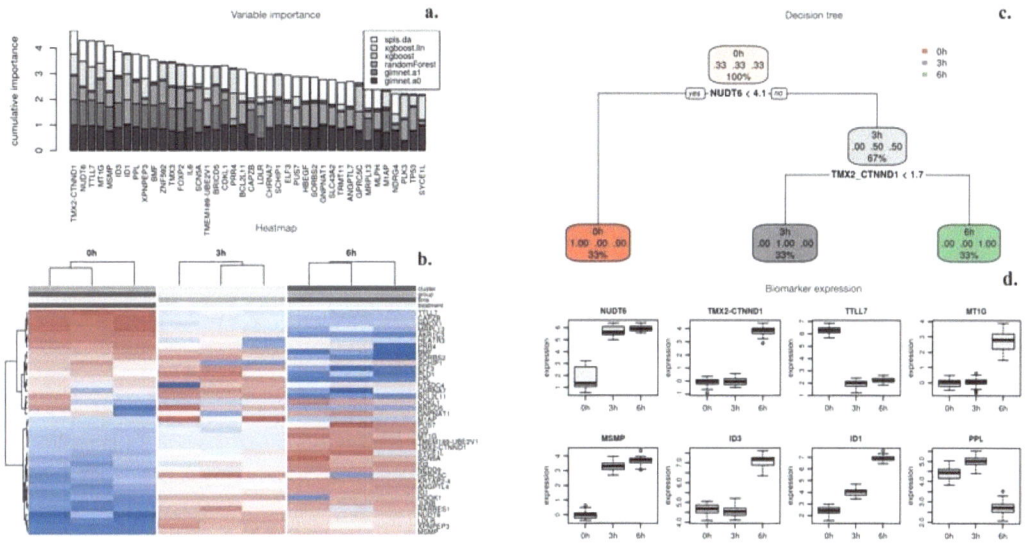

Fig. (12). Biomarker selection for classification or prediction purposes. The expression of specific genes may be used as markers to predict a certain phenotype such as response to a therapy. **(a)** An importance score for each feature is computed using multiple machine learning algorithms, including elastic nets, random forests, LASSO and extreme gradient boosting. The top features are plotted according to cumulative ranking by the algorithms. **(b)** The heatmap visualizes the expression distribution for the top most important features. **(c)** The decision tree highlights (one) tree solution for classification based on the top most important features. **(d)** Boxplots evidence the expression of biomarker genes across the groups.

ClueGO and CluePedia Analyses Produced Appealing Graphical Representation of Pathways and Enrichments Involved Clustered Genes

ClueGO result visualizations consisted of a functionally grouped network of terms/pathways, in which the most significant term of a group represented the "leader" and is evidenced on the network. Each term was represented as a node in the network, and all nodes were functionally grouped based on shared genes (kappa score ≥ 0.4) and highlighted with different colors. The size of the nodes reflected the degree of significance. When groups overlapped, the next most significant term was highlighted. Moreover, selected functional groups and terms were plotted in pie and bar charts, and a term included in several groups was multiple times counted in these charts. ClueGO analysis on input gene set highlighted 41 pathways, clustered in 11 "macro-pathways". The widest was "Phosphorylation of cohesin by PLK1 at centromeres", which was made up of 25 sub-pathways probably involved in major biological changes (Fig. **13**).

Then, CluePedia, in the WES dataset used for analysis, highlighted functional connections between about 30 already known causative RP genes, further enriched with about another 50, which resulted one carrying at least one variant in VCF output files (data under publication). These genes, thanks to deep enrichment analysis, could represent new putative associated or causative genes of orphan forms of RP. The main features of enrichment regarding input genes involved shared reactions, catalysis, expression and inhibition (Fig. **14**).

Fig. (13). ClueGO graphical representations. ClueGO results are illustrated as **(a)** Functionally grouped network of terms/pathways, **(b)** Pie chart with groups, **(c)** Bar chart with terms. The bars indicate the number of genes associated with the terms, while the percentage of genes per term is shown as bar label.

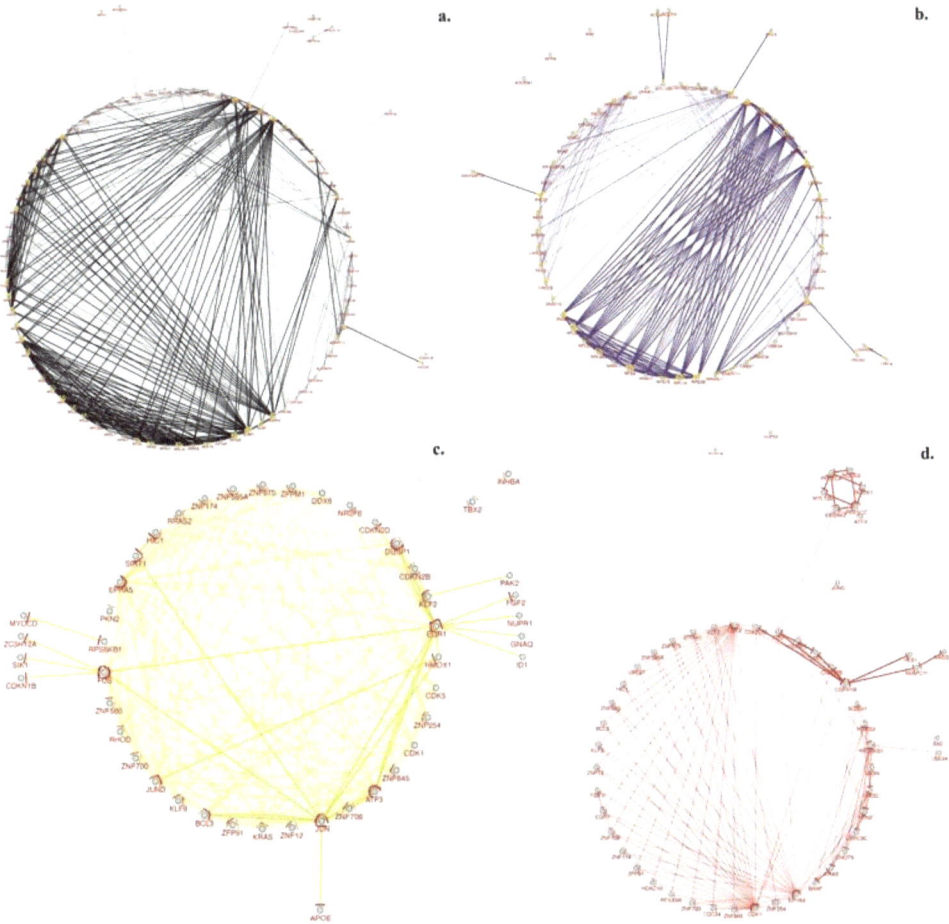

Fig. (14). CluePedia enrichment visualization. Represented panel shows several of CluePedia attributes that could emerge from an enrichment analysis with this tool. **(a)** Reactions feature. **(b)** Catalysis feature. **(c)** Expression feature. **(d)** Inhibition feature.

DISCUSSION

The age of reasonable, massive, high-throughput sequencing has exponentially increased the availability of genome, exome, transcriptome and other kinds of omic profiling data. Nevertheless, extracting biologically meaningful results and communicating these outcomes remains challenging [24]. The most important element is that despite the multi-scale nature of omic data, only a few tools take advantage of multiple linked view configurations that support efficient navigation and pattern discovery of the space [25].

Many tools are available not because there are many different visualization needs, but due to the necessity to access a wide range of incompatible data formats and sources, as well as the need to integrate them into common analysis workflows. These are also typically defined by the data formats they work on [26].

Genomic and exomic data were usually represented as tabular outputs, due to the amount of considered variables in their analyses. Modern software, commercial and not, developed graphical representation of these kinds of data, generally visualized as single tracks depicting individual outcomes as alignment quality of analyzed reads or variant localization in the genomic context. Recently, a more exhaustive plot was realized, with the main objective to collect the whole outputted data into one single informative representation [27]. This visualization method is the circular plot, best produced by the python-based algorithm Circos. Its flexibility of layout and formatting of graphical elements allows the production of different visualizations in various data domains, especially in graphical representation of the just cited tabular data. In this tool, the concept of ideograms is subverted, and they represent individual rows or columns of a table instead of regions of chromosomes [28]. So we were able to represent the exome sequencing read depth, the localization of variants in relationship to each human chromosome, the variant frequency in function of gene biotype or hereditary condition, the quality of the whole variant calling, the presence of variant in the dbSNP database and the putative effect of single variants on protein folding, all in the same plot.

Furthermore, in the case of single or multiple samples, it is useful to try to put all main information on an interactive map, as realized by the VIVA tool, suggesting the real impact of generated data [29].

Talking about RNA-Seq data, instead, not only is summarizing all big data produced (even bigger than genomic data) important, but the most difficult challenge deals with the possibility of visualizing all outcomes with specific plots, possibly from a full-featured software. Nearly all available tools are able to generate plots of transcriptomic data, from heatmaps clustering differentially expressed genes to Eulero-Venn diagrams [30]. However, a complete set of tools is generally exploitable only by experienced bioinformaticians after complex settings of workspace in a coding environment such as R [31]. The Omics Playground platform provides a unique combination of tools for more high-level analyses in a well-organized way, computing gene differential expression, gene set enrichment, functional and signature analyses, and biomarker discovery from a unique pipeline. In this way, for example, it was possible to identify the best dysregulated genes in an experiment involving RPE cells after exposure to an oxidant agent such as A2E, and from enrichment and functional analyses of them, to get to putative drug targeting of several of these genes.

Interestingly, both kinds of described omics data could represent an input for pathway analysis, frequently preliminary to translational discoveries correlated to both DNA and RNA data [32]. Pathway information is intrinsically redundant, as genes frequently play roles in numerous pathways, and several pathway databases organize them hierarchically by including general and specific pathways with many shared genes (e.g. "Phosphorylation of cohesin by PLK1 at centromeres" and "Kinetochore assembly"). Thus, realizing an enrichment map which collapses redundant pathways into a single biological theme simplifies interpretation [33]. ClueGO computes such a network representing pathways as circles (nodes) colored by enrichment score, connected with line (edge) size based on the number of genes shared by the connected pathways. Very usefully, multiple enrichment analysis results can be simultaneously plotted into a single enrichment map, differentially coloring nodes for each enrichment [34]. An enrichment map significantly improves the identification of interesting pathways and physiopathological themes. After an initial validation of enrichment analysis by identification of expected themes (positive controls), pathways not previously related to the experimental context are carefully evaluated as possible discoveries. This step is performed by examining enrichment scores, prioritizing from the highest to the lowest [35]. Finally, the most fascinating pathways are deeply analyzed, investigating the role of each gene involved. The latter process could be further improved by enriching master regulators of selected pathways with miRNAs and/or transcription factor target gene sets using an enrichment map post-analysis tool such as CluePedia. In this way, pathway enrichment analysis results can be published to support a scientific conclusion (e.g. discovery of putative genes associated/causative of an orphan disease), used for making hypotheses or designing experiments to support the identification of novel pathways [36].

CONCLUSIONS

Today, such an extensive variety of visualization tools is available to scientists that it can be difficult to select the right one. Data visualization users should mainly focus their choice on ease of use and whether a tool has the features they need.

The most powerful tool available does not always represent the best alternative: learning curves can be excessive, requiring more resources and time, while a simpler tool might be able to reach the hypothesized objective in an easier way. A tool is only part of the complex picture of a data visualization pipeline: it fits what the scientist would like to express. Thus, to achieve the maximum from data visualization the scientific community needs to be incentivized and enabled to study genomics visualization problems. This goal could be reached by improving infrastructure to provide handy access to genomic data and to enable efficient integration of new visualization tools into existing analysis frameworks. This will also permit the bioinformatics community to shift attention away from uselessly reimplementing basic functionality and, instead, focus on visualization problems, rather than data access difficulties.

REFERENCES

[1]   Ryan L, Silver D, Laramee RS, Ebert D, Rhyne TM. Teaching data visualization as a skill. IEEE Comput Graph Appl 2019; 39(2): 95-103.

[2]   Keim D, Qu H, Ma KL. Big-data visualization. IEEE Comput Graph Appl 2013; 33(4): 20-1.

[3]   Czauderna T, Schreiber F. Information visualization for biological data. Methods Mol Biol 2017; 1526: 403-15.

[4]   Keefe DF. Integrating visualization and interaction research to improve scientific workflows. IEEE Comput Graph Appl 2010; 30(2): 8-13.

[5]   Raidou RG. Visual analytics for the representation, exploration, and analysis of high-dimensional, multi-faceted medical data. Adv Exp Med Biol 2019; 1138: 137-62.

[6]   Souza AS, Rerko L, Oberauer K. Getting more from visual working memory: Retro-cues enhance retrieval and protect from visual interference. J Exp Psychol Hum Percept Perform 2016; 42(6): 890-910.

[7]   Abt E. Understanding statistics 1. Evid Based Dent 2010; 11(2): 60-1.

[8]   Fulton L, Mangelsdorff AD, Finstuen K. Using Anscombe's quartet plus one to illustrate data set matching, proper model specification, and relationships between inferential tests. J Health Adm Educ 2008; 25(2): 145-58.

[9]   LaPolla FWZ, Rubin D. The "Data Visualization Clinic": a library-led critique workshop for data visualization. J Med Libr Assoc 2018; 106(4): 477-82.

[10]   Weissgerber TL, Winham SJ, Heinzen EP, *et al.* Reveal, Don't conceal: Transforming data visualization to improve transparency. Circulation 2019; 140(18): 1506-18.

[11]   Shneiderman B. The big picture for big data: visualization. Science 2014; 343(6172): 730.

[12]   Gehlenborg N, O'Donoghue SI, Baliga NS, *et al.* Visualization of omics data for systems biology. Nat Methods 2010; 7(3) (Suppl.): S56-68.

[13]   Nusrat S, Harbig T, Gehlenborg N. Tasks, techniques, and tools for genomic data visualization. Comput Graph Forum 2019; 38(3): 781-805.

[14]   Chatterjee A, Ahn A, Rodger EJ, Stockwell PA, Eccles MR. A guide for designing and analyzing RNA-Seq Data. Methods Mol Biol 2018; 1783: 35-80.

[15]   Krzywinski M, Schein J, Birol I, *et al.* Circos: an information aesthetic for comparative genomics. Genome Res 2009; 19(9): 1639-45.

[16]   Tollefson GA, Schuster J, Gelin F, *et al.* VIVA (vIsualization of variants): A VCF file visualization tool. Sci Rep 2019; 9(1): 12648.

[17]   Akhmedov M, Martinelli A, Geiger R, Kwee I. Omics Playground: A comprehensive self-service platform for visualization, analytics and exploration of Big Omics Data. NAR Genomics and Bioinformatics 2020; 2(1).

[18]   Donato L, D'Angelo R, Alibrandi S, Rinaldi C, Sidoti A, Scimone C. Effects of A2E-induced oxidative stress on retinal epithelial cells: New insights on differential gene response and retinal dystrophies. Antioxidants 2020; 9: 4.

[19]   Donato L, Scimone C, Alibrandi S, *et al.* Discovery of GLO1 new related genes and pathways by RNA-Seq on A2E-stressed retinal epithelial cells could improve knowledge on retinitis pigmentosa. Antioxidants 2020; 9: 5.

[20]   Donato L, Scimone C, Alibrandi S, Rinaldi C, Sidoti A, D'Angelo R. Transcriptome analyses of lncRNAs in A2E-stressed retinal epithelial cells unveil advanced links between metabolic impairments related to oxidative stress and retinitis pigmentosa. Antioxidants 2020; 9: 4.

[21]   Shannon P, Markiel A, Ozier O, *et al.* Cytoscape: A software environment for integrated models of biomolecular interaction networks. Genome Res 2003; 13(11): 2498-504.

[22]   Bindea G, Mlecnik B, Hackl H, *et al.* ClueGO: A Cytoscape plug-in to decipher functionally grouped gene ontology and pathway annotation networks. Bioinformatics 2009; 25(8): 1091-3.

[23]   Bindea G, Galon J, Mlecnik B. CluePedia Cytoscape plugin: pathway insights using integrated experimental and in silico data. Bioinformatics 2013; 29(5): 661-3.

[24]   Lopez de Maturana E, Alonso L, Alarcon P, *et al.* Challenges in the integration of omics and non-omics data. Genes (Basel) 2019; 10: 3.

[25]   Subramanian I, Verma S, Kumar S, Jere A, Anamika K. Multi-omics data integration, interpretation, and its application. Bioinform Biol Insights 2020; 14: 1177932219899051.

[26]   Wani N, Raza K. Integrative approaches to reconstruct regulatory networks from multi-omics data: A review of state-of-the-art methods. Comput Biol Chem 2019; 83: 107120.

[27]   Nix DA, Di Sera TL, Dalley BK, *et al.* Next generation tools for genomic data generation, distribution, and visualization. BMC Bioinformatics 2010; 11: 455.

[28]   Gangwar K, Ramulu M. Dataset for interpreting the Circos figures used in the review of friction stir welding of titanium alloys. Data Brief 2019; 22: 164-8.

[29]   Williams JR, Yang R, Clifford JL, *et al.* Functional Heatmap: an automated and interactive pattern recognition tool to integrate time with multi-omics assays. BMC Bioinformatics 2019; 20(1): 81.

[30]   Conesa A, Madrigal P, Tarazona S, *et al.* A survey of best practices for RNA-seq data analysis. Genome Biol 2016; 17: 13.

[31]   Senabouth A, Lukowski SW, Hernandez JA, *et al.* Ascend: R package for analysis of single-cell RNA-seq data. Gigascience 2019; 8: 8.

[32]   Yang Q, Wang S, Dai E, *et al.* Pathway enrichment analysis approach based on topological structure and updated annotation of pathway. Brief Bioinform 2019; 20(1): 168-77.

[33]   Ghosh T, Ma X, Kirby M. New tools for the visualization of biological pathways. Methods 2018; 132: 26-33.

[34]   Liu L, Wei J, Ruan J. Pathway enrichment analysis with networks. Genes (Basel) 2017; 8: 10.

[35]   Lin SJ, Lu TP, Yu QY, Hsiao CK. Probabilistic prioritization of candidate pathway association with pathway score. BMC Bioinformatics 2018; 19(1): 391.

[36]   Mubeen S, Hoyt CT, Gemund A, Hofmann-Apitius M, Frohlich H, Domingo-Fernandez D. The impact of pathway database choice on statistical enrichment analysis and predictive modeling. Front Genet 2019; 10: 1203.

SUBJECT INDEX

www.ingramcontent.com/pod-product-compliance
Lightning Source LLC
Chambersburg PA
CBHW041714210326
41598CB00007B/643